THE GREAT TRANSFORMATION

Finding Peace Of Soul In Troubled Times

Ted Flynn

THE GREAT TRANSFORMATION

Finding Peace Of Soul In Troubled Times

Maxkol Communications, Inc.

Other works by Ted Flynn

The Thunder of Justice, The Warning, The Miracle, The Chastisement, The Era of Peace, Ted and Maureen Flynn, 1993, 2010

Hope of the Wicked, The Master Plan to Rule the World, The political and social ideology of the New World Order, 2000

Idols in the House, 2002

Prophecy and the New Times, (DVD), 1995

Key to the Triumph, The Final Marian Dogma of Co-Redemptrix, Mediatrix, and Advocate, DVD, 1997

We've had enough of exhortations to be silent!
Cry out with a hundred thousand tongues.
I see that the world is rotten because of silence.

—Saint Catherine of Siena,
Doctor of the Church

Declarations

Since the abolition of Canons 1399 and 2318 of the former Canonical Code by Pope Paul VI in AAS 58 (1966), p. 1186, publications about new appearances, revelations, prophecies, miracles, etc., have been allowed to be distributed and read by the faithful without the express permission of the Church, providing they contain nothing which contravenes faith and morals. This means no imprimatur is necessary when distributing new information on apparitions not yet judged by the Church.

In Lumen Gentium, Vatican II, Chapter 12, the Council Fathers urge the faithful to be open and attentive to the ways in which the Holy Spirit continues to guide the Church, including private revelation. We hear: "*Such gifts of grace, whether they are of special enlightenment or whether they are spread more simply and generally, must be accepted with gratefulness and consolation, as they are specially suited to and useful for, the needs of the Church... Judgments as to their genuineness and their correct use lies with those who lead the Church and those whose special task is not to extinguish the Spirit, but to examine everything and keep that which is good*" (I Thess. 5:19-21).

Written, compiled, and edited by Ted Flynn

MAXKOL Communications, Inc.
P.O. Box 307, Herndon, Virginia 20170
tflynn3@cox.net
703.421.1064

Acknowledgments

There are many people who have been a part of this process of thinking through the subject matter in this book, and offering valuable suggestions over many years. The conversations with many people have been fascinating. We are who we are, because so many people have touched us in so many different ways. Everyone who offered valuable suggestions did so in different genres of thinking and have contributed to the final product. I will thank those who helped alphabetically.

Dr. Gene and Barbara Conti have helped me understand the concepts of atheistic evolution and how it has bred widespread unbelief all the way to elementary school grades. This diabolical insidious agenda of disordered minds is to show the bible irrelevant and a work of fiction—or worse yet—fairy tales. It has opened my eyes to see just how effective the humanistic manifesto has worked its way into mainstream thinking. Father Joseph Esper provided valuable suggestions and corrections on a variety of subjects as the breadth, depth, and width of his knowledge is like few others. Page by page, suggestions were incorporated that made the book more accurate and readable. Colleen Flynn was tough on "dear old dad," which I didn't mind as it makes the book more relevant. Her comments were incorporated wholesale. Maureen Flynn for suggestions and edits. Martin Hartigan commented, added, deleted, and had substantial suggestions on a wide spectrum of topics few if anyone can match from a secular, economic, political, Marian, and faith point of view. He had his hand in every chapter.

Bud Macfarlane gave a balanced view of the big picture. He has the ability to stress the most important. It was the data on the Eucharist as the source and summit of the faith that will be the "*spiritual bail out plan*" for humanity that will save us. Susan Pohedra was a reader offering suggestions that were helpful and part of the whole process of watching it evolve. Father Ron Stone and the plan for the world by Our Lady we will all soon see to be majestic and true. Humble thanks to all. It has been a joy as we journeyed into the Immaculate and Sacred Hearts.

Ted Flynn

Dedicated to:

Soli Deo Gloria
To You Alone

TABLE OF CONTENTS

Introduction

We often hear the phrase, "*God has a plan.*" There is no question that is true, but discerning that plan, and coming to terms with "*that plan*" in our life is often very difficult. Things are not always as obvious as we would like them to be when we are in the midst of personal turmoil. Due to the mysteries of life, we don't always seem to understand what the Lord's plan actually is for us. A scripture is often recommended to people in times of stress—"*All things work together for the good of those who love God*" (Romans 8:28). Again, when a person is experiencing a difficult situation, that may bring some comfort, but answers are not always satisfactory when we have a troubled heart. Surrender to the Divine Will is the only solution as not much else makes sense. We must realize that God is in complete control and His plan for the salvation of mankind is always active.

We are watching a world in free fall morally, culturally, economically, and politically. Not just in the United States, but around the world. Man's disordered affections has created a world in "***diabolical disorientation***" as Sister Lucia of Fatima once said. Moral relativism has consumed and dominated our culture. People are confused and don't know where to turn. Little is working as designed, the safety net that used to provide some security is bursting, and the collapse of all that we have worked towards in the past is not just eroding, but so badly broken chaos is near on an unimaginable scale. We feel it in our spirits, and no matter our profession, social strata, income, education, or neighborhood, we see it in the daily news. This fear is the reason for our anxiety—and it is readily apparent. This fear is altering our lifestyle, and how we conduct our affairs. We know something is very wrong as the world is unraveling in nearly every social category.

Man has run out of answers trying to live without God, and people seem to be realizing it in greater numbers. As the babushka was asked in the Moscow streets after the October Revolution of 1917 how it all happened, her three-word response said it all, "*We forgot God.*" Our problems as a family, and a nation, are not political, they are moral. We have made bad choices that have allowed us to be in the situation we find ourselves. We have sought the answers in all of the wrong places. Since the data from just about everywhere supports this, it begs the question, "*Where are we headed? What precisely are we to do?*" The answers to those questions is not a neatly bundled package because the problems are so enormous, but we have historical and Scriptural precedents heaven takes care of their own—if we trust. This subject is a very large element of the content of this book. Heaven has given us clear prescriptions of how to live in difficult circumstances, and still maintain our composure and peace no matter the circumstances around us. Knowing and trusting in God's plan will sustain us. In the future we will either be "in or out" of the civil system. We must come to see this as a reality.

In times of stress there are only several actions to take. Retreat, take the offensive, or seek God's mind. After September 11, 2001, and the attacks on the Pentagon and the Twin Towers, people had two natural reactions. One group of people immediately tooled and prepped for war. This is what America has been doing now for many years, and in the process has been a large contributing factor to bankrupting the country and causing more problems in the world. Another group of people asked another question seldom if ever addressed in public policy circles, "*What did we do to allow this?*" This is much more of the Scriptural response, and the people who asked that question were believers. The hard question must be asked, "*Why did this happen?*" It is the Lord who puts a "*protective hedge*" when He blesses a nation due to obedience, and Scripture is clear, He also takes it down due to disobedience. But, because we are now a nation Scripturally illiterate, or see the bible as fairy tales, an unbeliever will not see this historical reality.

There are several immutable truths. God never abandons His people, and the Lord gives clear guidelines to His people. He always provides answers for His people to what ails them. As always, obedience is the key to the heart of God. To those who seek His will and trust, He gives consolation and hope. But, we cannot find the answers to those questions until we seek His ways. There is a quote from Pope Saint Felix III, "*Not to oppose error is to approve it, and not to defend truth is to suppress it, and, indeed, to neglect to confound evil men—when we can do it—is no less a sin to encourage them.*" We are in the moral quagmire we are in because we have remained silent when we needed to speak up. It is clear we have a moral obligation to speak the truth even if we are a minority. God plus one is a majority.

Because we have dug a hole so deep, heaven in their Divine Mercy will give mankind a last chance for repentance on a scale never known since the dawn of creation. The Lord told Sister Faustina we are now living in the Age of Divine Mercy. Here is the great Hope for mankind. It appears events are right around the corner that will be ultimate acts of mercy. We have been told in detail what they will be, and where they will take place. We have not been told exactly when, but we know we are getting close to that day.

This book is not the book of a political pundit just defining the problems. There is a heavy emphasis on very precise practical solutions for finding answers to achieve peace of soul in troubled times. All we need to do is stick to the fundamentals of the faith and we will be fine. No matter the circumstances for individuals and their families, heaven has given us the necessary tools we need for the journey. The solutions are not esoteric, but are very achievable as ordained by the Lord. They are tried and tested over millennia. They are eternal truths that don't budge for anyone or anything—ever.

The Lord didn't come to just define the problems of mankind, He came to redeem man and provide solutions to our fallen state, that man could live as he was destined to live under the Lord's authority, peace, and prosperity.

In all times there are people who seek the Lord, and those who don't. So from the outset in life, we have two groups of people. There are always those who seek His will, and those who are not really concerned with that thought. Good versus evil, Godly versus ungodly, Satan's cohort battling heaven's cohort. There are those in the know, and those who are not. As in the days of Noah, many will soon be pounding on doors as they did in Noah's time when it started to rain. There is still time to spiritually prepare, but for many who do not follow what the Lord is asking of them now, it will soon be too late to convert. The Blessed Mother has told us so. If the voices of the prophets are correct, there will be sea change events coming our way, and the world will be purified of its sin. We can hear the hoof beats now. Soon they will be deafening. The battle at dining room tables even by the best and most devout families and friends will be on a variety of serious subjects. There will be division. But, we have been told what to do and how to act to avoid these heated conflicts to maintain family unity and harmony. The guesswork has been eliminated if we follow His plan. We have been given a precise prescription for Peace of Soul in These Troubled Times of *The Great Transformation.*

We can expect some major events in the near future if what is prophesied comes true. There will be unprecedented acts where the Blessed Mother, the Lord's emissary for our age has said, "*it will be the greatest miracle in the history of the world,*" and she calls those now in the vineyard, "*the apostles of the last times.*" True to Scripture and tradition, there are many who know what to expect, and a deep majority who have not taken the time as it concerns the Lord's plan for the salvation of mankind. We can expect some dramatic events called *The Warning* and *The Miracle* that will alter history itself. These events have never happened in all of time and they will be spectacular. That is how great God's mercy is for all mankind. God's mercy is meeting the evil of the world on another dimension. "*Where sin abounds, grace abounds all the more*" (Romans 5:20).

These events will be the precursor to the New Jerusalem, the New Pentecost, the New Era, the Era of Peace, and the New Times that await us. Or as Saint John Paul II said, "*The New Springtime.*" All of the major apparition sites like Fatima and others speak precisely of our time being monumental.

We have been assured by the Lord Himself the gates of hell will never prevail against His Church. History has been cruel in the past and it may be cruel again. It has been our sin that has separated us from God (Isaiah 59:2), not an angry God punishing us. There are harsh repercussions to sin, the same way there are pleasant repercussions to virtuous living. It is our choice on a daily basis, and as a world we have turned our back on God. Our ease and comfort has caused a sloth of faith.

Jesus told Saint Faustina, we are living in the **Age of Divine Mercy,** and if one's sins are as scarlet, they can be washed away as white as snow with true repentance. Not one soul is beyond the Lord's mercy. As the Lord told the apostles, "*Fear not, it is I.*"

Ted Flynn
January 1, 2015
Feast of the Mother of God

one

Kingdoms In Conflict

I am the light of the world; he who follows me will not walk in darkness, but will have the light of life.

—John 8:12

When Jesus walked the earth in Israel, it was arguably the height of the power, might, and influence of the Roman Empire. Its dominance could not be challenged for any length of time by anyone. Those caught up in the wake of where Caesar wished to go and conquer, did so with little to no resistance. From the entire Mediterranean Sea to the outpost of the Roman Empire in Judea, the Romans ruled with an iron fist and those who stood in their way perished at the tip of a spear, or were soon Roman subjects on a slave ship chained to an oar.

In the western world, Rome was the first great empire. Many of the law-givers and Pharisees of Israel were expecting an earthly King to be the Messiah, as they knew the prophecies of Isaiah and others that an "*Anointed One*" was to appear from the Star in the East.

The single greatest issue for the Jews was Roman occupation and the payment of taxes. Jesus never addressed it until He was provoked into the conversation. When Jesus was asked about the payment of taxes, He gave a very simple and short response, "*Give to Caesar what is Caesar's, and give to God what is God's*" (Mark 12:17). This angered the law-givers, as they expected the Messiah to come on a white horse and free Israel as Moses had done from the years in bondage. Jesus disappointed many of the Jews as He never engaged in the political battle. His sole mission was the changing of hearts. By pouring Himself into twelve disparate personalities, and countless other ordinary souls of the time, He changed mankind forever. Jesus was perceived as a potential threat thirty years earlier, under the reign of Herod the Great. It was for this reason Herod commanded the slaughter of the innocents to take place as a safeguard that Rome not have any internal or external threats. All children under the age of two were slaughtered so Rome would not have a challenger from a God unknown to them, as they knew the prophecy in the Hebrew Scriptures of a coming Messiah. Time intersected eternity with the appearance of Jesus.

Change a heart, change a family, change a culture—one person at a time as Jesus did. That should be our model for the transformation of our culture. We have no better model than Jesus. From the time Jesus came and showed mankind a new paradigm of how to live and the meaning of life independent of foreign deities, the world went through unprecedented changes. God had become flesh and walked among us. No man ever had prophesied where He would be born and how he would die millennia in advance. No man had ever said He would rise from the dead—and then did. No grave had ever been guarded in world history for fear of a dead corpse rising. After the sign of Jonah had come to fruition, dead for three days in the belly of the earth (Matt.12: 38-4) the world had a new Savior.

The spiritual battle is two kingdoms in conflict. Jesus said, "*My kingdom is not of this world*" (John 18:36) and is clearly saying a new paradigm of love and values for how we look at life was being established. So after the death of Jesus, Christianity was in a state of constant persecution. The first thirty-three popes of the Church were martyrs. The Book of Acts is twenty-eight chapters long, and shows the violence of a new Church being born after the Holy Spirit descended at Pentecost. The change to a new paradigm of living under the new precepts of Jesus was so radical from the old established ways of the Israelites it bred violence. The old way of thinking was turned upside down and nothing would ever be the same again. All of the early popes died as martyrs, and the magenta/red vestments were a constant reminder to those who wore it of what may lie ahead, as clergy do not serve a temporal or social political power.

After Pentecost, a new church was emerging with a new agenda for living. Thousands were converted in a single day. Nothing had ever happened like this and a new experiment started for how man should live. The old way was seeing a total reformation of action for those following Jesus where Acts says, "*there was not a needy one among them*" (Acts 4:34), as the new believers shared their goods under the guidance of the apostles. As the Church moves towards greater persecution and littleness and becomes increasingly destitute, and has less of a voice in the marketplace, we will see more of this model among peoples of the world. Shared resources will be observed with greater frequency.

Persecution to Monarchy—The Existing Political and Social Power Merges and Forms a New Church

After the death of Jesus, for over the next three hundred years a battle was waged between the might of pagan Rome and the new gospel, given to the world by a simple carpenter with a message of peace, hope, love, trust, and faith. For almost four centuries before Christianity was accepted as a religion of Rome, the cities of the known world were lined with the blood of martyrs. There was great opposition from all established entities to the new way of life that was being introduced, and the new believers went into the catacombs. They did this for the freedom of worship according to the dictates of the new word of God imprinted on their hearts. A major shift in the geo political and religious landscape of the world began as a new way of living for the salvation of mankind. A New Era was emerging as Rome began to accept this new group called Christians. Saint Augustine in North Africa, and Saint Ambrose in Milan, had enormous influence in their regions.

The Edict of Milan by Constantine in the year 313, ending or at least easing the persecution of Christians, began to change Roman behavior. No immediate peace followed, but over the next several decades Christianity became more accepted by a pagan population. After Constantine allowed Christians to have more civil rights and not be under constant persecution, changes occurred. The circumstances of the acceptance of Christianity by him were as follows. After hundreds of years of blood, gore, guts, and martyrdom, a meeting took place between Constantine and Pope Miltiades. Constantine had been

Emperor of the western part of the Roman Empire, but not the eastern part. The evening before the meeting, Constantine saw a cross of Jesus upon the setting sun. Constantine said he heard an audible voice say, "*In this sign you will conquer,*" and the very next day Constantine won the Battle of Milvian Bridge, a decisive battle that solidified his sole leadership as Emperor. Constantine had become convinced he was a man of destiny.

In what is the defining moment for the next 1,600 years, an agreement was struck that aligned the new church structures to the Roman Empire so that this new religion called Christianity could spread without persecution. Popes would now be called the successor to Peter. With elevated temporal status came the trappings of Church, palaces, wealth, official responsibility and influence. Peter and the Apostles made Sunday a day of worship and a public holiday to honor the day Jesus was resurrected, and Constantine complied. Laws were instituted against the mistreatment of Christians, and crucifixions as a capital crime were forbidden. Many call the Edict of Constantine/Milan, the end of true Christianity as the persecuted church gained acceptance.

To bring order, control, and governance under the mantle of Christianity, the bishops and leaders of the Christian Church became the rulers of civil and ecclesiastical authority, with the new pope as the head. Popes and Church authorities had tried and failed to take control of a new kingdom that extended to the new capital of Constantinople, which was the catalyst for the separation of the Church in the East and the West. This merging of a political temporal power had economic consequences and ramifications. Thus, this model that Constantine laid out was the umbrella under which the Roman Catholic Church has governed. In the last several decades, we have seen dramatic changes to that model.

Even as bishops became involved in political matters, the Emperor involved himself in religious affairs—most notably in response to the heresy of Arianism, which denied the divinity of Christ. Realizing that this new and unorthodox teaching had the potential to rend the unity of the Church (an thereby undermine the political unity of the Empire), Constantine usurped the authority of the Pope by himself convening a Church council at the eastern city of Nicea in 325. With the Emperor in attendance, the assembled bishops formally condemned Arianism as heretical (though it would be many decades before the heresy finally disappeared), while formulating the statement of faith known to us today as the Nicene Creed.

The Monarchy Solidifies

Constantine chose a strategic piece of real estate where East meets West called Byzantium, located on the Bosporus Straits in what is now the bridge separating Asia Minor from Europe, for the church in the East. Turkey is on one side and Greece on the other, and a narrow waterway straight into what was Kiev Rus, much later to become Russia and the former Soviet Republics following the breakup of the U.S.S.R. In 381 another Ecumenical Council met, and from that meeting came famous Canon III which said, "*the Bishop of Constantinople shall have precedence in honor after the Bishop of Rome because Constantinople is the New Rome.*" The Bishop of Rome, Damasus I, never accepted any notion of being a subservient authority, and the split of Eastern and Western authority and rubrics which has ever since divided the two. The Patriarch of Constantinople governed through his collegial Patriarchs. When Charlemagne was near the height of his power in 800 AD, he proposed to Pope Leo III that he link the temporal power of the Emperor to that of the spiritual authority of the Pope, thereby solidifying the concept of monarchy. It is for this reason that monarchy emerged from the bishops in political, economic, and social matters.

Under Constantine the die had been cast. The Church became a monarchy. For over 1,600 years since the Church's early roots in the structure of Constantine it became a more formidable force under the formation of the Holy Roman and Apostolic Church. Under the leadership of Charlemagne, a new era or epoch in the Church was cemented. The consequence of these historical developments has defined the modus operandi of the Church up to the 21st Century.

Many hundreds of thousands of volumes have been written over the millennia about these historic developments. History is written through the eyes of the victor and there are many differing opinions as to how God would have ordained his earthly temporal Church to be formed and governed. In the Old Testament, the Lord set up a ruling body to help Moses guide the twelve tribes through the desert, even making sure the arms of Moses were raised in praise during battle so the Israelites could conquer in their wars. A leadership council emerged. The Sanhedrin emerged for the Jews; a Magisterium so to speak. The fact is, large entities need temporal government, which will always be inadequate when viewed against the purity of the gospel of Jesus. Detractors of the Roman Church point to these foibles of men and see a flawed institution and leave it. Martin Luther, Hus, and Calvin to mention a few, led the charge away from the Magisterium and believed they "reformed" the Church. It was men like Saint(s) Francis of Assisi, Vincent Ferrer, Dominic and Ignatius of Loyola who saw the mistakes of the fallen nature of man and their institutions, but worked within the existing Church structure to reform it. They decided to rebuild the Church from within, thus not allowing an internal fracture to ensue with all the negative elements that would pose. All of the Protestant offshoots have suffered from the same mistakes as the Catholic Church due to original sin and human weakness. The trappings of power and prestige are simply part of the formulae of men as institutions grow. It will never be any different as strong personalities fight for a political and ideological direction.

In recent times there has been a gradual rejection by some of the concept of the Pope as monarch. When John Paul I was elected on August 26, 1978, he gently pushed aside the tiara of Prince of the Church, but accepted the pallium. Saint John Paul II and Benedict XVI did the same. As Pope Francis stood on the balcony after the white smoke went up the chimney and the words *Habemus Papam* (we have a pope) were voiced on March 13, 2013, he appeared in just simple white vestments without any of the trappings of the more formal regalia of previous popes. He was sending a strong message from the outset that his pontificate would be different and would not have any of the regal formalities. In the Fall of 2013, Francis sent the message that the role of the pope "*was not that of a courtly prince.*" Approximately two weeks later at a formal concert where he would have sat in his honored chair with those sitting around him like court jesters, he was a no show. It was a new epoch, as the new Pontiff was sending a loud message that things would be different as Francis refused to live in the Papal Palace as previous popes. It was then reported in the early winter of 2013 that he had told many of the Vatican insiders they needed to go find a job and do something constructive rather than hang around the Vatican all day. Under Francis, a radical shift has taken place back to the local bishop and away from Rome much to the chagrin of those who prefer the Papal Monarchy of old. The ideological issue at the root of discussions is Monarchy versus the collegiality of "local rule." Governance from the center in Rome or from the local bishops is the issue. Many on the right prefer the Monarchy, and the left or progressives prefer the local level for church administration. Therein lies the primary difference of discussions about the direction of the Church at tables around the world.

When Honduran Cardinal Oscar Rodriquez Maradiaga of Tegucigalpa was being interviewed by Germany's Cologne's Kolner Stadt-Anzeiger he said,

> *"I am firmly convinced we are at the dawn of a new era in the Church, just as when Pope John XXIII opened its windows 50 years ago and let in fresh air. Francis wants to lead the Church in the same direction that he himself is moved by the Holy Spirit. This means closer to the people, not enthroned above them, but alive in them. Above all, a simpler life and leadership, from priests and bishops in line with the sometimes forgotten message of Jesus. Not sitting in our administrative offices and waiting for people to come."*

The Cardinal is head of the Council to advise Pope Francis on the reform of Church governance and reform of the Curia. The Cardinal went on to say that, "*the Pope's priority was that the Church should reach the common people, and show compassion through a different kind of care for the world, especially the needy.*"

For the time being, we see regal trappings of the institution taking a different direction from the historical type monarchy. Time will tell, but heaven is clear, changes are coming to all institutions of the world,—civil and ecclesiastical—and they are coming fast.

The Heart of the Matter: How the Papacy is Viewed

The discussion of how a Pontiff is to act, his tasks, his administration is an issue at the very heart of the Church. To those centered more on the right, it is viewed more in its magisterial power and might. This group sees the regal dominance of the papacy with a strong voice of authority in the world that should not tolerate anything to do with a more liberal agenda of collegiality and inclusive nature of issues which they consider to be heretical. Anything that leans away from this regal traditional aspect is shunned and rejected. Staying the course on matters of doctrine and what has been accepted and taught over the millennia of the Church are not to be interrupted. Anything less than that is a heresy. Many in the Church view the events of Vatican II as unacceptable or unfortunate to this day.

There are groups in the Church since Vatican II (1961-65) that believe the Seat of Peter is vacant (Sede Vacante). Although this may be the extreme on the issue of how the papacy is to be run, it is the very heart of the matter on Church authority and the response of the people. Many have a view of what they consider to be acceptable coming from Rome with their own worldview and social gospel. This issue will come to a head under Pope Francis. Especially with the more relaxed pastoral style of Pope Francis, this will drive a deep wedge with the more conservative right as they consider him to be lax in moral authority.

The left wants a more liberal church without the formal majesty, more folk music Masses, a less regal and formal structure, a more liberal view on divorced people being able to receive Communion, relaxed teachings on abortion, contraception, immigration, homosexual marriage, and women priests. They see God as accepting all people regardless of doctrine that has been taught since the formation of the early church. They believe the Church is outdated and obsolete in its present form, and presently does not meet the needs of the people. Many groups leaning left want a Church without borders and less of a regal structure. This more socially liberal gospel can find its roots in the Age of the Enlightenment of France and Western Europe, prior to the time of the French Revolution (1789) and beyond. The left wishes to do away with the official trappings of the Church and Peter's supremacy, while the right prefers the structure of monarchy and centralized control.

Who will win the short to medium term battle is unknown. However, with large governments and financed entities that are well organized continually chipping away at Church authority, the left is presently winning the battle. The decibel level of rhetoric rises when matters are brought up in the public square or the dining room table among friends and family concerning the direction of the Church, and what they think of any pontiff holding the Petrine Keys. Many may not be able to articulate the issues, but most people have an opinion where they want the Church to go.

Bishop Joseph Ratzinger in 1969 voiced an opinion where he saw the Church headed. It may have been a prophecy, prediction, or just insight based upon his knowledge of history. Nonetheless, here is what he said in 1969 four years after the final session of the Second Vatican Council:

> *"The Church will be restructured with far fewer members that is forced to let go of many of the places of worship it worked so hard to build over the centuries. A minority Catholic Church with little influence over political decisions, that is socially irrelevant, left humiliated and forced to start over. A Church more simple, and more spiritual." Bishop Ratzinger said he was convinced the Church was going through an era similar to the Enlightenment and the French Revolution. "We are at a huge turning point in the evolution of mankind. This moment makes the move from the Medieval to modern times seem insignificant." Professor Ratzinger compared the current era to that of Pope Pius VI who was abducted by troops of the French Revolution and died in prison in 1799. The Church was fighting against a force which intended to annihilate it definitively, confiscating its property, and dissolving religious orders.*
>
> *Today's Church could be faced with a similar situation, undermined by the temptation to reduce priests to* "social workers" *and it and all its work reduced to a mere political presence. From today crisis will emerge a Church that has lost a great deal.*
>
> *It will become small and will have to start pretty much all over again. It will no longer have use of the structures it built in its years of prosperity. The reduction in the number of faithful will lead to its losing an important part of its social privileges. It will start off with small groups and*

movements and a minority that will make faith central to experience again. It will be a more spiritual Church, and will not claim a political mandate flirting with the right one minute, and the left the next. It will be poor and will be the Church of the destitute."

One must remember that this was said when Father Ratzinger was an esteemed and respected professor of theology in Regensburg, Germany. He then went onto become Archbishop of Munich and Freising, Germany from 1977-1982 when appointed a Cardinal in 1977 by Pope Paul VI, and then head of the Congregation for the Doctrine of the Faith (CDF) under John Paul II, and then onto Dean of the College of Cardinals from 2002-2005 before becoming Pope Benedict XVI. He was pope from 2005 to his unexpected resignation in 2013. This is no small thing to say about the future direction of the Church by a man of Benedict's stature, and a Church that he was such an intimate part of his whole life. Benedict XVI is regarded as one of the greatest theologians of the Catholic Church in its history. The ramifications of his views have enormous implications for today and the direction of the church. In many alleged messages to mystics, the Blessed Mother has said that the Church would go through a tremendous trial and an ultimate outcome similar to what Bishop Ratzinger said in 1969. If Saint John Paul II spoke of a New Springtime coming to humanity, it indicates a major change is coming to the world and the Church.

Cardinal Karol Wojtyla (two years before becoming Pope John Paul II) said at the Eucharistic Congress in Philadelphia, Pa., August 3, 1976:

"We are now in the face of the greatest historical confrontation humanity has gone through. I do not think that wide circles of the American society or wide circles of the Christian Community realize this fully. We are now facing the final confrontation between the Church and the anti-Church, of the Gospel versus the anti-Gospel. This confrontation lies within the plans of Divine Providence; it is a trial which the whole Church, and the Polish Church in particular, must take up. It is a trail of not only our nation and the Church, but in a sense of 2,000 years of culture and Christian civilization,

> *with all of its consequences for human dignity, individual rights, human rights and the rights of nations."*

Due to the general instability in society with so many people dependent on government largesse to some extent, people will welcome a savior who they will look to solve their problems. Venerable Fulton Sheen gives what he thinks will be the type of ruler we may accept willingly:

"The false prophet will have a religion without a cross. A religion without a world to come. A religion to destroy religions. There will be a counterfeit church. Christ's Church (the Catholic Church) will be one, and the false prophet will create the other. The false church will be worldly, ecumenical, and global. It will be a loose federation of churches forming some type of global association. A world parliament of churches that will be emptied of all divine content and will be the mystical body of the Antichrist. The mystical body on earth today will have its Judas Iscariot and he will be the false prophet. Satan will recruit him from among our Bishops."

Persecution and the Church

Father Joseph Esper is a leading Catholic writer who understands the seriousness of our times and is articulate about the reality facing mankind. He writes of the stages leading to religious persecution:

> *"Persecutions, whether of religious, political or ethnic groups, generally unfold in five stages. First, the targeted group is stereotyped or stigmatized, making it an easier victim of bigotry, slander, or abuse. Secondly, the group is marginalized, or pushed to the fringes of society, so as to reduce its moral authority and influence, while emphasizing its member's differences from everyone else. Thirdly, the group is vilified, or viciously attacked and blamed for society's problems and accused of having a secret and sinister agenda. In the fourth stage, the group is criminalized by means of legal restrictions upon its membership and activities. The final stage is one of outright persecution, in which members of the group are subject to varying degrees of discrimination, repression, or imprisonment—and sometimes even harsher and more permanent measures. Many commentators claim America is in stage three of this process, and rapidly moving*

> *into stage four—and there is mounting evidence to support this assertion."*

To go into stage four or even five could happen with one significant event, and indeed happen very fast. We could see civil unrest escalating at a rapid pace bringing martial law. At that point anything is possible when people don't go along with the agenda demanded by the state. A public health hazard or virulent virus of some sort would be a good guess.

As the state becomes more dominant in virtually every area of life, martial law at some point is inevitable. The believer will be forced to comply to obtain goods and services, and a decision will need to be made, whom do you Trust—Caesar or God? This has led Cardinal Francis George of Chicago to say, *"I will die in my bed. My successor will die in prison, and his successor will die a martyr in the public square.*" As governments move to state supremacy over individual rights around the world, the war on Christianity will intensify.

Those thinking the days of comfortable and socially acceptable Christianity will continue are sorely mistaken. Throughout the world persecution of believers is taking place. There will be pain and costs to be a disciple. The esteemed German theologian Dietrich Bonhoeffer in his book The Cost of Discipleship, said in the very first line of the book, *"When Christ calls a man to Him, He bids him to come and die.*"

Through Scripture we know the voice of the prophets is lonely and often difficult. We will show in this book many examples of that dynamic. The prophet Jeremiah is just one who reflects the emotion of proclaiming the truth amidst the majority of the people who refuse to listen. He laments his calling when he writes, *"O Lord, thou hast deceived me, and I was deceived; thou art stronger than I, and thou hast prevailed. I have become a laughingstock all the day; everyone mocks me. For whenever I speak, I cry out, I shout, 'Violence and destruction!' For the word of the Lord has become for me a reproach and derision all day long. If I say, 'I will not mention Him, or speak anymore in His name,' there is in my heart as it were a burning fire shut up in my bones, and I am weary of holding it in, and I cannot*" (Jeremiah 20:7-9).

Here is a major prophet in time of doubt, stress and marginalization, wondering if God is near. We too, often feel this same emotion due to the circumstances around us. Know this, historically, you are in good company, and the emotion is a natural one. But, as Jeremiah, we cannot turn away from the calling to proclaim the truth no matter the pressure around us.

One can tell if there is fear in the air by what people will not talk about. Until just recently, people chose to stay away from "politically incorrect" topics while in social gatherings. Today, that has escalated to outright fear, as people are staying distant from subjects that could make them an enemy of the state or something that can cost them their job. From here forward there will be a cost for your views if you choose to be a critic of tyranny and the anti-God agenda of the state. To be a witness for Jesus Christ in the marketplace will place a bulls-eye on your back, and there will be a cost to pay in the form of lost opportunities in personal advancement. Due to ungodly policies in many places of business, finance, culture and areas of interest for the individual, opportunities for personal success will be inconsistent with the gospel message. Personal advancement will be blocked if a person following the Lord will not go along in many jobs due to what employers are asking. It has always been so in history because it is the believer who is the light of the world speaking out against injustice. As Solomon said, *"Nothing new is under the sun"* (Ecclesiastes 1:9).

Supreme Court Justice Antonin Scalia, speaking to law students at the University of Hawaii on February 3, 2014, said, *"Don't fool yourself into believing that the Supreme Court will never again allow a wartime violation of civil rights like it did allowing internment camps for Japanese Americans during World II."* This is an incredibly loaded statement from the Senior Associate Justice and longest serving member currently (since 1986) on the U.S. Supreme Court. Why would he bring this up? How much of what he said is code for those who have ears to hear? He used a Latin phrase for the events of interment that translated into English, *"In times of war, the laws fall silent."*

Then the peace of God that surpasses all understanding will guard your hearts and minds in Christ Jesus.

—Philippians 4:7

JESUS, I TRUST IN YOU

two

The Stages Of the Decline Of Church and State

In those days, like a fire there appeared the prophet Elijah whose words were as a flaming furnace.

—Sirach 48:1

People today are constantly bombarded with sports and media entertainment which has successfully driven God from the market place. This state of affairs has now been steadily growing for nearly three generations. There is an inordinate emphasis on the physical side of preparation in life, but not the spiritual. We buy gym memberships, new clothes and luxuries, we travel, and pamper the flesh to no end decade after decade, but when it comes to spending a Holy Hour in church for Eucharistic Adoration, few can say they have ever done it. When upheaval and societal collapse come, those who have not been in spiritual formation will crumble in an instant, while looking in vain for human solutions. They will not have seen what God has been doing with His plan for the salvation of the world because they were never properly formed in the faith. We should know this, "*the Lord is in total control.*" It won't take much now to tip the world over the edge as the world is so interconnected.

At the World Economic Forum (WEF) at Davos, Switzerland in 2014, the general theme was the world is going through seismic changes that will have profound ramifications for generations to come. When the global elite gather in private in secret observing the Chatham Rules (not divulging who was there or what was said), to discuss world global policy, you can be assured they have an agenda to perpetuate their financial and political empires. To think otherwise is to be naïve about human nature and political philosophy. Such groups like the Bilderbergers have been meeting in private since the early 1950's, and they now explicitly recognize the world is at a unique juncture with the present confluence of events. The state of the world is like a giant termite infestation that has been festering for generations. It won't take much to have the rotted beams just come tumbling down in an instant as the generational rot is so great.

A seasoned Ob-Gyn doctor will tell you that when a woman's womb becomes toxic, the doctor must remove the baby. If the baby stays in the toxic womb, the baby will die. There comes a time in the birthing process when the doctor takes charge to save the baby, which at that time will usually be an emergency C-section. We are going through events similar to a birthing process that will bring forth a New Era of Peace. A mother will not let her child be in danger, and heaven at some point in the near future is going to say, "e*nough is enough,*" as in the times of Noah, Sodom and Gomorrah, Ezekiel, Moses, Jonah, and many others. As the birth pangs increase in severity and intensity, the baby is crying forth to be removed. Our world is groaning with labor pains and the hour is late. Even the earth itself is in revolt due to man's sin. It is the dawn of a new day.

The Blessed Mother and the mercy of heaven are about to shower the world with grace to save mankind lest we all be lost. No mother will allow her children to be harmed if she can help it. This is exactly what the Blessed Mother and heaven are saying as we approach THEIR agenda of going toe to toe with the evil one for the soul of mankind. Heaven has their cohort and the devil has his cohort—and that is the battle. Most people will be caught unaware and unprepared. As you walk away from the Son (sun), your shadow lengthens. There will be pain for all in the process, but after the birth of a new child, all pain will be forgotten.

The American Empire is coming to an end. We are witnessing in real time, the death of a nation. We chose materialism over following God and are now paying the price. We chose the easy way and will have to fight like never before to preserve the freedoms that have been recently lost. There will be bloodshed over this issue at some point. What will trigger the chaos no one knows for sure, but it is coming. Popular guesses are currency devaluation, another major war spreading our troops thinner than we've seen already, a nuclear device of some sort, extreme weather, an electromagnetic pulse (EMP), and anything of another hundred possibilities. A revolution is brewing as the strong arm of reckless tyrannical government is suppressing people to where they feel they will have no alternative but to fight. When government takes away the right for a family to provide for themself, that is when the violence will start. As Thomas Jefferson said, "*When the government fears the people that is democracy. When the people fear the government, that is tyranny.*"

Confluence of Events Around Us

As we look around we see the rapid deterioration of western civilization in real time. Sister Lucy of Fatima said the times in which we live are of "***diabolical disorientation.***" If there was ever a loaded phrase, that lets us know in the clearest possible terms that something is not right in the world, this is it. If there ever was a term that lets us know why we have a troubled spirit as we lay our head on the pillow at night, and offend God with little remorse as a nation, this is it. *Diabolical disorientation!* First, it is Satan himself who orchestrates the onslaught on a daily basis. Here lies the reason for our uneasiness in our spirit. It is an epic battle over every last soul.

No nation can defy natural and God-given laws for an extended period of time before it is judged harshly. The entire history of the Hebrews as God's chosen people with a covenant is one where Israel as a people experiences God's faithfulness. When they drifted from the standards He gave them, they were dealt with harshly. At first it may have been a warning, then a stronger admonition, then a more direct command because of disobedience, then outright admonishment through an enemy victory and other means to bring them into submission to His laws again. It is a general theme of the entire Old Testament between the Lord and His chosen people. God is a God of love with no evil in Him. We bring judgment upon ourselves through our sin and that in turn passes through the permissive will of the Father. The issue is of countless conversations, "*is God a God of wrath*" who gets angry and punishes us? The answer to that question is emphatically no, He is not. We allow His judgment through our disobedience and sin, and then this gives Satan room to take control as we are not under the mantle of God's protection.

Sins That Lead to Captivity

There are sins that lead to captivity as we see in the times of Daniel, Jeremiah, and innumerable stories of Scripture. One can nearly indiscriminately just open the Bible and see these themes chapter after chapter, book after book. Sin has repercussions. The sins that led to Israel's captivity were:

1. Idolatry
2. Rampant Immorality
3. Child Sacrifice

If the people do not heed the voice of God against sin, then the Lord gives His people a Divine reprimand. Idolatry is putting anything ahead of worshipping God alone. Any false idol like sports or anything that consumes your time away from the most important aspects of what God desires in our life is idolatry. However, an idol to one is not necessarily an idol to another.

We see the rampant immorality of Sodom and Gomorrah where fire rained down from heaven upon the people. Their sinfulness was so great the cities were destroyed. One would have to be living a very isolated life not to observe the gradual decay of our culture through accepted immorality, and fail to see what it has done to the basis of all civilization—the family.

Then there are the means of captivity. They are:

1. Capture from an outside enemy
2. Moral decay from within
3. Weather to get the attention of His people
4. The Lord gives Israel a bad king, or in other words bad leadership

Little explanation is necessary on the above points. We see them every time we turn on the television, step outside the safety of our home, go to work, and venture on trips. Add the above with the chapter in this book on the *Judgment of Nations and the United States* called *The Blessings and the Cursing of a Nation,* and you can be the judge where America and the world are headed. It is God's point of view in Holy Scripture. To those who say that is an Old Testament God who no longer exists, should be reminded, "*God is the same yesterday, today, and forever*" (Hebrews 13:8).

The Lord is in control and He will use any means necessary to get the attention of His people. It is the love of God where He brings His people back to Him through any means. We are experiencing a merciful chastisement, and it is not just America undergoing hardship, but the entire world. Famines, conflicts and fratricidal wars are occurring all over the world, not just America. We must look at the bigger perspective to see what God is doing.

All of us fall short of the glory of God, but some look to hear His voice and abide by His commands. It was the Irish writer Oscar Wilde who said, "*All of us are in the gutter, but some of us are looking at the stars.*" Yes, we are all sinners, but some recognize the Supremacy and Divinity of God.

Staying the Course

David Stockman, former Congressman, head of the Office of Management and Budget (OMB) under President Ronald Reagan, and investment banker for nearly thirty years, is speaking out about the complete dislocation and the soon to collapse institutional banking world. He said in 2014 the derivative bubble of unfunded liabilities and debt is over $500 trillion worldwide. The Bank of International Settlements (BIS) in Basel, Switzerland put the derivative bubble at over $700 trillion. This number is incomprehensible. No one can accurately point to who is really liable for the debt due to computer-traded transactions and the amount of derivatives. To put that number in perspective, it means it is the end of the world as we financially know it. It is a train wreck in the making. The coming financial collapse will be something completely unknown and it will not be friendly. We are in uncharted waters. When the system crashes, nothing will be the same ever again. There will be no alternative but a one-world government and one world financial system because the world is so interconnected and joined at the hip. Debt has been trading freely via the internet recklessly for the last fifteen plus years. What is even more fascinating is that the most senior investment people in the world over the last few years are increasingly speaking in language that is not usual business protocol and etiquette. They are now speaking about a total financial apocalypse. Due to the enormity of data supporting their claims that something terrible is about to happen, more senior investment professionals are speaking out about the existing financial system's inability to survive much longer.

Traditionally, rattling the markets is not good for business, and spooking your client base is not good for any brokerage house. The people in the financial system pretend that all is fine for people to invest. Most large institutional banks lie about the truth from the opening of the bell to close— from sun up to sun down. As long as the status quo is maintained, people hope things will be fine. Recently, an increasing number of the most sophisticated people in the banking and the investment world are saying that the present system cannot last. With the very fabric of society unraveling in so many areas, things will not continue with the cliché, business as usual.

> *The premise of this entire book is that life won't continue as it now is and the Lord is using societal and economic breakdown of our world to break the will of a very stiff necked sinful world into submission to His will. He will use all means possible to get man's attention.*

Those people who already understand and accept, even welcome what the Lord is doing, will have an easier time than those who are young in the faith or without any strong spiritual practices. The Lord is allowing these calamities due to our collective sin and the lack of virtue among us. As a world we are far removed from truth emotionally, intellectually, financially, and spiritually. Before something new is introduced, the existing structures will collapse.

Plagues

The Blessed Mother has said to the Marian Movement of Priests that AIDS is the angel of the first plague, and what Revelation 16:2 refers to. She says, "*So the first angel went and poured his bowl on the earth, and foul and evil sores came upon the men who bore the mark of the beast and worshipped its image.*" Our Lady explained to the Marian Movement of Priests, "*AIDS results from impure acts against nature itself*" (#402).

The last two plagues on mankind described in book of Revelation are homosexuality and drugs, and the openly stated goals of global government are to promote immoral behavior, including homosexuality and drug abuse. What is most disconcerting is that many believers do not understand the nature of evil. First, evil never sleeps and has the sole goal of destroying mankind. Second, the Church must always be militant, never ceasing to speak the truth. For the most part, believers are woefully naïve about how evil operates. As God operates through chosen souls and the Church for His purpose, evil has the same structure. Satan has chosen souls and organizations where he seeks to destroy heaven's agenda. There are organizations like the Bilderbergers, secret societies of all kinds, ungodly people, foundations, and entities of all sorts like Planned Parenthood seeking to kill, destroy, and steal with an anti-God agenda. These organizations are organized and highly financed. In May of 2014 financier Warren Buffet made a donation of $1.2 billion dollars to pro-abortion organizations. A billion dollars will buy a lot of votes in Congress. There are one thousand two hundred millions in $1.2 billion. We can see why so many political and social policies have decimated our way of life with that kind of money going to ungodly candidates.

The term "*Church Militant*" is not a negative or aggressive phrase. It is a phrase that is specific to a Church that cannot rest and expect the truth to be spread unless it teaches the faith. Each generation must be taught the faith to maintain the culture of a Christian family so it can be preserved. Light has no association with the darkness. You are either hot or cold and cannot be lukewarm in your faith. As a result of the slumber and sloth of the Church leadership, we see so many blank faces in the pew.

Civil law is the foundation of civilization, as natural law is founded on nature. In the last several generations, civil and natural law have been progressively violated and corruption has become rampant. Because law is broken, Satan is closer to accomplishing his goal through his cohort of a one world currency, a one world financial system, a one world government, and a one world religion. Godless governments do brutal things. The Lord instituted diverse and sovereign governments as a means to prevent one government from overtaking and dominating the other. The existing trend in government will be one strong single body dictating public policy for all peoples of the world with global dictatorship. It will be precipitated and then justified by ever greater crisis and natural disasters.

The Four Stages in the Decline of the Church

Confusion

Confusion is seen everywhere one looks. Catholic colleges promoting a homosexual agenda, grade school children taught sin is permissible, leading clergyman are silent on important issues, and heinous pagan practices unthinkable years ago are now aggressively taught. Programs are openly being promoted by school administrators corrupting youth with outright immorality in schools to lower grades each passing year. Schools openly promoting acceptance of homosexual lifestyles in grade schools is the norm in many states. The onslaught continues to bombard our families to a point where believers are overwhelmed by it. It is for this reason we see so much cynicism with people tired from the assault. People no longer know where to go for sound doctrine and many have quit being involved in the fight due to fatigue. After being deluged with so much information day after day, our senses are overloaded. The Church is walking Calvary and the time of purification is here. The Word of God is being questioned, and sacred doctrines are challenged that have stood the test of time for nearly 2,000 years. Spiritual mysteries that will never be fully understood are now inaccurately being explained beyond all logic and reason. It will be through humility and trust that heaven will grant us the full and entire truth of the plan for the salvation of mankind in due time. Error has crept into every area of the Church. Discord reigns nearly everywhere. We see the fulfillment of the Blessed Mother's messages at the apparition of LaSalette, France in 1846 that said: "*Cardinal against Cardinal, Bishop against Bishop, priest against priest, and confrere against confrere.*" Darkness has penetrated to the very summit of the Church and contributed to much of humanity being in a confused state. With the faith of the Patriarchs, Fathers of the Church, and Saints who came before us, we are asked to live in humility, docility, truth, prayer and quiet preparation for the Son's return in Glory.

Lack of Discipline and Apostasy

People now flock in great numbers to places where eternal truths are openly questioned. In no place is this more obvious than the university. Right is wrong, and wrong is right. Virtue is openly mocked. People do not make an outcry when Notre Dame University (we forget the name means Our Lady in French) gives an Honorary Doctorate (2009) to President Barack Obama, the most openly hostile and pro-abortion president in U.S. history. Fancies of the day prevail over rational and logical thought everywhere we turn. Obedience to the eternal truths of the Magisterium is often scoffed at by some clergy who lack the fortitude to direct the flock because they have submitted to the whims and cultural norms of the day. The desire to be inclusive without obedience to the Church is false ecumenism. As a result of the lack of a strong gospel being taught, we see relativism accepted as a more normal trend. There is a fear of "offending" someone if one speaks the truth, especially on morality. Many clergy and laity alike are fearful about giving strong admonitions on moral issues. Christians and especially the youth are wandering around in a moral vacuum taking the position of the secularist rather than the view of the gospel. Politically correct language over the last generation has become the gospel for many. Jesus said there was only one way when Thomas asked, "*Lord, we do not know where you are going; how can we know the way?*" Jesus said to him, "*I am the way, and the truth, and the life; no one comes to the Father but by Me*" (John 14:5-6). He said, *The Way, The Truth, and The Life.* There is no other way to the Father but Jesus Christ.

All around us is the rise and constant bombardment of social media. If you are anything short of a hermit, it cannot be avoided. By and large the youth today are not attending church on a regular basis—if at all. Facebook and other forms of social media supplant what church used to be for people of all ages. In the past it was the parish that provided fellowship, interaction, meetings, activities, inspirational guest speakers, sports, camping trips, day trips, volunteering, and generally a wholesome atmosphere meeting new friends and having fun while learning your faith. Facebook and other forms of social media is now the equivalent of church. Sin is not recognized, so youth don't even know where to turn for solutions to cravings that emanate from the depth of their soul. Over time as more people in the materially advanced nations have ceased even going to Church, or recast as merely social or cultural value, the spiritual void has grown. The odd thing is, when the truth is delivered in love and humility from the pulpit, people will journey great distances to hear it. It has the opposite impact one would expect. In strength of truth the people flourish and order is maintained.

Many people today have become their own master with no beacon of light pointing north.

The apostasy of faith in the Unites States has caused an enormous shift in important data points over the last generation. Only several will be provided that were compiled by CARA Services at Georgetown University in Washington, D.C. We see why we are in this situation today because the teaching of the faith has been so watered down there is no longer any flavor to the gospel. See the below data from the years 1965 to 2014.

	1965	**2014**
Total priests	58,632	38,275
Priestly ordinations	994	494
Graduate level seminarians	8,325	3,631
Religious brothers	12,271	4,318
Parishes without a resident pastor	549	3,496
Active diocesan priests per parish	2.0	1.0
Religious sisters	179,954	49,883
Catholic elementary schools	10,667	5,399
Marriages in previous year	352,458	154,450
Mass attendance	55%	24%
Catholic hospitals	800	549

Extrapolate this data out another generation with youth today having virtually no formation or very limited development in the faith, and you have a far larger crisis on the horizon.

Division

Pope Paul VI said, "*The smoke of Satan has entered the Sanctuary.*" We have the Word of God written on our hearts and we know truth when we hear it. Truth is indelibly written on our soul. Satan is strong at this point and is particularly aggressive against marriages and the priesthood. No one is safe from his snares and deceit. Doctrine is unclear because people don't know where to turn for truth and direction. The end result is people have tuned out leadership and hierarchy because people in the pews have turned cynical. Fear of speaking out or cynicism is the widespread public traits of many today.

A large number of people, perhaps no longer the majority, make an attempt to see the world through the gospel. However, they see their personal salvation or justification largely through a political and social agenda. This ideology of state and human rights becomes the sacred ground they walk on. Extreme environmentalism is just one expression of this thinking. It has become the driving force in their life, giving them meaning and a sense of self-worth with a place in the world. The state and its societal function has largely replaced the family dining room table as the incubator of ideas motivated no longer by what is best for the family, but the collective public good or socialist agenda. Although the term socialist may never be used, that is what it is. Seldom is socialism taught in schools using the word socialism, but its practices are openly promoted. This group usually lacks a sense of the superior "*God rights*" and His due in the equation. Government has had a diabolical and relentless organized agenda to replace the role of mother and father in the family as authority figures. This liberal group with each new social program relies more heavily on the state, with the state eclipsing the roles of religion and faith in the family to make decisions regarding human welfare. As a group they are largely intolerant of any view other than their own.

Persecution

The Blessed Mother has said to numerous mystics, "*we are apostles of the last times,*" and "*The refuge is The Sacred Heart of Jesus and my Immaculate Heart.*" We should look nowhere else for safety. All over the world today Christians are being persecuted and dying for their faith. The Church has its enemies from within and without. Satan has an agenda to dismantle the Church and eliminate the Eucharist as the "*perpetual sacrifice*" (Daniel 12:11). The Church has its betrayers and faithful servants. The Church will continue to suffer, and its faithful numbers will decrease. Those who stay faithful will struggle, but with that struggle will come purification, and in the end, the Triumph of the Immaculate Heart. But, the Lord was very clear from the outset teaching His apostles, "*the gates of hell will not prevail against it*" (Matt. 16:18).As gold is refined, residue is swept from the surface.

As it is put under heat again, another layer of dross or residue is wiped off again. This process continues until the gold is ready to be cast.

Only when the refiner can see his reflection in the gold, is it suitable to be made into a bar. It is the same with us. Only when the Lord can see his reflection in us, will we be ready to meet Him face to face. Trials bring purification. As Jesus encountered Gethsemane, we too will have our Good Friday. Good Friday precedes His glorious return of Easter Sunday. The birth pangs increase in intensity and severity near the birth of the child, and right at birth, the pain is most intense. We are at that point now, as Jesus is soon to shower graces on all mankind in unprecedented ways through what the Blessed Mother has said, "*will be the greatest miracle in the history of the world.*" What exactly that is, we don't know for sure, but she says "***the greatest.***" This trial we must endure by concentrating on the most basic elements of the faith, not looking left or right, but living a Christ centered life focused on the most essential spiritual necessities. All else must be placed aside or we will perish. It will be a difficult time, but heaven has promised the Divine Will or New Era is soon to come.

Stigmatist Therese Neumann's Prophecy and Disasters About America

German stigmatist Therese Neumann had something to say about the fate and destiny of the United States. Neumann was born in 1898 in Germany, and died in 1962. She was not persecuted during World War II, but many members of her family endured hardship, as she was vocal against the Third Reich. She had the very rare spiritual gift of inedia, where she did not need food or water to live. From 1923 to her death in 1962, she took no food or water and existed solely on the Eucharist. This is a fact substantiated and verified by countless people and news organizations over decades who investigated her life. In 1995, I interviewed an American man who lived in San Jose, CA., and had met her. He had been amongst the first GI's to liberate Germany after World War II. I had heard the stories about her, but he told me something interesting that I have watched for many years gradually come true. He said he personally asked her what was the future of America, and he was told that, "*America would be destroyed by natural disasters at the turn of the century.*" What is the turn, before or after the year 2000? If one looks at the heavy economic destruction that has happened to the United States due to natural phenomena, it begins principally with Hurricane Andrew in 1992, and goes to this very day. Each year another part of the country is devastated by some form of extreme weather costing local, state, and the federal branches of government hundreds of billions cumulatively. Fires, floods, cold, heat, mud slides, tornados, drought, hurricanes and other natural events, which have had a ripple effect through the entire economy continue to chip away at the U.S. economy. They are continual occurrences nearly everywhere in America. The end result is less economic efficiency, and government printing more money to just meet demands. This does not factor in the cost to private business, lost employee time, and the tens of thousands of personnel needed to help with search and rescue efforts, first responders, fire and police, state emergency crews, increased insurance premiums, lost business, and many costs involved in the long term totals of government and private loss. Here are just five hurricanes of multiple dozens of the natural phenomena and the estimated damage:

1. Hurricane Andrew in 1992 was the costliest hurricane in U.S. history at that time with damage estimated at $26-32 billion
2. Hurricane Katrina, 2005, $81 billion
3. Hurricane Wilma, 2005, $29 billion
4. Hurricane Ike, 2008, was over 600 miles wide and had the largest evacuation in U.S. history, a cost of $29.5 billion
5. Hurricane "Super Storm" Sandy, 2012, $65 billion

The above list includes only a few hurricanes and not the lesser ones, nor hundreds of other events costing tens of billions over the last 20 plus years. Major tornadoes in the south and Midwest, great ice storms affecting the eastern and northern U.S. and Canada, Mississippi floods, and fires all over the west and southwest U.S. must be added to this total. Tsunamis, and natural disasters of all kinds are not just in the United States, but are worldwide. There are numerous large natural disasters where the cumulative total cost far exceeds just hurricanes. The prophet Isaiah speaks of a "protective hedge" the Lord puts around a nation when it is blessed. The Lord tells Israel He is taking the protective hedge down due to sin. He says, "*Now I will tell you what I am about to do to My vineyard. I will remove its hedge, it will be consumed; I will tear down its wall, and it will be trampled*" (Isaiah 5:5). Sin has consequences. For a person not versed in Scripture it is a bizarre and foreign thought that God judges nations due to sin.

Every country of the world is undergoing birth pangs. The phenomena of the Great Transformation are happening worldwide. It is not just America experiencing this. However, we have made more bad choices than other nations because we have had free will and we have not had to exist under the duress of oppressive regimes like North Korea, China, or Russia, and other nations. We are fast moving in the direction of a planned socialist state that could bring America to martial law. Government regulations are now on the books that make us a police state with the stroke of a pen. The USA has been lulled to sleep through the bread of easy credit, and the circus of entertainment. What the East has lost through suffering and oppression, the West has lost through materialism and self-indulgence. Because the world is so collectively lost and drowning in sin, Our Lady's appearances and apparitions are a global occurrence.

Global Elites and Change

The problem with the global elites is they fight any major change in thinking coming from the grass roots. The cabal of leading bankers, policy makers, heads of Non-Governmental Organizations (NGO's) with a humanist agenda, the United Nations, bilateral organizations, and world policy makers are in a final push to remake the world without God. They are attempting to mold the future to their way of thinking. The elites need to maintain the status quo and optimism about the existing political structure, because the last thing they want is change they cannot manipulate and control. New regimes bring disruption because the old guard has the most to lose. It is for this reason revolutions begin from the ground up, not the top down. As with all other people, they too find resistance in their own ranks, and those out of step are ridiculed and isolated. Clergy are as affected by peer pressure as any other group. They also have the added dimension of a superior called a bishop. If a bishop doesn't like what the priests say, there are various means to "*bend his will*" if he does speak out not in accordance with the bishop's agenda.

The Bachelor—A Barometer

If one wants to gauge the shallowness of our culture, and take a good look at our pagan society masquerading as elegant sophistication, one need to look no further than a popular program on prime time network TV. It is a program called "*The Bachelor.*" It now has a female component that came on stream several years after The Bachelor premiered called, "*The Bachelorette.*" This program has been on prime time for approximately fifteen years. In its simple elements it goes like this. A guy meets approximately 22-28 gorgeous young women. They dress up as fancy as possible to impress the bachelor with the hope they are given a proposal for marriage. That's what the show is about. Marriages have taken place amongst participants. There is no question there is scripted staging going on, as this is entertainment with sponsors paying only if there are viewers, but some of it is very real. As the man and the woman spend time together, emotional attachment grows. If a woman is not given a rose, they go home. Some go tearfully, somewhat angry, or disappointed. As the show progresses with just 6-8 women, the cat fights begin. Some of the women really want a proposal to marry. Meanwhile the bachelor is kissing all the other women in view of the other contestants still remaining. They try to put themselves in position to curry favor. TV drama entertainment to some extent yes, but emotional bonding is definitely is taking place as the weeks progress.

There is entertainment at the most plush settings on the planet designed to be romantic. Boats, candles, exquisite food, dining, planes, helicopter rides, water sports, palatial settings, international cuisine and travel, beaches, and all the trappings of the romantic. Each passing week a woman is sent home if the bachelor finds no chemistry. As things move along and the field narrows, the couples decide if they want to get "intimate" to determine compatibility in the Fantasy Suite. Some of the women participate, some do not. From that point forward, no cameras are allowed and the couples behave as they choose. The show makes it clear that the Fantasy Suite is an option.

What is most striking is that this represents what many people in America really think constitutes a marriage courtship. Another mind numbing observation is how many of the women think that they are actually falling in love and vice versa, as they both sit together on some exotic beach resort in the middle of the Pacific Ocean or some Caribbean island paradise. Some of these women actually believe they love the guy after having a dinner, as the white spray of the surf hits the rocks twenty-five yards away. Many women lose it emotionally and break down if they are not given a rose by "The Bachelor." Some go into an emotional meltdown.

If anyone wonders why the divorce rate is so high, look no further than what the media thrusts into our homes under the aura of reality. The show is just one of a multitude of cultural barometers of how degenerate the United States has become in the last generation. What is designed by God to be a monogamous sacramental union has been reduced to trite games and entertainment for so many. Nothing could be further from the truth as God ordains a marriage based upon Biblical principles. Year after year we become increasingly numb to the media and its immoral agenda. In May of 2014, the homosexual community called for a network to air the *Gay Bachelor*, saying it is a double standard to not have one, as they said, "*it is about damn time to do it.*"

A Drug Culture of All Ages

Due to our abysmal disregard for sin in today's culture, few even recognize the signs that our nation and so many others like it are suffering under divine judgment. In the days of Noah, people were making merry, divorcing, and remarrying before the flood. The similarities in Scripture to the time of Noah, and the times today, are striking. The historian will often view events solely through the eyes that history repeats itself, and goes in cycles. This is true that history is a constant rhythm of cycles. Nations rise and nations fall. What this group fails to recognize is that it is not just a normal cycle operating in a vacuum. It is God amidst this cycle who raises up a nation because of His blessings due to the virtue of His people, and brings it down by withdrawing His protection due to sin. It is the blessings of God which bring forth fruit to a nation.

No matter where we turn, we see drugs of some sort. A generation ago school grounds were relatively safe from drugs; now school is the primary portal to gateways drugs. The Greek word for "witchcraft" is *pharmakeia*, which is where the word pharmacy originates. The more accurate word in Scripture for pharmakeia is the word "*sorcery.*" To participate in sorcery in the Old Testament was punishable by death. Centuries ago it was the pharmacist who made elixirs for licit medical reasons, and illicit means as poisons and potions. An industry emerged into what it is today is a very large business called pharmaceuticals with very positive and negative aspects. Out of this pharmaceutical industry a behemoth has been born that is nearly in outright control of medicine. There is no legislator safe from the wiles of their far-reaching tentacles of unlimited cash contributions to sway favorable legislation. "Big pharma" is merely meeting a need of America and a world that is demanding more drugs. Modern medicine has done many wonderful things for humanity and continues to do so. Drugs have their legitimate uses, but what is being discussed here is the abuse of drugs that industry knows is destructive to the body, mind, and soul of humanity that is continually thrust upon people.

If anyone doubts how drugged up and medicated America really is, look no further than the data below that was posted on the Infowars.com website. Drugs of all types for many are the attempt to fill the spiritual void in their lives. They temporarily alleviate the anxiety and what ails them through prescription and other drugs in massive quantities. We are a nation of approximately 315 million people.

- **a.** 70 million Americans are taking legal mind altering drugs.
- **b.** According to the Center for Disease Control (CDC) and Prevention, doctors wrote more than 250 million prescriptions for antidepressants in 2010.
- **c.** According to a study by the Mayo Clinic, nearly 70% of Americans are on at least one prescription drug.
- **d.** Americans spent more than $280 billion on prescription drugs in 2013.
- **e.** According to the CDC, 9 out of 10 Americans 60 years or older took at least one prescription drug within the last month.
- **f.** There are 60 million people who abuse alcohol.
- **g.** According to Health and Human Services (HHS), 22 million Americans use illegal drugs.
- **h.** More than 11% of Americans admit that they have driven home under the influence of alcohol at least once during the last year.
- **i.** According to the Center for Disease Control and Prevention, there is an unintentional drug overdose in the U.S. every 19 minutes.
- **j.** In the U.S. today prescription painkillers kill more Americans than heroin and cocaine combined.

k. According to the CDC, approximately 750,000 people a year are rushed to the emergency room due to adverse reactions to pharmaceutical drugs.

l. According to Alternet, "11 of the 12 new to market drugs approved by the Food and Drug Administration (FDA) were priced at over $100,000 per patient per year in 2012."

m. The percentage of women taking antidepressants in the U.S. is higher than any country in the world.

n. Many of these "antidepressants" contain warnings that suicidal thoughts are one of the side effects that should be expected. The suicide rate for Americans between the ages of 35-64 rose by close to 30% between 1999-2010. The number of Americans that are killed by suicide now exceeds the number of Americans that die as a result of car accidents every year.

o. In 2010, the average teen in the U.S. was taking 1.2 central nervous system drugs. Those are the kind of drugs which treat conditions such as ADHD and depression.

p. Children in the U.S. are three times more likely to be prescribed antidepressants as children in Europe.

q. The Government Accountability Office (GAO) report discovered that approximately one-third of all foster children in the U.S. are on at least one psychiatric drug.

r. A survey conducted for the National Institute on Drug Abuse found 15% of all U.S high school seniors abuse prescription drugs.

s. The eleven largest pharmaceutical drug companies combined made approximately $85 billion in profits in 2012.

In the documentary film titled, *Doctored,* by Jeff Hays, he states, "*America consumes an incredible fifty percent of Big Pharma's drugs, yet have only five percent of the world's population.*" His documentary claims drugs are meant to imprison us in poor health rather than heal us due to the profitability of the products. Seven in ten Americans are taking medications, over 100 million Americans are taking five or more prescriptions, eighty percent of people say they are affected by some sort of chronic pain, sixty million say they don't sleep well at night, and every nineteen minutes a person dies from a prescription drug overdose. April 25, 2014 the Center for Disease Control (CDC) as a part of the National Health Interview Survey said, "*7.5 percent of children ages 6-17 are being prescribed psych meds for emotional or behavioral problems.*" Research from Natural News in May of 2014 published an article saying that over the last twenty years all mass shootings have one thing in common—and it is not guns. They say overwhelming evidence points to the single largest common denominator of all mass shootings is the shooter(s) had all been taking psychotropic drugs or had been in the immediate past before they committed the crimes. Combine drugs with a high divorce rate, disenfranchised youth, loneliness, lack of purpose, and other forms of vice kids are exposed to at young ages, and you find a fuse waiting to be ignited in homes and on the streets of America.

Every doctor knows he cannot cure the ills of society, so many take the path of least resistance. Doctors will never lose their license by prescribing drugs approved by the FDA that are in line with the American Medical Association (AMA) guidelines. The medical profession is "pill happy" as it is an immediate solution as there is big money in it for everyone. There is little legal liability for a doctor prescribing medicine approved by the FDA with a seal of approval from the AMA for the above reasons. If a doctor goes outside the system there is a price to pay on several fronts, so with those options, prescriptions are written by the hundreds of millions annually. However, the doctor is not solely at fault here. It is the individual person who has abdicated personal responsibility who is most liable. Individually, we are responsible for our own health. In no way should this be misinterpreted by anyone if they are taking a good and beneficial prescription drug for a very valid reason that they are at fault in a personal way. The issue being addressed here is the abuse of drugs where a person is looking for peace of soul from an artificial substance. The more there is a neglect of God, the more the illicit drug consumption.

Harvard University and the Wharton School, the University of Pennsylvania

Just before Christmas of 2013, Harvard University released the findings of what had been a $20 million dollar undertaking for a longitudinal study on why people were happy. Harvard Business School, and the

Wharton School of Business at the University of Pennsylvania released a study saying that their graduates were successful financially, but not as human beings and wanted to know why this was the case. Their conclusions were:

1. Alcohol destroys relationships and marriages
2. People do best when they have solid relationships in their life
3. Being around people who love you and vice versa matters most in life

Again it gets back to the message of the gospel for peace of soul.

The USA is a Spent Bullet

President John Adams, one of the chief framers of the U.S. Constitution, wrote about the experiment that the United States was going through attempting to live in a democracy. He said, "*Our Constitution was made only for a moral and religious people. It is wholly inadequate to the government of any other. We have no government armed with power capable of contending with human passions unbridled by morality and religion.*" Adams is clearly saying, a nation can only attempt to have civilized self-rule if there is an authority greater than the individual through voluntary compliance with the law. In the Constitutions of all 50 U.S. states, there are references to the Almighty God of the Universe. The framers of the Constitution of the United States knew it was a strong belief in God that would make America work.

We obey the law because it is what is best for us and God asks it. Once the law breaks down, democracy ceases to work. It will take a totalitarian governmental regime to enforce a democracy out of control. That is what we are seeing evolve. We are in decline as a nation. Law on top of law is making us unable to be governed. Today our government is not working and is not accountable to its citizens because we have abandoned God, which means it has no chance of working. The wholesale breakdown in our culture is because morality and spirituality are not at the center of our laws—thus we are failing miserably.

A democracy ceases to exist when the legislators realize they can give themselves largesse from the treasury with no repercussions from the people. When law-makers continue to raid the public treasury to simply satisfy their constituents demand for free goods, it is no longer sustainable. It becomes fiscally impossible to have civil self-rule. The system will collapse. From the time of ancient Greece and her philosophers, to modern day empires, this type of behavior ensues. The USA is the twenty-third great empire in world history, and our role as world leader is coming to and end. The ancient Greeks spoke of a democracy being capable of lasting only approximately 200 years. As the United States approaches its 250th year of existence, we are beyond our allotted time.

Our country since its founding has had a run similar to those great civilizations before us. See the sequence of stages for the rise and the decline of an empire as articulated by Scottish philosopher Alexander Tyler of the University of Edinburg in 1887.

1. From bondage to spiritual growth
2. From spiritual faith to great courage
3. From courage to liberty
4. From liberty to abundance
5. From abundance to complacency
6. From complacency to apathy
7. From apathy to dependence
8. From dependence back to bondage

Tyler wrote, "A democracy is always temporary in nature; it simply cannot exist as a permanent form of government. A democracy will continue to exist up the time the voters discover that they can vote for themselves generous gifts from the public treasury. From that moment on, the majority always votes for the candidates who promise the most benefits from the public treasury, with the result that every democracy will finally collapse over loose fiscal policy, which is always followed by a dictatorship."

Depending on your vantage point, you can decide what stage we are in, but a good guess would be somewhere near complacency to apathy. Some would say dependence because the only thing propping us up at the moment is the printing of fiat money by the trillions. With millions of people on the public dole, we are on the verge of disaster. When the printing stops, it is anyone's guess where we will end up as a nation. From complacency, apathy, and dependence it can spiral down very fast. The nation that is caught up in these last stages is so out of touch with reality, it doesn't even recognize it.

The USA is Broke

Trade imbalances show how unsustainable our business practices are with just one nation—China. The Chinese, like other nations of the Middle East, and Far East have been less prone to adapt blithely the economics of John Maynard Keynes, the notion that deficit spending leads a nation to prosperity. No nation can print trillions of fiat dollars and expect to survive for very long. The destruction of the United States from within has been intentional. In 2013, the U.S. spent over $2 trillion on entitlements and benefits from the Federal Government. Just one indicator of trade with China shows the general trend. U.S. yearly trade deficits with China have been increasing enormously for the last twenty-five years. In 1990 the annual deficit was $10 billion, and by 2013 it had grown to $318 billion—a year.

The overall strategy of think tank and public policy global elites in the United States has been to manufacture a crisis to bring about change. Every great crisis will have an equal or greater reaction in social change and new policy. In 1968, American sociologists and political activists at Columbia University devised the Cloward-Piven Strategy to implement a crisis by overwhelming the U.S. Public Welfare System. This was done so government could gain control of the entire political and social welfare system through its default of financial obligations, and usher in a new aggressive socialist policy. Increase taxes and regulations of all sorts, and you only exacerbate the problem. Factor in the language engineering of social justice and equality, you have a formula few understand is the agenda of the global elites. This has been the model used to gain control. By overwhelming the system, there is a new crisis weekly that deserves attention by Congress and policymakers. However, with the constant onslaught of crisis situations thrust upon law-makers in Congress, nothing is able to get accomplished. When the problems are no longer even remotely manageable, legislation will come that will destroy our way of life and bring us to a place we have never been before. Social unrest will be the norm. Out of chaos will come a New Order—that is the agenda being deliberately and strategically implemented.

But, know this, God does not abandon His people and the woman clothed with the sun (Rev. 12) will play a key role. It is Our Lady who will end the present carnage we see going on in a mystical way the Berlin Wall and the former Soviet Empire fell without a shot being fired. In a message speaking from Slovakia to the Marian Movement of Priests titled In the Name of Mary (#456) she says,

> *"In the name of your heavenly Mother, yes, in the name of Mary, the Turks were defeated, when they laid siege to the city of Vienna and threatened to invade and destroy the whole Christian world. They were far superior in strength, in number and weapons, and they felt that their victory was assured. But I was publicly invoked and called upon; my name was inscribed upon their banners and shouted out by the soldiers, and thus through my intercession, there took place the miracle of this victory which saved the Christian world from its destruction. It is for this reason that the Pope instituted, on this day, the feast of the Name of Mary. In the name of Mary, Marxist communism, which for decades has been exercising its rule and holding so many of my poor children in oppressive and bloody slavery, has been defeated in these countries.* ***Not because of political movements or persons, but through my personal intervention, has your liberation finally come about.*** *It will again be in the name of Mary that I will bring to completion my work with the defeat of Masonry, of every diabolical force, of materialism, and of practical atheism, so that all humanity will be able to attain its encounter with the Lord and be thus purified and completely renewed, with the triumph of my Immaculate Heart in the world."*

In the beginning was the Word, the Word was with God, the Word was God.

—John 1:1

JESUS, I TRUST IN YOU

three

It's Amazing How God Agrees With Me

My people perish for lack of knowledge.

—Hosea 4:6

What are the reasons for the demise of a culture? Why do they change towards virtue or vice? Why do some societies endure for a long time while others collapse suddenly? There are many answers to these questions, but historians agree that cultures self-destruct and commit suicide. Societies decay from within morally. Wherever you go, people who say they are spiritual promote their own political and social agenda. They envision how their views should be applied socially. Was Jesus a philosopher, God, a socialist, a communist, a revolutionary, a peaceful leader, a wise man, and so on? A person will act according to how they answer that question. If one has no orientation or is hostile towards the gospel, the result is a totally secular worldview, absent of any mention or awareness of Jesus Christ and what He is asking or expecting of us.

When a government itself is openly hostile towards Christianity, good civil government becomes a casualty. There is a fierce battle to remove God from our nations classrooms and institutions. We have an openly hostile virulent group in society straining for authority in all domains against the message of the gospel. Then there are those wishing to have God placed at the forefront of the culture. Herein lies the battle. When we encounter Jesus Christ in our heart, mind, and soul, we are asked to die to self.

When a person is "*in Christ,*" as Saint Paul so often said, a deep conversion takes place and the life is reordered. When a person decides on a personal relationship with God and makes Him the center of their life, then issues are looked at differently. Life can no longer be viewed in the same way after a person makes a commitment to God. The new behavior looks at the world through spiritual eyes, and heaven's agenda is not our previous worldly way of thinking. Believers engaged in the secular order typically face an on-going struggle of "*not being able to serve two masters*" (Matt. 6:24). Due to social pressures many buckle under to the secular order and try to compartmentalize their lives and value systems. But we can't have it both ways. As the author C.S. Lewis said, "*God was either who He said He was, or He was a raging lunatic.*" To follow Him means accepting His truths and trying to keep His word above all. Life is about the choices we make.

If there is a true conversion of the heart there will be change. Ingredients of this lifestyle include fasting, Mass being the center of our life, quiet time for listening to God, prayer, Scripture reading, confession, and a life more of simplicity serving others. However, we often get in the way with our bad actions and block what God is attempting to do. If there is not a proper formation in the gospel, often a radical agenda develops taking many different avenues veering towards an overemphasis on social justice, to the neglect of the Sacramental life. There is a subtle dichotomy: God-based pursuit of social justice and equality, and godless pursuit of it, often with the latter being secular humanism. If not Christ-centered, the compassion that drives action can drift into what euphemistically could be labeled "misguided compassion." One example of this confusing hallmark of our day seen most graphically is the ideological split between the 'pro-life' and 'pro-choice camps,' both numbering professed Christians among their proponents. There is no doubt listening to Pro-death politicians and other advocates feel they are on the correct side of the gospel message being compassionate helping a woman abort.

As Israel deteriorated under the Judges, the Lord gave the answer of what went wrong with their thinking when He said, "*every man did what was right in their own eyes,*" (Judges 21:25). Saul of Tarsus thought he was doing as God asked when he was out persecuting the new Christians; as he was present at the stoning (killing) of Saint Stephen. Saul of Tarsus absolutely believed he was on the right side of the Lord's prescription of the law as he sought to persecute those who were following Jesus. Saul never thought he was doing evil or following the devil; he believed he was being righteous before God. Only when Saul was knocked off his horse and blinded, did he hear a voice asking why he was persecuting God. It was then he realized the error of his ways (Acts 9). Saul then became Paul of Tarsus, the Great Lion of God. More people need a Damascus Road experience. Jesus said, "*if you love Me, keep My commandments*" (John 14:15). The hallmark of a believer is "*keeping His commandments.*" Those who say they are following the Lord, yet advocate an ideology of sin, think they may be doing right, but are not.

The people who are promoting evil in the world in their own minds think they are doing what is right and just. This is very common with the secularist and humanist who believe they are doing God's work. It is as if they are saying, "*it is amazing how God agrees with me.*" Strident disregard for a life not centered in Christ will only bring ruin to the individual, and tyranny to a nation's citizenry. In a world where there is such a lack of respect for spiritual things, should we expect the culture to heal when governed by those who have so little regard for the mind of God? As the saying goes, "*the road to hell is paved with good intentions.*"

Babylon in Scripture refers to the world with all its allures and vices. In contrast, the Holy Spirit is truth, light, and wisdom, peace, justice, love, and all that is good and virtuous. When a person sees a tyrannical government or a godless agenda being legislated, he can be assured the Holy Spirit has been extinguished from that government, knowingly or not. When one is living in the light of the Holy Spirit, good emanates from that root. Believers often become disappointed when a godless value system or despotic ruler does bad things. A misguided value system or despot does not legislate for the good, but for the cadre of people who share their same agenda, to the detriment of the long term good of the people. These people honestly believe they are doing the right thing as did Saul of Tarsus. It is for this reason the framers of the U.S. Constitution built in checks and balances to counter-act man's lower nature. The wisdom of these men were clear their guidance drafting documents came from Scripture. This was the genius of America's founding fathers.

Pope Pius XII and Tyranny

Heinous unjust laws are the byproduct of godless leaders. There is the story about Pope Pius XII when he was interviewed after he became Pope in 1939. The interviewer was the U.S. Consul General of the Vatican by the name of Alfred Klieforth. The Pope had this to say about tyrannical leaders and specifically Hitler and his policies. "*I oppose unalterably every compromise with National Socialism, and Hitler is a not only an unworthy scoundrel, but a fundamentally wicked person, who is not capable of moderation.*" People today have forgotten that type of fundamental judgment on truth is the gospel message. There should be no mincing of words on black and white issues. Hitler was an antichrist with a small a. Not the big Anti-Christ who is to come according to Scripture. The world is full of people who have an antichrist agenda.

As a result of the churches in Germany not speaking out when they should have against Hitler, the end result was worse for all concerned. This is where many believe the United States is today. Fear is prohibiting people from speaking the truth, and the moral slide just continues. Fear of what must be asked?

By not speaking out today, nothing will be left for tomorrow. We will shortly be left on the ash heap of history like other great civilizations that have preceded ours if we do not speak out. Historian Will Durant, considered one of the great historians of the Twentieth Century, wrote in his book, *Lessons of History*, that it is clear from all he had observed as a historian over a lifetime of study that one person at the right time speaking out can alter the destiny of a nation, and thus history itself. We are now at that point where all will soon be lost unless this happens.

There are truths of life where there is no negotiation. After speaking the truth, the chips must fall where they may. This principle is true in politics, faith, social and financial aspects of living. There are truths that are eternal, contrary to what so many people think. Accepting that there are no moral absolutes is harming those coming up behind us and putting them in moral jeopardy. In the U.S., we are kicking the proverbial can down the road because we lack the resolve to confront responsibility and state the truth to the powerful and influential. There are deeply moral issues today where many in the Church are silent when they should be speaking out forcefully. History shows the result is far more destructive and chaotic in the future if believers do not proclaim the pure unadulterated truth in boldness today. The pews are largely empty because the pulpits have a watered-down message. When the gospel is spoken strongly and challenges people, people flock to that church as their hearts, minds, and souls desire the truth. It is a commitment to prayer and conviction that sends the message. When the Cure d'Ars arrived in his parish, few souls were attending church. He then prayed before the Eucharist non-stop for them and made himself available to hear confession. That's why he's the model for pastors of Christ's wayward flock. He would often tell people, "*not to have time for God is to live wasting time.*"

In the depths of man's soul, he desires truth and is desperate to hear it. Jesus could gather 5,000 on a hot remote hillside because He had a bold message. His message rang true to people because He practiced what He preached, prayed constantly and stood by His Truth all the way to the cross.

The Importance of Faith

The inequality of man increases as faith takes a subordinate role to secular behavior. As faith and religion decrease, government, secularism, humanism, and communism grow. When faith is openly under attack with some appreciable result, depression and despair increase among the general population. Faith-based initiative is then incrementally destroyed. The human heart and soul aspire to the Glory of God and love of neighbor. It is men and women of God who have given the most to civilizations. Medicine, architecture, hospitals, social programs, mission work, care for the disadvantaged, and discoveries of all kinds can attest to the fact that people who are devoted to God, and give rather than take, do the most to benefit their fellow man.

Saint John Eudes said, "*Faith penetrates God's shadows and His darkness to go straight to the infinity of His perfections. It makes you know Him as He is, infinite in His Being and all His divine perfections. Faith shows you that God is true in His words and unfailing in His promises. It shows you that He is all goodness and gentleness and love to those who seek Him and put their trust in Him.*"

The believer is the glue that holds society together. Take the God-fearing believer from society, and chaos will soon develop. A nation's sovereignty comes from its goodness. That goodness then protects from internal and external threats. Goodness breeds wisdom, self-donation, and the desire to do what is right and just before God. This brings a civilized order for all participants. Due to this God-fearing righteousness, the Lord '*puts a protective hedge*' around that nation to preserve its integrity. When a nation ceases to be good, it is only a matter of time before it decays from within, and thus falls to ruin. As we see repeatedly in Scripture, when Israel obeyed God, their land was blessed. As the Chosen People became prosperous and veered off the prescribed path directed by the law, calamity after calamity came Israel's way. In prosperity, nations forget the foundation for the blessings they received from God. In that prosperity, the neglect of God leads to a downfall. Civilizations appear and disappear for this simple reason.

When a nation ceases to seek God, a culture of death becomes inevitable. Once innocent life is taken, that society will legitimize reasons to enable the culture to move more easily legislatively towards euthanasia and other forms of death and convenience. Shortly after the acceptance of this position, the general population assumes death is then their right, with little or no constraints or standards. The health of a democracy is directly proportional to its view on the sanctity of life. Once a culture of death is sanctioned by the state, and also given financial support, that government ceases to deserve and receive the blessings of God and is without hope. Protection in the womb is the most basic of all human rights. The violation of human rights on a subjective basis by a government is tyranny. Once that tyranny evolves into something more commonplace, collapse is inevitable. The primary reason for the collapse of western democracies is the violation of this most basic principle. Our financial woes are due to our moral laxity. The United States has political and financial problems because it has moral problems.

Saint John Paul II in a homily at Cherry Creek State Park, Denver, Colorado, 1993 said, "*This struggle parallels the apocalyptic combat described in Rev. 11:19- 12:1-6, 10 on the battle between 'the woman clothed with the sun' and the 'dragon.' Death battles against Life: a 'culture of death' seeks to impose itself on our desire to live, and to live to the full. Vast sectors of society are confused about what is right and what is wrong, and are at the mercy of those with the power to 'create' opinion and impose it on others.*"

At the time of Noah, his was the only righteous family to escape the punishment of moral decadence to the Ark. Genesis gives us a graphic account of the sin. We see the same in Sodom and Gomorrah, when it was only Lot, his wife, and two daughters who escaped the wrath of God. What most people do not see is that Lot's daughters were both betrothed, but neither of his daughters' potential new sons-in-law made the journey. Lot's wife disobeyed the Lord's command by turning around, and turned into a pillar of salt. You cannot minimize the sin that is rampant in our culture, no matter how you wish to sanitize it with elegant and sophisticated language.

Spiritual or Religious?

An increasing percentage of the population says it is spiritual, but not religious. They are clearly saying they want nothing to do with a framework of organized religion. It is not hard to understand this with the lukewarm messages and demonstrable lack of conviction coming from many pulpits across America. Many pastors fall prey to the spirit and fads of the day rather than fidelity to the Eternal Word of God spoken in boldness. As Blessed Fulton Sheen said, "*Marry the age, and you become a widow in the next.*" Embrace the age too tightly, and you will shortly lose all of your moral standards. If people try to mold themselves and take security in the times in which they live by adapting to the thinking of the day, it is not long before they become a blur with a bland message and possess little of lasting value.

The word of God does not bend to the modern whims of the people. We are all fallen sinners and it is intellectual fraud to have an argument on the issue of *spiritual versus religious,* as it is often a circular argument with no end. On the other hand, it is understandable why so many people do not attend church. So little of relevance is generally said that has any application in daily life versus being mere 'genuflection' to an esoteric God. The person who says they are "spiritual," but not religious is usually not reading Scripture, going to church, in fellowship with other believers, praying to find the mind of God, not into some form of self-donation, not volunteering time anywhere, not giving of themselves, not going to confession, not fasting, and other ingredients necessary for spiritual growth. They are like a tree planted in the desert not being watered. In time, they die spiritually. Year after year they drift into relativism. Yet, they often say they are spiritual, but not religious. They begin to think they have the answers in a humanistic doctrine that will ultimately fail without God at the center. This is usually the same group that finds their "spiritual" activity in the gym and golf course on the Sabbath. After they are done with that, it is often a day of running errands and doing the shopping. After they are then finished with that, it is watching sports on television the rest of the day. It is Scripture that enables us to put the world in context according to God's design. The Lord was clear in the Old Testament that a house not built on His foundation is doomed to failure.

A person going to church every Sunday will not necessarily be seated at the right hand of God the Father on the day of judgment. But, a person who attends church living a sacramental life creates the environment for a better life in Christ. It is an earnest step to fight our fallen nature. If a person is not following the rubrics of the faith, they more easily slide into a place where they cannot recognize who God is, as they will not know how to hear His voice. For the non-believer, it is often all about the passions, pleasure, cuisine, self-aggrandizement, the flesh, and generally self-gratification. As this secular group moves into positions of leadership, they project a humanistic view of the world. It is then only a matter of time before their plan fails and societal chaos consumes all it was designed to serve. When we see ourselves in the light of a Divine Absolute Truth, we see our imperfections. Only when we look at a painting up close, we see the brush strokes and imperfections. When we see ourselves in the light of Divine Truth, we too more easily see our imperfections. The unbeliever has no framework to construct something that will endure. It is just that simple: without God we fail.

The Protestant Church is in a similar situation of fracture and confusion over many of the same issues as the Roman Catholic Church. Gordon Cromwell Seminary in Massachusetts conducted a longitudinal survey on off shoots of denominations. The survey said in the year 1900 there were 1,600 denominations. In the year 2000 there were 34,000, and by the year 2012 there were 43,000. This again is showing the widespread fracture due to different interpretations of the Scripture and authority. The confusion today over doctrine is severe in nearly all denominations as people pick and choose what dogma to follow. A virtual cafeteria exists for everyone to choose a church to attend and feel "*comfortable.*" However, Jesus was clear that he was building His Church on Peter (Matt. 11:33-36), and the gates of hell would never prevail against it.

Where are the Shepherds?

It is estimated in the USA the Roman Catholic Church to date has paid $2.6 billion in payments to victims of sexual abuse by clergy. This does not include undisclosed out of court settlements not made public. Many inner city parishes and land were sold in the 1990's beginning the process of quiet payouts. Since the inner city parishes had less resources to fight closure, they were the first to compensate victims. To date, the total is estimated to be over $3 billion that has been spent to sexual abuse victims.

The Public Religion Research Institute (PRRI) on March 31, 2014 released some findings on Catholics from 1990-2013. Results of the survey are as follows:

- In 1990 nearly 8 in 10 Catholics were white. Today 60% are white.
- Of all the major religious groups, Catholics have experienced the largest loss of membership. Three in ten said they were raised Catholic in 1990, but now 20% now identify that way. It would be a larger loss were it not due to Spanish immigrants who are Catholic.
- 57% favor allowing homosexuals to marry.
- 61% favor same sex couples being able to adopt.
- 65% believe that a homosexual orientation cannot be changed.
- 54% agree that homosexuals should be eligible for priestly ordination with no special requirements.
- 56% of white Catholics believe having an abortion is morally wrong. 77% of Hispanics believe abortion is morally wrong.

Even if the results were skewed by the samples chosen and the ways questions were asked, the findings still suggest an awful state of spiritual formation and moral life in the Catholic family over the last two generations. The only group to vote more liberal, than liberal Catholics, are atheists. This is a direct result of improper formation and a watered down message form the clergy. Does one wonder looking at the above why we get the laws we do from our elected leaders?

The divorce rate for Catholics is 50%, the same as for everyone else. The divorce rate for couples who cohabitate before marriage is approximately 75%. Catholic couples who claim to have been chaste before marriage, practice their faith devoutly, pray as a family, and follow Church's teaching on God's Divine Will for the transmission of life, have a divorce rate of less than 1% according to data from Natural Family Planning. An estimated four thousand babies in their mother's womb are legally murdered by a medical doctor every day in the USA. Few people are aware that abortifacient hormonal contraceptives (the Birth Control Pill, Depo-Provera, Plan B, Norplant and IUDs) also kill 20,000 to 35,000 babies every day in the USA alone. Mother Teresa said: "*There will be no peace in the world until there is peace in the womb,*" and more ominously she warned us that, "*The fruit of abortion will be nuclear war.*" Saint John Paul II, while visiting Detroit in 1987, warned us, "*America, your very survival as a nation depends upon how you treat the weakest among you, especially the babies in their mother's womb.*" At World Youth Day in Denver in 1993 Our Holy Father implored the United States, "*America defend life, defend life!*" At Castel Gandolfo, Italy in 1996, Saint John Paul II warned the world, "*A nation that kills its own children is a nation without hope!*"

At the Nuremberg Trial in Germany after World War II, there was a conversation that took place after the sentencing between the leading jurist of Germany by the name of Ernst Janning, and the American judge Dan Haywood. It was depicted in the film *Judgment at Nuremberg*. After the trial, Janning asked that Judge Haywood visit him in prison before he left to depart to the United States. The German asked if Haywood would like copies of his most prominent legal decisions. Haywood politely declined. Janning then said, "*I never knew it would come to that. You must believe me.*" Judge Haywood replied, "*It came to that the first time you sentenced a man to death you knew to be innocent.*" So too, with the USA and its acceptance of abortion. We sentence ourselves every day as a nation with government payment, acceptance, and promotion of abortion.

The Sins of Apostasy and Relativism

It is the loss of faith that incubates apostasy. They are brother and sister and have the same spiritual DNA. Following a lack of spiritual formation for individuals, we then move immediately to relativism. Relativism in a general sense is a form of humanism that says there is no absolute truth. It is a world absent of a Divine Standard. Pope Benedict XVI (Emeritus) has always spoken eloquently and forcefully on this subject, reflecting on the profound impact of its evil on the world. Below are several quotes from him.

"*No one who looks realistically at our world today could think that Christians can afford to go on with business as usual, ignoring the profound crisis of faith which has overtaken our society, or simply trusting that the patrimony of values handed down by the Christian centuries will continue to inspire and shape the future of our society.*" (Pope Benedict XVI, September 18, 2010, England).

"*The dictatorship of relativism that recognizes nothing as definite, and which leaves as the ultimate measure only one's ego and desires. Having a clear faith, according to the credo of the Church, is often labeled as fundamentalism. Yet, relativism, that is, letting oneself be tossed and 'swept along by every wind of teaching', appears the sole attitude acceptable to today's standards.*" (Cardinal Ratzinger in a pre-conclave homily, Pope Benedict XVI April 18th, 2005).

"*In our days, when in vast areas of the world the faith is in danger of dying out like a flame which no longer has fuel, the overriding priority is to make God present in this world and to show men and women the way to God. The real problem at this moment of our history is that God is disappearing from the human horizon, and, with the dimming of the light which comes from God, humanity is losing its bearings, with increasingly evident destructive effects*" (Letter from Pope Benedict XVI to all the Bishops of the World, March 10, 2009).

"*Today the prospect that the world might be reduced to ashes by a sea of fire no longer seems pure fantasy: man himself, with his inventions, has forged the flaming sword of the angel of justice that appeared in Fatima*" (Cardinal Joseph Ratzinger, Pope Benedict XVI, Emeritus).

For I know the plans I have for you, says the Lord, plans for welfare and not for evil, to give you future and a hope.

—Jeremiah 29:11

JESUS, I TRUST IN YOU

four

The Judgment Of the United States

Lastly, all angels, good and bad, all men, just and sinners, elect and reprobate shall be summoned to the presence of the Judge before whose Divine Majesty every knee shall bow in profound adoration. We must all stand before the judgment seat of Christ, that every one may receive the proper things of the body according as he has done, whether it be good or evil.

—2 Cor. 5:10

As covered previously, the confluence of events surrounding us on all levels is beyond our grasp to understand. The disordered affections people have embraced over the last several generations has left many feeling empty and without purpose. The excessive noise and distractions in our lives are principal reasons for our anxiety. We simply can't manage the data and distractions anymore and people are confused and lacking direction.

In March of 2014, there was considerable press given to the issue of the first openly homosexual college football player going to the NFL draft. Homosexual groups were celebrating him as the new Jackie Robinson who broke the color barrier in professional baseball in 1947. Homosexual advocates started wearing T-shirts that said, "*Who Am I to Judge,*" echoing the words of Pope Francis. Upon hearing the news of the football player, Cardinal Timothy Dolan of New York remarked, "*Good for him…I would have no sense of judgment on him…God bless ya. I don't think, look, the same bible that tells us, that teaches us about the virtues of chastity and the virtue of fidelity, and marriage also tells us not to judge people. So I would say, Bravo.*"

Upon being selected in the draft, the football player kissed his boyfriend on national TV. Those who dissented from his conduct were criticized in the press. Since these events, it is the Christian conservatives who are defending themselves against the position of not accepting homosexuality.

Cardinal Dolan made no mention of sin or amendment of life, but said, Bravo! In essence, Cardinal Dolan was saying, "Yes, it's about time." Immediately after the comment, academic administrators around the U.S. warmly welcomed the homosexual lifestyle to schools and campuses saying they felt they were in no position to judge either. People then said, "if leading Catholic clerics like Pope Francis and Cardinal Dolan support this, we can now promote this view as well." Within weeks, schools all over the U.S. were allowing homosexual advocates a greater voice in school activities on school properties. Cardinal Dolan then said he would serve as Grand Marshal of the 2015 Saint Patrick's Day Parade in New York City which would allow gays to march under their own banner for the first time. Dolan said, "*the organizers have my confidence and support. I know there are thousands of gay people marching in the parade, I know it, and I am glad they are. It is a sign of inclusiveness and unity.*"

The late Cardinal O'Connor of New York previously did not allow it, and said, "*Irish Catholics have been persecuted for the sole reason that they have refused to compromise church teaching. What others call bigotry, Irish Catholics call principle.*"

The Franciscan Friars of Boston's Saint Anthony Shrine joined the chorus when members of the same Capuchin religious order as Cardinal Sean O'Malley, had an information booth at the city's homosexual Pride Festival. The event was held at City Hall Plaza on June 14, 2014. The booth distributed T-shirts, buttons, and banners that read, "WHO AM I TO JUDGE." The Boston Archdiocese was silent as they were the month before regarding the satanic black Mass that was scheduled to be held on Harvard University property. Nothing of dissent came from the Diocese or Chancery, but one priest from MIT who organized a procession that gathered momentum that swayed public opinion to not have the Mass anywhere in Boston. Neither Pope Francis nor Cardinal Dolan brought up the issue of sin in the conversation. Had Pope Francis or Cardinal Dolan simply said, "*go and sin no more*" (John 8:11) as Jesus said to the adulterous woman without condemning her, it would have removed some fears of the faithful about the direction of the Church. Jesus privately judged her conduct as sin, but He would not condemn her to the public. Jesus was worthy and entitled to judge; but He told us not to judge because we are all sinners.

At the very heart of this matter is the issue of tolerance or intolerance. The Lord is compassionate to all. He turns no sinner away. However, due to the lax teaching over the last several generations on matters of faith, we find minimal conviction to sin—and a willingness to call it sin lest we offend someone. The aggressive homosexual agenda has had an affect where few are willing to publically speak against it. If we remain silent on this as well as other grave moral issues, society will soon have little left that has any resemblance to a Scriptural, traditional or sane approach to living. Chaos and judgment is the historical precedent for this attitude and behavior. Does one wonder why the person in the pew is confused? As the late G.K. Chesterton said, "*tolerance is a virtue to those of no conviction.*"

However, no one single denomination is alone credited with mediocrity and not proclaiming the gospel from the housetops without compromise. In 2014, pollster George Barna released the results of a two-year survey concerning church leadership. Pastors admitted they knew that the bible addresses areas of sin and key issues of the day, but would not address them. Barna said less than ten percent of pastors were willing to speak about flashpoint cultural issues for fear of causing controversy. The question was then asked why did they not speak about them? The pastors answered they did not think it was key to a "successful" church. Pastors listed the five things that they felt constituted a "successful" church and they said, "*Attendance, giving, number of programs, number of staff, and square footage.*" Speaking the truth of Jesus Christ did not make the list.

Watching While it Burns

The world is under the judgment of God. The Transition and Transformation that is taking place is bringing the world to a New Era, a New Epoch of time. This is a concept spoken about for many years by leading mystics in the Catholic Church. This is not the "end of the world" as some people often derisively mock. But it is now readily apparent to many that something is very wrong in the world and getting worse. Global governance is out of control and chaos is not far away. It is hard to see a way out with human solutions. Heaven has told us that we are living in the "end times," meaning the end of Satan's rule as prince of the world. Spiritually, politically, financially, Scripturally, and sociologically, all data points to major events on the near horizon. It must have been extraordinarily difficult, despite the signs, for the Jews to believe that it was the Messiah in their midst when Jesus walked among them. Jesus spoke of a radical departure from what had been known previously, challenging the people of His day to accept a new paradigm for mankind. As prophesied, Jesus had come and changed the world. The End Times dialogue today is just as emotionally charged, and a concept that divides good people.

Some may say this is an Old Testament concept of the wrathful God that is no longer relevant today, but the word of God does not change. One does not need to look very far into the Old Testament, New Testament, or history, to see that people, families and nations experience positive or negative repercussions for virtue or sin. If a child starts stealing bikes as a seven year old and is not stopped, the natural progression is to move onto cars, and so forth. The Lord does judge nations, much to the chagrin of progressives and liberals who deny the very existence of God. We bring problems upon ourselves. Do we think we will grasp the mind of God listening to un-churched unbelieving, agnostic, or an atheistic media? Yet, this is where most people get their quotable information. Not that going to church makes everyone a saint, but it does show there is a desire to first seek His Kingdom and know the things of God.

The reasons for our anxiety are numerous, but there is one main reason why we lose peace of soul. It is that we have become separated from God. Isaiah says, "***it has been your sin that has separated you from God***" (59:2). This verse is very clear. It is not God judging us, but our decisions often bring grief upon ourselves. Sin allows Satan room to take over our life. When things get more difficult in the world, remember that verse from Isaiah. It is not God who is causing the pain, but our sin that has allowed it. When things get difficult, we often blame God for the pain. But, this verse must be remembered to stay the course because hard times are coming.

Economics has trumped spirituality in the United States in much the same way the people of Germany chose Hitler as their economic savior in times of stress. On paper, Hitler gave Germany an economic and industrial solution after World War I. Education and career advancement has trumped the need for the confessional. The mania over entertainment, sports, leisure, and other diversions is a major contributor to our nation's departure from God. Sports and entertainment have swamped the things of God, with faith and belief no longer welcome in many places in our culture. The Worship of God on the Sabbath has been bumped to provide time for Sunday sports, with people often sitting in front of the television all day watching sports and inane entertainment and barely participating in their children's lives.

Alexis de Tocqueville and America

Early in the nineteenth century, the French philosopher Alexis de Tocqueville was commissioned by the French government to travel in the U.S. to seek answers about what made America work, and what made her unique among nations. He wanted to find what made America great. Tocqueville visited the cities, the rural areas, farming communities, schools, factories, and businesses. It wasn't until he visited America's churches that he found what made America great. Writing from France in his book called Democracy in America (published 1835) he said, "*America is great because America is good. And if America ceases to be good, America will cease to be great.*" A study on the United States Constitution conducted at the University of Houston, sponsored by the American Political Science Review and published in 1983, concluded that 94% of the Constitution's provisions were based directly or indirectly on the Bible.

Writing the Apocalypse on the Isle of Patmos, Saint John the Apostle in Revelation chapters 2 and 3 the Holy Spirit speaks about the seven churches that have contemporaneous spirits in all of history. To each church the Holy Spirit has something to say that is laudatory, and then a rebuke on something where that church is amiss. All but the Church of Philadelphia have a mild rebuke—as Philadelphia is the church of love, where there is no fault. The church of Sardis was told something very interesting; "*And to the angel of the church of Sardis, write: These things saith he, that hath the seven spirits of God, and the seven stars: I know thy works, that thou has the name of being alive: and thou art dead. Be watchful and* ***strengthen the things that remain,*** *which are ready to die*" (Rev. 3:1-2). Here is a Church where God is telling the people to remain steadfast and "strengthen the things that remain," and not buckle under pressure from anyone, or any civil entity. This in history is called the remnant, and that remnant today closely resembles the Church in Sardis.

Your View Of The Word—Or God's Eternal Word?

There is general distrust all around us and few know what to do. All sides have dug their ideological heels in, and their respective views preclude answers from surfacing for the general welfare of the people. Political and social ideologies have become sacred and have replaced divinity and God's rightful place. The environmental and green movement is a god and religion for many, as are other causes. Talking about saving whales and baby seals is fine, but woe and behold if you dare say abortion is wrong to this crowd. Political positions are so polarized there are no solutions in sight. Political pundits and writers of social commentary continue to look at the problems of the U.S. and the world with diagnostic astuteness. However, they rarely if ever deal with the root issue that our problems are moral, and not political. Rarely, if ever, do they point to a solution. Many refuse to clearly say that adherence to moral and spiritual guidelines is what makes a nation good. The problems of our culture start first in our family, and then go directly to the schools. In many high schools in America, our children may be learning more about Buddha and Islam than Jesus Christ. It is no wonder the kids are lost as they are not taught the rubrics of the faith. Archbishop Fulton J. Sheen said, "*it may be better to send your children to a secular college where they might have to fight for their faith, than to send them to a Catholic college where they might risk having their faith stolen away.*" That was said in the 1960's. Children learning their faith makes them more responsible citizens.

Many students today, if taught purely a social gospel tend to become social activists rather than disciples of Jesus because the seed in formation in the faith was sown on thorny or rocky ground. Social activism must branch out from the heart of what Jesus is asking of us, to love one another through good works and make God's love for humanity credible as a basis to share His message and make disciples of others.

There may be a realistic political remedy on paper to fix things, but it is simply not a politically realistic solution. Many things seem logical on paper for what ought to work, but in practice, they don't. We are increasingly defenseless against the onslaught of dysfunction and filth coming our way. We all feel most comfortable around people who share our views. This is normal and we gravitate to it for ease of the day in a like-minded community. When people get too comfortable without being challenged, they will race off a cliff together, not to mention shed creativity and zeal. This is human nature. In that comfort is a resistance to new ideas, and new thinking. Few people see change coming, and even fewer are willing to confront that reality. If you need a fresh realistic outlook, it may not come from your local church.

People now see that many of the support groups and social structures they have become so accustomed to over the last several generations are disintegrating. This is another reason for our anxiety. If one looks for what may be a genesis of when America lost its innocence, it may be the day President John F. Kennedy was shot. After President Kennedy was assassinated on November 22, 1963, author Norman Mailer said, "*For a time we felt the country was ours, now it's theirs again.*" Mailer is saying there is a power elite in control of the destiny of nations. There was a quote from Ernest Hemingway that was also often quoted about President Kennedy where he said, "*If people bring so much courage to the world, the world has to kill them to break them, so of course it kills them. The world breaks everyone, and afterward many are strong at the broken places. But those that will not break, it kills. It kills the very good and the very gentle, and the very brave impartially.*"

Those who wish to do as Christ is asking of us in life, and be a counter sign to the world as Jesus was, will be hurt. This is a significant nuance from the mega church pastors who neglect this side of the gospel message. This concept of pain is in the equation of battling the original sin of fallen man. The day of unlocked cars and unattended purses has long passed. No one is safe from the onslaught of a nation on its way to control by a few elites with a global agenda of control. The desire to implement the agenda for control is driven by Satan. Increasingly people don't see a safety net supporting them anymore. Previously, it was families, churches, schools, and neighborhoods that supported them. Because the sound nuclear family unit is now in the minority, most people do not have the family support they once enjoyed.

You Are the Salt Of the Earth

When the Holy Spirit is extinguished from a culture through sin, that culture is left to its own devices. It is then no longer possible to maintain order. Jesus said about believers, "*you are the salt of the earth*" (Matt. 5:13). When the Lord used His parable of salt, people knew just what it meant. Salt was more important to a mariner than gold, as there was no way to preserve food on a long voyage without it. People would starve if they were not in possession of salt. Also, remember, there was no refrigeration in those days. Christopher Columbus could not have sailed without it. It was an essential.

Salt is a preservative and when salt is not present, society collapses into disorder. If you take the believer out of society, you will have an accelerated breakdown. The believer is salt to a society, and when the salt is no longer present to perform its intended function, light is extinguished and there is chaos. Saint Paul in Romans (1:28), speaks of how people are given over to depraved minds. He said, "*In other words, since they refused to see it was rational to acknowledge God, God has left them to their own irrational ideas and to their monstrous behavior.*" Once the light of the Holy Spirit is gone, there is no light, truth, or wisdom. This is where we are today, and don't expect logical rational thinking from a government that is out of control and given over to godless or depraved behavior. In the USA, many of our political leaders and citizens have a depraved mind, thus spiritually blind without the guidance of God. We are no longer a nation of liberals or conservatives. We are now a nation of those ignoring God's precepts and commandments, and those trying to maintain them. This is the battle. The believer must make a mental transition that it is not business as usual. There is a tremendous shift taking place as the Lord is doing away with the old, and ushering in the new. It will be extremely disruptive, and we must be grounded spiritually if we are to maintain peace of soul.

Social Indices That No longer Function as Designed—A Broken System

People are justified in their anxiety. Whether you are a longshoreman on the docks of New York, or an accountant in Kansas, people see the dysfunction. U.S. governments at all levels are leveraged and broke, Social Security is being used as a giant Ponzi scheme by the Federal Government, Social Security Disability Income (SSDI) is being used as long term unemployment relief rather than as a temporary program, union and state pension plans are severely underfunded to the tune of billions and many are bankrupt.

Major U.S. cities are bankrupt living on borrowed Federal dollars, and the U.S. welfare program is broken so badly no one knows what to do with it. Job insecurity is rampant, severe unemployment and inflation understated by government reporting agencies that fudge the measures and the numbers. U.S. infrastructure is in an increasing state of disrepair that would take trillions to remedy, a broken godless school system, home mortgages underwater, more than 48 million people on Food Stamps forming a permanently unemployed and underemployed class of people, even as the elderly are losing all types of funding that were reserved for them after a lifetime of saving. Meanwhile, the U.S Federal Government is still sending tens of billions of aid to foreign nations.

An inordinate number of vaccines are being forced upon young children by a Federal government and medical professionals and a public school system bullying young mothers, excessive government regulation is destroying initiative in nearly every area of living, we have international currency wars, drones, consequences in all forms of extreme weather and climate change, and natural phenomena eroding budgets of all kinds, 100 year droughts, 500 year droughts, reservoirs drying up, 100 year cold, 100 year rain depending on the part of the world in which we live, and whole states, cities and towns that will lose water.

We have tax payers funding abortions as sanctioned by our government, states that now allow the purchase of marijuana with Food Stamps, a U.S. prison system bursting at the seams, a U.S. banking system that is over $250 trillion in debt when one looks at derivatives and other bizarre financial instruments, an estimated $700 trillion or more in worldwide derivative debt, emerging markets that are sliding into insolvency, and approximately 100 million Americans who are not employed either voluntarily through retirement or loss of jobs, a liberal political ideology for the most part that means we have a godless agenda and don't want God in the culture, income inequality growing so fast that eighty five of the wealthiest people in the world now have more than the poorest 3.5 billion people, powerful groups with undisclosed agendas and participation at meetings like the World Economic Forum (WEF) meeting annually in Davos, Switzerland, the Bilderbergers, the Council on Foreign Relations (CFR), the Trilateral Commission (TC), and secretly framed new global treaties like the Trans Pacific Partnership (TPP) designed to circumvent U.S. law, politicians who bypass the Constitution, a clash of world views so disparate no government can bridge the gap, a dysfunctional political system where there is no political will to curb spending, big banks, big government, and big bureaucrats dictating life for all of us, severe race issues, a dysfunctional Church saying little, lack of courage among leadership to speak the truth, the U.S. increasingly losing its sovereign creditworthiness and value of the U.S. dollar, a culture of sex, drugs, and rock n roll, casinos and marijuana being legalized by state governments to fund state programs and pensions. All are clear signs America, if not much of the world has lost its way.

Years ago widespread casinos were unthinkable and gambling was centered in Las Vegas and Reno, Nevada. States now see the financial benefits coming to their coffers, and more states open casinos rather than let neighboring states grab the revenue. An added incentive for the states to pursue casinos and marijuana sales is to allow exorbitant state and local pension plans to continue. Government does it because thy can. There is no longer accountability, in government, and as English historian Lord John Acton (1834-1902) said, "*Power tends to corrupt, and absolute power corrupts absolutely.*"

The U.S. dollar has become untrustworthy as the U.S. Federal Reserve prints dollars by the trillions. Many nations are actively moving away from the U.S. Dollar as the international reserve currency for world trade and investment. Germany, the economic powerhouse of the

Eurozone, and other nations are moving towards the East for economic survival and away from the west as they are dependent on Russian oil and gas for their own survival. Clergy of all faiths are racked with sexual problems that have been covered up by their leaders who were meant to protect the people they serve. Along with the general loss of morality, there is intrusion of a venomous virulent homosexual agenda down to the U.S. grade school level, boys being allowed to use girls bathrooms and vice versa in schools, schools educating children in a moral vacuum, and tens of thousands of high school graduates each year reading several grades below where they should be, food and water quality become less trustworthy with the growing prevalence of GMO seeds, environmental degradation and distrust of governments, high divorce rates, drugs amongst the young, and pornography in viewing habits even by the very young which science shows alters the chemistry of a brain much in the same way drugs do. There is a pervasive moral confusion of the general population, and the younger one is the less anything is seen wrong with it due to media brainwashing and other influences around them.

Leaders give up handling the big issues or sell out on serving the public good, immigration issues remain unsolved as the resources of state and local budgets dwindle trying to deal with reckless federal policies, the impact that race in the Middle East and Israel will have on life in western democracies and the price of oil, the Arab Spring redefining borders, the desire for the caliphate to promote violent Islam throughout the world, the Muslim Brotherhood and mid-east jihadist insurgencies infiltrating society and government agencies, the coming worldwide decades long war between Muslims and Christians, gun registration which will lead to gun control, the shredding of U.S. Constitutional Law which has stood for centuries, school shootings, civil wars everywhere, the War on Poverty which has been an abysmal failure, creating a permanent class of people unwilling or unable to work as the system pays them more staying home than they can earn in employment, fear of the U.S. Federal Government defaulting on its financial obligations, federal, state, and local governments so bloated they just sap the life from the working population, the rudeness and lack of civility law abiding people encounter when outside the safety of their homes, banks and the International Monetary Fund (IMF) talking openly about "bail ins" which will confiscate X percent of personal funds as a 'wealth tax' to further pay for excessive government that refuses to live within its means, the United Nations pushing hard for a climate tax from all citizens of the world so they can have a slush fund to distribute as they see fit to nations abiding by their socialist policies, ebola and other virulent strains of virus, U.S. IRA's and pensions to be confiscated by government for use as the government dictates, the U.S. National Security Agency (NSA) and other intelligence and private corporations snooping into private affairs virtually obliterating the concept of privacy, radiation from the Fukushima nuclear power plant in Japan causing fall out and seafood contamination in the Pacific Ocean and western North American shores. The United States has an estimated 5% of world's population, yet has 25% of the world's inmate population. No matter where you work and live, you see a breakdown.

The Blessings and the Cursing Of a Nation—The U.S. Case

Few doubt the United States is in a steep economic and moral decline. It is generally acknowledged around the world that the United States cannot continue to sustain itself due to its reckless policies. There are approximately 2 million Federal workers, a demoralized military, an aging population, manufacturing which has heavily been relocated offshore. State, local, and municipal government continues to squeeze tax-payers to fund public pensions and support outdated inefficient programs, and there are millions more government contractors operating in the private sector, but supported financially by Federal and State government money.

The Cato Institute in Washington, D.C., released a study in 2013 that shows how much more welfare benefits pay than a minimum wage job in 33 states and the District of Columbia. In 13 states, welfare pays more than $15.00 an hour. According to the study, welfare benefits have increased faster than minimum wages. In other words, it is more profitable to sit at home than work, and millions of Americans have figured this out. Hawaii is the biggest spender, where welfare "earns" $29.13 per hour. The study calculated a pre tax equivalent "salary" that welfare recipients receive. When there is no longer the ability to pay and the well runs dry with government largesse, this will cease and there will be violence as we have seen in Greece and other countries. When a nation has well over 50% of its citizens dependent on some form of government subsidy or welfare payment, that nation is living on borrowed time. See the compilation below on welfare spending by state, per beneficiary.

1. Hawaii: $60, 590
2. District of Columbia: $50,820
3. Massachusetts: $50,540
4. Connecticut: $44,370
5. New York: $43,700
6. New Jersey: 43,450
7. Rhode Island: $43,330
8. Vermont: $42,350
9. New Hampshire: $39,750
10. Maryland: $38,160
11. California: $37,160
12. Oregon: 34,300
13. Wyoming: $32,620
14. Nevada: $29,820
15. Minnesota: $29,350
16. Delaware: $29,220
17. Washington: $28,840
18. North Dakota: $28,830
19. Pennsylvania: $28,670
20. New Mexico: $27,900
21. Montana: $26,930
22. South Dakota: $26,610
23. Kansas: 26,490
24. Michigan: $26,430
25. Alaska: $26,400 …and so forth.

The average middle class family income is $50,000, down from $54,000 before the recession of 2009. Hawaii and Massachusetts welfare recipients earn more than the average middle class family makes. If anyone doubts that America is bankrupt, they need only take a look at this Cato Institute study. In addition, the salaries of:

A. All retired U.S. Presidents is $180,000 for life.
B. Retired House and Senate members is $174,000 for life.
C. The Speaker of the House is $223,500 for life.
D. The Majority and Minority Leader is $193,400 for life.

If you are now feeling dizzy after all the issues listed above, you should be. It was designed to show the reader the severity of the dysfunction, and how broad the problems are, because it is a reality and needs to be intellectually and emotionally confronted. The constant barrage of negative data is crushing the human spirit and it is why people are exhausted and filled with anxiety about the future. As a result, many are medicating to deal with the stress.

It is time to realize the Lord has a plan for the salvation of mankind. The above litanies were not meant to be depressing, but to show the cold hard facts that stare us in the face. The reasons for our anxiety are real and numerous. A nation that has allowed fifty five million abortions (the killing of the innocents) is under judgment. That is not happy talk. As Dorothy said in the Wizard of Oz, "*Toto, I don't think we're in Kansas anymore.*" The sooner we realize we need to have trust and hope in His plan, the sooner we will achieve peace of soul. Coming to this realization is a very difficult thing to do. The Harvest of the Lord will be great during this time of The Great Transformation because people will fall into the arms of God, as there will be no other place to go. When people realize there is no other option, but seek Jesus and His Kingdom, it will be the beginning of the New Springtime of the Church. When we know the final outcome, it gives us the ability to fully understand why we should have no fear.

In 1922, five years after the Bolshevik Revolution, it was asked of the babushka (in Russian this means "old hat," but loosely translates to old woman) in the streets of Moscow how it happened? Her simple three-word response said it all, "***we forgot God.***" Simply three words define our life. The world is in the situation it is, because we forgot God.

Much more could be said here, but the point has been made that changes are coming at us fast, and in the near future they will come at us like box cars one after another. If you don't have a well-developed spiritual life, you will find it tough going. We will at best struggle, and at worst perish without spiritual formation. As Moses told the Hebrew people to sprinkle blood on the doorpost so the angel of death would "Pass Over," we too have been told where our refuge and safety lies. We have a very dangerous situation fast emerging for a one-world leader poised to come on the scene. When chaos reigns worldwide, the world will look to an economic and political savior, much in the same way people look for a political leader to turn things around in times of stress. The Blessed Mother said to the Marian Movement of Priests, "*you will know the time is here, by the events themselves.*"

As God Says

Below is the entire Chapter 28 of Deuteronomy. The entire chapter has been included because it is in the Lord's words why He chooses to bless or curse a nation. Depending on your version of the Bible it is called, Blessings for Obedience, or The Blessings and the Cursing of a Nation. There are several things to specifically notice. The first 14 verses are blessings, and note the blessing of verse 11. Notice how simple one blessing is and the benefit to all who receive it. There is a protective hedge around the nation that observes the laws and statutes of God. There are only 14 verses of blessings and all live in prosperity and peace as a result. In verse 15 there is a radical departure to the famous, "if then" or the transitional clause. The cursing of a nation continues for 54 verses. The blessings are general and easy, and the cursing is long and complicated. God's ways are always easier than those of the world as Jesus said, "*my burden is easy, and my yoke is light*" (Matt. 11:30). It is clearly stated there is a requirement of obedience for God's blessings.

There are many preachers who teach the "prosperity gospel" which has a very good message of hope, trust and faith. This message is central to Scripture and extraordinarily important. It is the essence of God communicating His love and fidelity to His people—Faith, Hope, Trust, and Love. However, with this repeated message of God's blessings and how we deserve them, seldom is obedience ever mentioned by the ministers of the prosperity gospel. Obedience is the prerequisite to enjoy God's blessings few speak about.

Fidelity to the tenets, precepts, statutes and commandments of God as ordained in Scripture are required for blessings. Over time this prosperity message becomes hollow as it becomes a social or cultural exchange. The mystery of suffering, mortification, the mysteries and paradox of living, and life's struggles are seldom if ever taught. Seldom is anything ever mentioned how to deal with the complex mysteries of heaven, and so many elements of the gospel we are confronted with at different times in our lives. Embracing the cross to endure the dark night of the soul is avoided and considered negative to this crowd.

Does God want us to live in a state of poverty? No, He does not. But living in extravagance is another matter. In Deuteronomy 28 we see the repercussions of sin and how it affects every area of living. If there is repentance, as with Jonah walking through Nineveh there can be restoration. Today there is little talk of repentance from any pulpit. Sin is not mentioned by many pastors because it is not a popular message. People push back when the local pastor or minister speaks as Jesus spoke. To the down and out, Jesus spoke love and never bruised a reed. To the self righteous, He was very hard calling them "*white washed tombs*" (Matt. 23:27), and "*you serpents, you brood of vipers*" (Matt. 23:33).

See if you recognize anything that has happened to America as you read Deuteronomy 28? Have we turned our face and hearts from God? Chapter 28 is lengthy—a total of 69 verses. When read in its entirety, ask yourself if we have abandoned the principles of God, rather than God who deserted us? Do we deserve God's justice because we left Him? This will be a big issue in the near future as people in distress often ask if God abandoned them in time of need, but fail to ask the question, "*Did we leave God first?*"

Chapter 28—Deuteronomy

But if you faithfully obey the voice of the Lord your God, by keeping and observing all his commandments, which I am laying down for you today, the Lord your God will raise you higher than every other nation in the world,

2 and all these blessings will befall and overtake you, for having obeyed the voice of the Lord your God.

3 'You will be blessed in the town and blessed in the countryside;

4 blessed, the offspring of your body, the yield of your soil, the yield of your livestock, the young of your cattle and the increase of your flocks;

5 blessed, your basket and your kneading trough.

6 You will be blessed in coming home, and blessed in going out.

7 The enemies who attack you, the Lord will defeat before your eyes; they will advance on you from one direction and flee from you in seven.

8 The Lord will command blessedness to be with you, on your barns and on all your undertakings, and he will bless you in the country given you by the Lord your God.

9 'From you the Lord will make a people consecrated to himself, as he has sworn to you, if you keep the commandments of the Lord your God and follow his ways.

10 The peoples of the world, seeing that you bear the Lord's name, will all be afraid of you.

11 The Lord will make you abound in possessions: in the offspring of your body, in the yield of your cattle and in the yield of your soil, in the country which he swore to your ancestors that he would give you.

12 For you the Lord will open his treasury of rain, the heavens, to give your country its rain at the right time, and to bless all your labors. You will make many nations your subjects, yet you will be subject to none.

13 The Lord will put you at the head, not at the tail; you will always be on top and never underneath, if you listen to the commandments of the Lord your God, which I am laying down for you today, and then keep them and put them into practice,

14 not deviating to right or to left from any of the words which I am laying down for you today, by following other gods and serving them.

15 'But if you do not obey the voice of the Lord your God, and do not keep and observe all his commandments and laws which I am laying down for you today then all these curses will befall and overtake you.

16 'You will be accursed in the town and accursed in the countryside;

17 accursed, your basket and your kneading trough;

18 accursed, the offspring of your body, the yield of your soil, the young of your cattle and the increase of your flock.

19 You will be accursed in coming home, and accursed in going out.

20 'The Lord will send a curse on you, a spell, an imprecation on all your labors until you have been destroyed and quickly perish, because of your perverse behavior, for having deserted me.

21 The Lord will fasten the plague on you, until it has exterminated you from the country which you are about to enter and make your own.

22 The Lord will strike you down with consumption, fever, inflammation, burning fever, drought, wind-blast, mildew, and these will pursue you to your ruin.

23 The heavens above you will be brass, the earth beneath you iron.

24 Your country's rain the Lord will turn into dust and sand; it will fall on you from the heavens until you perish.

25 The Lord will have you defeated by your enemies; you will advance on them from one direction and flee from them in seven; and you will be a terrifying object-lesson to all the kingdoms of the world.

26 Your carcass will be carrion for all wild birds and all wild animals, with no one to scare them away.

27 'The Lord will strike you down with Egyptian ulcers, with swellings in the groin, with scurvy and the itch, for which you will find no cure.

28 The Lord will strike you down with madness, blindness, distraction of mind,

29 until you grope your way at noon like a blind man groping in the dark, and your steps will lead you nowhere. 'You will never be anything but exploited and plundered, with no one to save you.

30 Get engaged to a woman, another man will have her; build a house, you will not live in it; plant a vineyard, you will not gather its first-fruits.

31 Your ox will be slaughtered before your eyes and you will eat none of it; your donkey will be carried off in front of you and not be returned to you; your sheep will be given to your enemies, and no one will come to your help.

32 Your sons and daughters will be handed over to another people, and every day you will wear your eyes out watching for them, while your hands are powerless.

33 A nation hitherto unknown to you will eat the yield of your soil and of all your hard work. You will never be anything but exploited and crushed.

34 You will be driven mad by the sights you will see.

35 The Lord will strike you down with foul ulcers on knee and leg, for which you will find no cure—from the sole of your foot to the top of your head.

36 'The Lord will send away both you and the king whom you have appointed to rule you to a nation unknown either to you or to your ancestors, and there you will serve other gods, made of wood and stone.

37 And you will be the astonishment, the byword, the laughing-stock of all the peoples where the Lord is taking you.

38 'You will cast seed in plenty on the fields but harvest little, since the locust will devour it.

39 You will plant and till your vineyards but not drink the wine or gather the grapes, since the grub will eat them up.

40 You will grow olive trees throughout your territory but not anoint yourself with the oil, since your olive trees will be cut down.

41 You will father sons and daughters but they will not belong to you, since they will go into captivity.

42 All your trees and the whole yield of your soil will be the prey of insects.

43 'The foreigners living with you will rise higher and higher at your expense, while you yourself sink lower and lower.

44 You will be subject to them, not they to you; they will be the ones at the head, and you the one at the tail.

45 'All these curses will befall you, pursue you and overtake you until you have been destroyed, for not having obeyed the voice of the Lord your God by keeping his commandments and laws which he has laid down for you.

46 They will be a sign and a wonder over you and your descendants for ever.

47 'For not having joyfully and with happy heart served the Lord your God, despite the abundance of everything,

48 you will have to serve the enemy whom the Lord will send against
you, in hunger, thirst, lack of clothing and total privation. He will
put an iron yoke on your neck, until he has destroyed you.
49 'Against you the Lord will raise a distant nation from the ends of
the earth like an eagle taking wing: a nation whose language you
do not understand,
50 a nation grim of face, with neither respect for the old, nor pity for
the young.
51 He will eat the yield of your cattle and the yield of your soil until
you have been destroyed; he will leave you neither wheat, nor
wine, nor oil, nor the young of your cattle, nor increase of your
flock, until he has made an end of you.
52 He will besiege you inside all your towns until your loftiest and
most strongly fortified walls collapse, on which, throughout your
country, you have relied. He will besiege you inside all the towns
throughout your country, given you by the Lord your God.
53 During the siege and in the distress to which your enemy will
reduce you, you will eat the offspring of your own body, the flesh
of the sons and daughters given you by the Lord your God.
54 The gentlest and tenderest of your men will scowl at his brother,
and at the wife whom he embraces, and at his remaining children,
55 not willing to give any of them any of his own children's flesh, which
he is eating; because of the siege and the distress to which your
enemy will reduce you in all your towns, he will have nothing left.
56 The most refined and fastidious of your women, so refined, so
fastidious that she has never ventured to set the sole of her foot to
the ground, will scowl at the husband whom she embraces, and
at her son and daughter, and at the after-birth when it leaves her
womb, and at the child to which she has given birth.
57 she will hide away and eat them, so complete will be the starvation
resulting from the siege and the distress to which your enemy will
reduce you in all your towns.
58 'If you do not keep and observe all the words of this Law, which
are written in this book, in the fear of this glorious and awe-
inspiring name: The Lord your God,

59 The Lord will strike you down with monstrous plagues, you and your descendants: with plagues grievous and lasting, diseases pernicious and enduring.

60 He will afflict you with all the maladies of Egypt which you used to dread, and they will fasten on you.

61 What is more, the Lord will afflict you with all the plagues and all the diseases not mentioned in the book of this Law, until you have been destroyed.

62 There will only be a small group of you left, you who were once as numerous as the stars of heaven. 'For not having obeyed the voice of the Lord your God,

63 just as the Lord used to delight in making you happy and in making your numbers grow, so will he take delight in ruining you and destroying you. You will be torn from the country which you are about to enter and make your own.

64 The Lord will scatter you throughout every people, from one end of the earth to the other; there you will serve other gods made of wood and stone, hitherto unknown either to you or to your ancestors.

65 Among these nations there will be no repose for you, no rest for the sole of your foot; there the Lord will give you a quaking heart, weary eyes, halting breath.

66 Your life ahead of you will hang in doubt; you will be afraid day and night, uncertain of your life.

67 In the morning you will say, "How I wish it were evening!," and in the evening you will say, "How I wish it were morning!," such terror will grip your heart and such sights you will see!

68 The Lord will send you back to Egypt, either by ship or by a road which I promised you would never see again. And there you will want to offer yourselves for sale to your enemies as serving men and women, but no one will buy you.'

69 These are the words of the covenant which the Lord ordered Moses to make with the Israelites in Moab, in addition to the covenant which he had made with them at Horeb.

Teachings Of the Ages

Below are writings from the Old Testament, New Testament, and the Blessed Mother on sins against nature that bring judgment to the nations.

Leviticus 20:13 states, "*If a man lies with a male as with a woman, both of them have committed an abomination; they shall be put to death, their blood is upon them.*"

Saint Paul addresses immorality and how one should conduct their life in the Book of Romans. Romans 1:18-32 reads as follows:

> *"For the wrath of God is revealed from heaven against all ungodliness and injustice of those men that detain the truth of God in injustice: because that which is known of God is manifest in them. For the invisible things of him, from the creation of the world, are clearly seen, being understood by the things that are made; His eternal power also, and divinity: so that they are inexcusable. Because that when they knew God, they have not glorified Him as God, or given thanks; but became vain in their thoughts, and their foolish heart was darkened. For professing themselves to be wise, they became fools. And they changed the glory of the incorruptible God into the likeness of the image of a corruptible man, and of birds, and of four-footed beasts, and of creeping things. Wherefore, God gave them up to the desires of their heart, unto uncleanliness, to dishonor their own bodies among themselves. Who changed the truth of God into a lie; and worshipped and served the creature rather than the Creator, who is blessed forever. Amen. For this cause God delivered them up to shameful affections. For their women have changed their natural use which is that use against nature. And, in like manner, the men also, leaving the natural use of the women, have burned in their lusts one towards another, men with men working that which is filthy, and receiving in themselves, the recompense which was due to their error. And as they liked not to have God in their knowledge, God delivered them up to a reprobate sense, to do these things which are not convenient; Being filled with all iniquity, malice, fornication, avarice, wickedness, full of envy, murder,*

contention, deceit, malignity, whisperers, detractors, hateful to God, contumelious, proud, haughty, inventors of evil, disobedient to parents, foolish, dissolute, without affection, without fidelity, without mercy. Who having known the justice of God, did not understand that they who do such things, are worthy of death; and not only that they do them, but they also that, consent to them that do them."

We see more of the same when Saint Paul writes throughout the New Testament when he says if we have ungodly practices and the consequences of sin upon the flesh, "*Do not be deceived; God is not mocked, for whatever a man sows, that he will also reap. For he who sows to his own flesh will from the flesh reap corruption; but he who sows to the Spirit will from the spirit reap eternal life*" (Galatians 6:7-8).

Our Lady to the Marian Movement of Priests speaking from Seattle Washington in message 354 titled, *How It Makes His Divine Heart Suffer said,*

> *"Jesus is today again despised, scourged and wounded in His Mystical Body. How the permissive attitude of many priests and of some bishops who justify even the gravest acts of impurity makes His Divine Heart suffer. Precisely here, in this very place, the Heart of Jesus has been despised, wounded and outraged by the welcoming of so many of my poor children, consumed by this terrible vice and by the public encouragement given to them to continue along the road of impure sins against nature. Impure sins against nature are sins which cry for vengeance in the sight of God. These sins draw down upon you and upon your nations the flames of the justice of God. The time has come to proclaim to all, with clarity and with courage, that the sixth commandment given by God to Moses: 'Do not commit impure acts' (Ex. 20:14) still has its full force and must be observed even by this corrupted and perverted generation. Every pastor who, in any manner whatsoever, would justify these sins, draws down upon his person and upon his life the fierce fire of divine justice. The cup of iniquity is now full, is more than full and is flowing over everywhere."*

A man's steps are ordered by the Lord, how then can man understand His way."

—Proverbs 20:2

JESUS, I TRUST IN YOU

five

The World Wide Warning: An Unprecedented Act In History

And I will work wonders in the heavens above, and signs on the earth below; blood, fire, and a cloud of smoke.

—Acts 2:19

People who have followed what the Blessed Mother said at Garabandal, as well as messages from other apparition sites, are waiting in joyful hope for several events they believe will alter history as we know it. There are millions of people who have been exposed to these messages and what has been foretold. The events will be difficult for everyone, but for the believer living in a state of grace and receiving the sacraments worthily, it will be easier. It is natural to conjure up different scenarios of what the future may hold, but when events unfold as heaven has said, it will be exactly as prophesied. God is a God of order, and He speaks to us gently and in small doses over a long period of time so we can internalize what He is conveying.

When Jesus walked on the water in the Sea of Galilee in the midst of a storm, His words to his spiritually young apostles were, "*Fear not, it is I*" (Matt. 14:27). Very early in his pontificate Saint John Paul II would often say especially to the young, "*There is nothing to fear,*" and "*Fear not.*"

The Beginning of Garabandal

The story began on the evening of June 18, 1961 when the Archangel Michael appeared to four young girls in a remote village called Garabandal in northern Spain. The Archangel made eight silent appearances the following twelve days. On July 1, the Archangel Michael finally spoke to announce that on the following day, the

Blessed Virgin Mary would appear to them as Our Lady of Mount Carmel. At that time, San Sebastian de Garabandal was a tiny village with only about three hundred people in the Diocese of Santander, Spain. By any standard in the world even for that time it was simple, not impoverished, but primitive. There were approximately 70 small stone houses, no electricity, heat only from home fireplaces, and not one motor with moving parts of any kind. About one quarter of a mile to the north of the tiny local church, the nine pines tower over the village, where the Blessed Mother frequently appeared. Over the next four years, the Blessed Mother appeared over 2,000 times accompanied by frequent miraculous phenomena.

The visionaries were Conchita Gonzales (age 12), Jacinta Gonzales (12), Mari Cruz Gonzales (11), (none related), and Mari Loli Mazon (12). They described the Blessed Mother as about eighteen years of age. The apparitions were preceded by three interior calls, which the girls described as joys, each one becoming stronger. After the third call, the girls would come running from different parts of the village and would arrive at the same time in the place designated by Our Lady and they would fall to their knees in spiritual ecstasy. Frequent phenomena occurred that denied natural law.

Our Lady revealed the first message for the world. She told the girls to announce the message publicly on October 18, 1961. On this day, the children made known the message: "*Many sacrifices must be made, much penance must be done. We must pay many visits to the Blessed Sacrament...but, first of all we must be very good...if we do not do this, punishment awaits us...already the cup is filling, and if we do not change, we will be punished.*" The messages given to the young girls were heavily centered on conversion and amendment of life. The Blessed Mother had a continual theme of the urgency of our times and what would happen, IF man did not repent. However, what made Garabandal unique from all apparition sites in history is the visionaries spoke about two events that would happen: *The Warning and the Great Miracle.*

On January 1, 1965 the Blessed Mother told Conchita Gonzalez that the Archangel Michael would appear to her on the following June 18 to deliver a final message in Mary's name for the entire world because her messages were not heeded. He delivered the final message which said,

> *"Since my message of October 18 (1961) has not been complied with, and has not been made known to the world, I will tell you that this is the last one. Before the chalice was filling, now it is overflowing. Many cardinals, many bishops and many priests are on the path of perdition and they take many souls with them. To the Eucharist, there is given less and less importance. We should avoid the wrath of God on us by our good efforts.*
>
> *If you ask pardon with a sincere soul, He will pardon you. It is I your Mother, who through the intercession of Saint Michael, wish to say that you amend, that you are already in the last warnings and that I love you much and do not want your condemnation. Ask us sincerely and we will give to you. You should sacrifice more. Think of the Passion of Jesus."*

Our Lady appeared wearing the Brown Scapular, an indication we should wear it, and taught the children how to pray the rosary. Her greatest emphasis was placed on the importance of the Eucharist and the priesthood. The last apparition for Conchita was on November 13, 1965 at the nine pines.

The number 18 is significant at Garabandal as some very important messages were given on that date. In the Jewish culture 18 means "*life*," and in the future, the Jews will not be able to deny what happens at Garabandal.

The Story

Garabandal is an extension of heaven's plan for the salvation of mankind—and to prepare the world when the messages were given in 1961. It had been expected that Saint Pope John XXIII would reveal the Third Secret of Fatima in 1960 and he did not, to the disappointment of the faithful. Is it a coincidence that just a year later the Blessed Mother came to Garabandal and gave messages dealing specifically with the Eucharist and the Priesthood, exactly the same time period when Vatican II was meeting and many in the church were deliberately undermining those traditions?

For many people in the Church, the truth about the Third Secret of Fatima is as elusive as the location of the Ark of the Covenant. Many believe the Church has never officially released it in total. We know a portion of it deals with a Pope dressed in white being killed. Yet, that has not happened. There is continual dialogue on the Third Secret that has grown more intriguing with each passing year. It is a never-ending story that grows, and continues to grow as Pope Francis consecrated the world October 13, 2013 from Rome, yet never mentioned Russia by name. Russia was central to Mary's call for consecration at Fatima in 1917. Everyone has an opinion and is aware of certain facts. The Blessed Mother has said to the Marian Movement of Priests it is now "*My Time*" due to the lack of cooperation of God's people to fulfill her plan for peace.

There are powerful forces within the Church blocking the full release of The Third Secret. The political maneuverings inside the Vatican are as significant as any issue in the Church over the last several hundred years. Why? Because we have been told The Third Secret deals with communism, the destruction of the Church from within, deep apostasy of the Church, widespread calamities such as "*fire from heaven,*" millions of humanity perishing, and Satan reaching the very summit of the Church.

There is widespread opposition to the Secret being released for obvious reasons. Cardinal Ratzinger (Pope Benedict XVI Emeritus) while head of the Congregation for the Prefect of the Faith (CDF) and having read the Third Secret of Fatima, said the church-approved messages of Akita, Japan and Fatima are essentially the same. No messages in the entire history of the Holy Roman Catholic and Apostolic Church are as apocalyptic as those from Akita. Pope Benedict XVI while speaking at Fatima on May 13, 2010 made an interesting point when he said, "*May the seven years which separate us from the centenary of the apparitions hasten the fulfillment of the prophecy of the Triumph of the Immaculate Heart of Mary to the glory of the Most Holy Trinity.*" This would put the centenary at 2017.

The Illumination of Conscience

Pope Paul VI (Papacy from 1963-1978) called the struggle of good and evil going on in the world "apocalyptic." Pope Paul at the time quoted

Luke 18:8 which says "*when the Son of Man returns will He find faith on earth*" adding that the "*smoke of Satan had entered the sanctuary.*" The Blessed Mother said at Fatima, "*In the end my Immaculate Heart will Triumph...*" The Triumph of her Immaculate Heart is the return of Jesus in glory. It is never about Our Blessed Mother, as she always points to her Son Jesus. As the Blessed Mother said at Cana when instructing the servants, "*Do whatever He tells you*" (John 2:5). The Holy Trinity has appointed her for this task specifically at this point in time. She says, "*The Refuge is My Immaculate Heart.*" Looking for safety anywhere else will be of no value. Our Lady does not take away from the authority of Jesus in the least, but leads people to glorify and love His Sacred Heart. We are called to be co-redeemers with her in His salvation plan for mankind. What better vessel than Jesus' mother who came into the world without the stain of sin. Her role has been to bring us to Him—and Him to us.

The messages at Garabandal as well as at other authentic apparition sites are simple and direct. They speak in the most basic language about the essential tenets of the faith. The messages are easily understood and speak of truth, goodness, and beauty—not philosophy that few can understand, but always to the heart of a life changing experience. When the message is heard and absorbed, there is a transformation of the soul. Saint (Padre) Pio, Pope Paul VI, Saint John Paul II, Mother Teresa, Father Stefano Gobbi, and many other contemporaries of our time believed in what happened at Garabandal, and were public in affirming it.

The Warning—Seeing the State Of Our Soul

Amen, I say to you, unless you become like a little child, you will not enter the kingdom of Heaven. Whoever humbles himself like this child is the greatest in the kingdom of Heaven (Matthew 18:3-4).

The WARNING is an event where we will see the state of our soul as God would judge it upon our death. There will be nowhere to run and nowhere to hide from the divine truth revealed to us. It will be a line of demarcation in all of history. Satan's lies will be exposed for who he is and the deception he has done. His grip in the world will be lessened. There will be sin in the world after the event, but a line will be drawn in the sand where the fear of Satan is not there. The Free Will of man will still be evident, but the neutrality of people will largely be gone. One will either be for God, or not.

As the Jews wandered in the desert for forty years after they left behind four hundred years of slavery in Egypt, it was not long before they forgot what God had done for them. What was supposed to be an eleven day journey turned into forty years due to disobedience. Shortly after leaving Egypt they were making a golden calf in the desert. While manna and quail were falling from the sky to feed the migratory people heading to the promised land they still were offering up pagan rituals. It will be the same here. Some people will soon forget the graces they have been given at "*The Illumination,*" and will go back to their old ways because they were not properly formed in the faith. It is for this reason that formation in the faith is so important while times are relatively tranquil compared to the turbulence ahead. "*Faith comes by hearing, hearing by the Word,*" and as the Psalmist said, "*I have hid the word of God in my heart that I may not sin against thee*" (Ps. 119:11). If we live Scripture now, we will have a much better chance of understanding the future of God's present plan for the world. The Lord communicates with His people in His own language.

The first of the two events will be a worldwide warning from God. Conchita wrote in a letter dated January 1, 1965, "*Our Lady said that a Warning would be given to the entire world before the Miracle in order that the world might amend itself. It will come directly from God and be visible throughout the entire world. People forget that the Warning will be seen and felt. So that assumes there must be some sort of cosmic or heavenly event in the skies that can be seen on a worldwide basis.*" There is great speculation on what this event will entail. Conchita said it will be like "*two heavenly bodies colliding.*" Conchita wrote on June 2, 1965, "*the Warning, like the chastisement is a fearful thing for the good as well as the wicked. It will draw the good closer to God and warn the wicked the end of times is coming. These are the last warnings.*" Conchita explained "*that the warning is a purification to prepare us for the miracle. Each person on earth will have an interior experience of how he or she stands in the light of God's Justice. Believers and non-believers alike will experience the Warning.*" Conchita said, "*Those living in a state of grace will have less severe impact.*" Mari Loli who died in 2009, was the only visionary to know the year of the Warning, but she did not know the day of the Great Miracle. Mari Loli said, "*We will see it and feel it within ourselves, and it will be most clear that it comes from God.*"

The Lord in His infinite love and mercy for humanity continues to provide every opportunity for His people to make amends. Much evidence, from many sources in the Church today, indicates that the day of reckoning is soon to come upon us. Just as prophets like Amos, Ezekiel, Jeremiah, Jonah, and Isaiah warned the people of impending judgments, we too are being warned by the prophets. The great multiplicity of Our Lady's apparitions shows the urgency of our times. The Warning will be an event on a scale unprecedented in world or Church history. There are miraculous things like days of darkness that have happened several times in Scripture, but not the Warning or Great Miracle.

The Warning will allow every man, woman, and child to see the state of their own soul through the illumination of conscience, or as God sees them in the fire of Divine Truth. The fire of divine truth will enable all of God's people to "see" their lives in the form of a "*judgment in miniature.*" This will be one of several acts of mercy coming from Heaven to allow us to change the direction of our lives. If one is not moved by this, and what it would mean to the world, there is either an insensitivity of spirit or a general unawareness of the profound meaning of these events and their impact on the world.

The Warning Is the Second Pentecost

Message number 383 of the Marian Movement of Priests is titled, *The Holy Spirit Will Come.* The Blessed Mother says something absolutely breathtaking on the significance about The Warning. She said it is the **Second Pentecost.** The message is delivered on the Solemnity of Pentecost May 22, 1988. "*This is the day which recalls the descent of the Holy Spirit upon the Apostles, gathered together in prayer with me in the Cenacle of Jerusalem. On this day of Pentecost of the Marian Year, consecrated to me, I am calling upon you to unite your prayer to that of your heavenly Mother, to obtain the great gift of the second Pentecost. The time of the second Pentecost has come.*

The Holy Spirit will come, as a heavenly dew of grace and of fire, which will renew all the world. Under His irresistible action of love, the Church will open itself to live the new era of its greatest holiness and will shine resplendently with so strong a light that it will attract to itself all the nations of the earth. The Holy Spirit will come, that the Will of the Heavenly Father be accomplished and the created universe once again reflect His great glory. The Holy Spirit will come, to establish the glorious reign of Christ, and it will be a reign of grace, holiness, love, of justice and of peace. With His divine love, He will open the doors of hearts and illuminate all consciences. Every person will see himself in the burning fire of divine truth. It will be like a ***judgment in miniature.*** *And then Jesus Christ will bring His glorious reign in the world.*

The Holy Spirit will come, by means of the triumph of my Immaculate Heart. For this, I am calling upon you all today to enter into the cenacle of my Heart. For this, I am calling upon you all today to enter into the cenacle of my Heart. Then you will be prepared to receive the gift of the Holy Spirit which will transform you and make you the instruments with which Jesus will establish His reign."

The message above has enormous similarity to the Warning that is described at Garabandal, Spain. The Marian Movement of Priests addresses in elegant and majestic language heaven's master plan for transforming the world. Words alone cannot convey the significance of this event. The apostles were frightened men after the crucifixion of Jesus and feared for their lives due to persecution. After Pentecost they left the Cenacle room and went to the streets like roaring lions for the faith. The apostles had been infused with the Holy Spirit in a supernatural way. This will be a similar event with the second Pentecost. We will see ourselves in the "*burning fire of divine truth, a judgment in miniature, and illuminate all consciences.*"

The Blessed Mother is mother and Queen of the Universe. In this time she has taken a more exalted role and speaking to her movement, her people, in her time and her Heart. She is giving very specific instructions that the safety for the future is in her Immaculate Heart under the guidance of the Most Holy Trinity. When the Second Pentecost happens, believers will be operating with preternatural gifts as the apostles did after Pentecost. As the Jews sprinkled blood on the door posts in Egypt so the angel of death would Pass Over them, the Blessed Mother tells us our safety and refuge lies in her Immaculate

Heart. It is for this reason all people are encouraged to have Cenacles including their own families.

The Warning –Conchita

Conchita told us that the Warning will be like "*two heavenly bodies or stars colliding that make a lot of noise and a lot of light, but they don't fall.*" We are going to see it. It will horrify us because at that very moment we will see our souls and the harm we have done. In that moment we are going to see our conscience, everything wrong that we have done, and the good we are not doing. It will be as though we are in agony, but we will not die by its effects, but perhaps we will die of fright or shock to see ourselves. The Warning is a purification to prepare us for the Miracle. Conchita said the Warning is a type of catastrophe. It will make us think of the dead, that is, we would prefer to be dead than to experience the Warning. Conchita revealed to us that it would be very fearful, a thousand times worse than earthquakes. It will be like fire. It will not burn our flesh, but we will feel it bodily and interiorly. Conchita said that if she did not know what the Chastisement was, she would say that the Warning was worse than the Chastisement. Conchita seems to be saying that the Warning coincides with celestial phenomena of some sort when she says, "*two heavenly bodies or stars colliding...*"

During an interview, Conchita said the duration of the Warning is about five minutes. In an interview in October 1968, in answer to a question about the Warning, Conchita said: "*The Warning is something supernatural and will not be explained by science. It will be seen and felt.*" According to Conchita: "*The Warning will be a purification, a preparation for the Miracle, and everyone will see it. It will make people aware of the evil that they do with their sins.*"

Father Joseph Pelletier, the noted Marian scholar, asked Conchita about the Warning of Garabandal. Conchita's answer on June 19, 1965, is as follows:

> *"Here in writing is the warning that the Blessed Virgin gave me when I was alone at the pines on January 1st of this year, 1965. The warning that the Blessed Virgin will give us is like a chastisement. Its purpose is to draw the good nearer to God and to warn the others. I cannot reveal what the warning will*

> *consist of. The Blessed Virgin did not tell me to announce it. Nothing further. God would like that through this warning we amend our lives and that we commit less sins against Him."*

To the question posed by Marian and Garabandal scholar Father Laffineur, whether the warning would cause death, Conchita replied in writing: "*If we die from it, it would not be from the warning itself, but from the emotional shock that we would experience in seeing and feeling the warning.*"

September 13, 1965 Conchita's statements were said in response to questions put to her:

> **Q.** Will the warning be a visible thing or an interior thing or both?
>
> **A.** The warning is a thing that comes directly from God. It will be visible all over the world, in whatever place anyone might be.
>
> **Q.** Will the warning reveal personal sins to every person in the world and to persons of all faiths, including atheists?
>
> **A.** Yes, the warning will be like the revelation of our sins, and it will be seen and felt equally by believers and non-believers, and people of any religion whatsoever.

October 22, 1965 Conchita's statement to a Spanish woman is in reply to a question whether the warning might be a comet that was approaching the earth, Conchita said: "*I don't know what a comet is. If it is something that depends on man's will, I answer—no. If it is something that God will do, it is quite possible.*" When the woman expressed fear and asked Conchita to pray for her, the latter replied: "*Oh, yes, the warning will be very fearful, a thousand times worse than earthquakes.*" To an inquiry concerning the nature of the warning, Conchita answered: "*It will be like fire. It will not burn our flesh, but we will feel it bodily and interiorly.*" She added, "*We shall comment on this later. All nations and all persons will experience it in the same way. No one will escape it. Even the non-believers themselves will experience the fear of God. Even if you hide in your room and close the blinds, you will not escape it. You will feel and see it just the same.*" And again, "*Yes, it is true. The Blessed Virgin gave me the name of the* *phenomenon. It begins with an '*A*' but she did not tell me to reveal it to anyone.*"

As the lady again expressed her fear, Conchita added: "*Oh, but after the warning, you will love the good Lord very much.*" To the question: "*What about the miracle?*" She said, "*The miracle will not delay in coming.*" Conchita added an interesting observation: "*Although it is taking time to come, it will not be late. God's time is always the appropriate time.*" An important note should be added. When Conchita describes the warning as being "*like fire,*" she means that in some way or ways it resembles fire but that it is not fire.

The Warning—Mary Loli

Mary Loli said: "*When the Warning occurs everything will stand still, even planes in the sky, but just for a few moments. At the moment everything stops, the Warning will occur. The Warning will last just a few minutes. It is important we prepare ourselves because it is a terrible thing. It will make us feel all the wrong we have done. Everyone will experience it wherever they may be, regardless of their condition or their knowledge of God. It will be an interior personal experience. It will look as if the world has come to a standstill, however, no one will be aware of that as they will be totally absorbed in their own experience. It is going to be something like an interior feeling of sorrow and pain for having offended God. God will help us see clearly the harm we are causing Him and all the evil things we do.*"

The Warning—Jacinta

Jacinta Gonzalez said, "*The Warning is something that is first seen in the air, everywhere in the world and immediately is transmitted into the interior of our souls. It will last for a very little time, but it will seem a very long time because of its effect within us. It will be for the good of our souls, in order to see in ourselves our conscience...the good that we have failed to do, and the bad that we have done. Then we will feel a great love towards our heavenly Parents and ask forgiveness for all of our offenses. The Warning is for everybody since God wants our salvation. The Warning is for us to draw closer to Him and to increase our faith. Therefore, one should prepare for that day, but not await it with fear. God does not send things for the sake of fear, but rather with justice and love. He does it for the good of all His children so they might enjoy eternal happiness and not be lost.*" The Warning will coincide with celestial phenomena of some sort.

The Game Changer

Right when it appears all is lost, heaven will intervene. *The Warning* or the *Illumination of Conscience* is an event that was given more detail at apparitions in Garabandal, Spain from 1961 to 1965 than at any other place. Many who have experienced such phenomena come back and tell of having seen heaven, hell, and purgatory. There are different degrees of sin, and the more one is away from confession and a Christ centered life, the more difficult it is to hear God and receive grace.

We will be stripped naked before God and we will see our lives like a slow motion movie and we will have no rebuttal before a Divine God. Serious mortal sins will go slower so we can see the hurt we have caused. We will be in the presence of such Divine Light, we will have no response. Sins that are serious will go slower (what Catholics call mortal sins). Sins of omission and commission will have no response from us, as we will know our faults. We will be in the presence of such Divine Light and truth, we can have no response.

The Transition Of Civilization Will Take Place

There are also important links among Mary's messages at LaSalette in France (1846), Fatima in Portugal (1917), Akita Japan (1973), Amsterdam (1940's and 50's), Medjugorje in Bosnia (1981-present), Kibeho in Rwanda (1981-1989), and Garabandal in Spain (1961-1965). They affirm and amplify one another, with similar themes on the importance of the Rosary, the Eucharist, the Mass, the Sacraments, and all that entails living a daily life in communion with God. Many who follow such events, however, make a mistake in thinking that what has been said at one apparition site will automatically carry over to another. This is not necessarily the case and causes confusion. Each apparition site is separate and distinct in message—it stands on its own. The events revealed at Garabandal will show the world God's faithfulness to mankind. What will come to pass in the not too distant future will shake the very foundations of the world. It will bring all peoples of the world to a place we have never been before physically, spiritually, or emotionally. The deterioration of the old ways is now accelerating into decay, allowing a New Era to begin.

Heaven has an agenda and it is filled with grace. We can either accept it, or fight it—the choice is ours. If a person is unsure whether the apparitions at Garabandal, Spain are true, wisdom would say remain quiet and not quench the work of the Holy Spirit. If it is not true, it won't matter. If it is true, nothing you can do or say will stop it. This conjures the similar situation described by the Rabbi Gamaliel when the Jews were fighting amongst themselves after Pentecost. Addressing the Sanhedrin Gamaliel said, "*What I suggest, therefore, is that you leave these men alone and let them go. If this enterprise, this movement of theirs, is of human origin it will break up of its own accord; but if it does in fact come from God you will not only be unable to destroy them, but you might find yourselves fighting against God*" (Acts 5:38-39). The supernatural events that will take place at Garabandal are of such breathtaking scope, it is actually impossible to really comprehend them.

Our Sins Revealed

Sin is our resistance to becoming the loving person God wants us to be. Sin is the result of unloving thoughts, deeds, decisions, and attitudes. Our sin will be vividly clear in the brilliant light, which God shines upon our souls. Our consciences will be thoroughly illuminated at that moment, exposing all the self-deception we indulge in so often, pulling out the dead memories that have never been leavened with love, uncovering the lies we told ourselves and the compromises we made.

We will see the many harsh, stubborn, and unkind decisions we have made, the times we cruelly trod on others feelings, coveted their possessions, envied their good fortune, rejoiced at their failures, or any harm we have done them, especially to the vulnerable or the unborn. We will groan with anguish when God reveals to us the neglect, the refusal to help, the deeds done or undone, and the unfulfilled plans. We will hear God say to us as He did to Saul, "*Why have you persecuted Me.*" All we ever did will be before our eyes, seen all at once, in a single glance. We will know then and see the true universalism of heaven with no barriers of space and time that grasps the uttermost secrets. We will see the true internationalism of Heaven with no barriers of color, race, or creed. He will share with us how He sees us, and in a mercifully brief instant, whatever in us that displeases Him. We will understand our eternal state and the lightness or blackness of our souls. We will suffer for a moment the pain of our sin, the pain of separation from God, the pain of purgatory or hell. We will see it all whether we wish to or not.

Over the last twenty plus years, more than a dozen people who have experienced the Warning have called me regarding their own personal experience of what it was like. Priests, seminarians, and lay people alike tell a similar story—some self- proclaimed people of little virtue, others the most devout daily communicants. All speak of seeing their lives like a motion picture going on before them. In what seems to be a great deal of time, but actually not, some have fallen to the floor and wept for hours as they have seen sins in their lives. When this has happened they have been away from the Church and not lived a life of faith. In every instance, it has been the single biggest life-changing event that they have experienced. With no exceptions, everyone speaks of this "*Illumination of Conscience*" the same way—the single defining moment of their lives. All speak of unconditional love and purity in their midst, which gives them virtually no way to refute their sins. All know they are in the presence of God and His judgment. What I have noticed is that those who went to confession regularly and generally tried to live in a state of grace experienced far less trauma. For those who have lived in a state of sin, we are told by mystics, it will be a very hard day indeed.

Garabandal Is Key

The Warning is a sign for the future and will be a major turning point in world history. The parting of the Red Sea and manna from Heaven were powerful divine interventions for small numbers of people. The world wide Warning and the Miracle will be much greater interventions, for they will affect every man, woman, and child on earth. The Warning will prepare all of the world's people for the message of the Gospel, prepare them all for Jesus and His life. We will know we need a Savior. Without knowing our own sins, we would never understand how much we need Jesus and His forgiveness. The Warning is a direct intervention from God. This "sign" shows again the depth of His love for us. Never before has God acted directly and universally to make every person in the world completely aware of his or her sinfulness and His holiness.

The Warning will be the first dramatic sign to all that the old age is ending. We will be Transitioning to a New Era, a New Epoch, a New Age of time. It is not God's wish that we be among those who refuse to repent in time. Never is it His wish that even a single one of His little ones be lost. Before Jesus went to the cross, in John 17, which is often called the High Priestly Prayer, Jesus prayed "*that not one be lost*" (17:12). We have made the choices, and in the past we have not chosen the way of the Cross. For this reason He has intervened, so that the danger would be manifest, the evil of the present age unmasked, and the darkness of false enlightenment exposed. If the world has not wanted to listen to the truth, and the Father's little ones are being misled, He, in His sovereign majesty and power, will ask us to listen. With the Warning, He will sweep away all the sophistry and deception with which Satan has obscured the light of the Gospel. All of our acquired refinement will be stripped away and we will see ourselves as God sees us.

The Warning As Preparation for the Miracle

A Great Miracle has been foretold by Our Lady of Mount Carmel, which will take place in the little village of Garabandal. A similar miracle, also predicted in advance, was granted at Fatima in 1917, in what has come to be known as The Miracle of the Sun. The sun spun in the sky and hurtled toward earth. Some 70,000 spectators witnessed it. Marvelous as that may sound, even more amazing, the miracle will be experienced by so many more people. Millions will undoubtedly journey there to behold its glory, to be healed, converted, and comforted. They will travel there because they have been prepared to accept the Miracle with faith. The Warning will prepare people for the Miracle and will send unknown multitudes to Garabandal. In 1994, I had a meeting with Conchita's brother while in Garabandal. He told me at the time of the Miracle it would be difficult to travel there. Why, I don't know and can only speculate that the situation in the world will make it difficult to travel.

The "*Illumination of Conscience*" will prepare us to hear God together at Garabandal, where His people will be gathered once again, just as they were on Sinai, where the protective covering of the Shekinah Glory—the cloud or pillar of smoke by day and a fire by night—offered a protective shield and guidance for the people of God. The place of the Miracle will become a destination place.

Blessed Anna Maria Taigi

Blessed Anna Maria Taigi (d. 1837) and others spoke of a Great Chastisement that would come to the world, preceded by an *Illumination of Conscience* in which everyone would see themself as God sees them. She indicated that this illumination of conscience would result in the saving of many souls because many would repent as a result of this "warning," this miracle of "self illumination." Beatified in 1920, and a model for women and mothers, Anna Maria Taigi was not only a prophetess, but one of the most extraordinary mystics in the history of the Church. From the time she was twenty years old until she died at the age of sixty-three, she was accompanied by a mysterious light in which she saw past, present, and future events. Some related to struggles among nations, some related to individual souls. Blessed Anna Maria gazed into that light only when she felt an interior impulse, a sort of direction from Our Lord and the Holy Spirit. When she looked into the light, she was asked to offer some special suffering for a special need of the Church or an individual.

In that light, Blessed Anna Maria saw a Great Chastisement coming upon the world in the future, but at the same time a great blessing. She spoke about the illumination of the consciences of men, just as though suddenly every man was given the same kind of light that accompanied her, in which they would see themselves as God sees them. Blessed Anna Maria Taigi's body in Rome is incorrupt (has not decayed) in a church dedicated to the Most Holy Trinity.

Saint Faustina Kowalska—Divine Mercy

Saint Faustina Kowalska (1905-1938), of Krakow, Poland, experienced on a personal basis a "judgment" where she was allowed to see her sins as God sees them. She wrote about this spiritual experience: "*Once I was summoned to the judgment [seat] of God. I stood alone before the Lord. Jesus appeared such as we know Him during His Passion. After a moment, His wounds disappeared except for five, those in His hands, His feet and His side.* ***Suddenly I saw the complete condition of my soul as God sees it. I could clearly see all that is displeasing to God. I did not know that even the smallest transgressions will have to be***

accounted for. What a moment! Who can describe it? *To stand before the Thrice Holy God!*" "Jesus asked me, '*Who are you?*' I answered, "*I am Your servant, Lord.*" '*You are guilty of one day of fire in purgatory.' I wanted to throw myself immediately into the flames of Purgatory, but Jesus stopped me and said, 'Which do you prefer, suffer now for one day in Purgatory or for a short while on earth?' I replied, 'Jesus, I want to suffer in Purgatory, and I want to suffer also the greatest pains on earth, even if it were until the end of the world.*'

Jesus said: '*One (of the two) is enough; you will go back to earth, and there you will suffer much, but not for long; you will accomplish My will and My desires, and a faithful servant of Mine will help you to do this. Now, rest your head on My bosom, on My heart, and draw from it strength and power for these sufferings, because you will find neither relief nor help nor comfort anywhere else. Know that you will have much, much to suffer, but don't let this frighten you; I am with you*' (Diary 36).

Saint Faustina's writings were silenced by the Church for over twenty years. The Diary of Saint Faustina, called *Divine Mercy in My Soul,* is considered a spiritual classic today. Saint John Paul II initiated the reinvestigation of her life and writings while he was Archbishop of Krakow. She was canonized as the first saint of the new millennium on April 30, 2000 by Saint John Paul II, on the Feast of Divine Mercy before a crowd of 200,000 people in Saint Peter's Square.

British Jesuit Saint Edmund Campion referred to the Warning as "*the day of change" when "the terrible judge should reveal all men's consciences.* Servant of God Maria Esperanza of Caracas, Venezuela called The Warning, "*a great day of light when the consciences of the world will be shaken, and the hour of decision for man," and "the light of the new dawn of Jesus.*"

Night Of the Screams

Over the decades information has been gleaned, interviews given, and more information has been provided about the forthcoming events of Garabandal. The visionaries experienced something called the "*Night of Screams.*" The first night of screams took place on June 19, 1962. Jacinta and Mari Loli saw visions where Russia would have dominion over the world, and communism would rule Europe. Priests would go into hiding, churches would be destroyed, and there would be many martyrs. This vision lasted approximately fifty minutes.

On June 20, 1962 on the Vigil of Corpus Christi there was another horrifying vision that lasted for three and a half hours. They saw destructive things happening in the world at a future time. Mari Loli Mason said, "*We saw rivers change into blood...fire fell from the sky...and something worse still which I am not able to reveal now...*" Three of the girls were shown the Great Chastisement of Fire that would come if humanity reverts to its evil ways after the grace of the Great Miracle. This vision and language is similar to the message of Akita, Japan.

The girls begged the Blessed Mother not to let these things happen, and that people be allowed to go to confession first. They asked that the events would not take place, as it was worse than being burned alive. This strongly suggests that the chastisements are cumulative and there may be several events to occur in some sequential pattern.

A recurring theme of the apparitions all of the young girls spoke about was at the time of the Warning, communism would have engulfed the earth to such a degree that it would make the Mass impossible. To date, this has not happened. When these events occurred from 1961-65 communism was very different than it is today. Now the United Nations and other sovereign government bodies have a concerted, well funded, and organized agenda to remove God from our culture. This is happening today on a far wider basis than in the past, as we see even the West expelling God from society. There is a silent war on Christianity at a policy level over the last several generations. A slow strangulation of Christianity is taking place in the world. One must remember that for communism to be effective, it can be implemented by enforced government public policy year after year, decade after decade until people no longer know their rights, and their liberties have been stripped from them. The Blessed Mother revealed to Father Stefano Gobbi of the Marian Movement of Priests that the "*Red Dragon*" of biblical prophecy is atheistic or Marxist communism, which has succeeded in conquering humanity with its widespread error of theoretical and practical atheism (Message 404).

The Complete Transformation Of a Soul

The Warning will be our *road to Damascus* moment like that of Saint Paul the Apostle (Saul), when he was knocked from his horse and penetrated by the same light we will soon endure. Saul was on his way to Damascus to persecute the new Christian converts. Saul's self righteous bigotry was so strong, it took the Lord Himself to knock him off his horse. In a glorious vision Jesus revealed to him that he was assailing not only the members of the Church, but persecuting Jesus Himself. The blinding light of the Risen Christ convicted him of sin. Saul heeded the warning Jesus had given him; he repented and became the Lord's faithful follower. A follower of Jesus in Damascus named Ananias was told in a vision to lay hands on him to restore his sight and fill him with the Holy Spirit (Acts 9). Saul, one day an enemy of the Church who approved of the stoning the first Christian martyr, Saint Stephen, soon became the great Paul, a saint, after the "*illumination of soul.*" The same grace granted to Saul will penetrate every human heart in a single sudden burst of divine light. Saint Paul became the first "visionary" of the New Testament as his teaching came from infused knowledge because he never met or walked with Jesus. Many of us who have our own rigid views will shortly be knocked off our horse as well.

Communism Disguised, But Still Communism

In 1988, on the 1,000 year anniversary of Kiev Rus, General Secretary of the Communist Party of the Soviet Union Mikhail Gorbachev said the mistake of the Bolshevik Revolution was they tried to remove God from the Russian soul too abruptly. He said this was not possible in a short period of time, and it was for this reason the revolution failed. What a striking truth he articulated. Gorbachev later said, speaking from the Presidio in San Francisco, California that communism needed more of the approach of socialism with small steady incremental changes, because with this strategy the people would not notice what the government was really doing. If we had followed that incremental approach, Gorbachev said, we would have achieved our goals.

If communism continues to develop as revealed to the children of Garabandal, it will come in the way we are seeing government takeover today. The government of the USA has been a good learner and observer of what worked and what failed over the last one hundred years. The government takeover has not been violent thus far, but many freedoms have already been legislated away by the usurping of Congressional, Executive and Judicial powers. Most people don't realize this because entertainment and easy credit have overcome all reason, logic, and spirituality. It will only take one large event of some kind for the U.S. and other governments of the world to treat believers very harshly. What could make the Mass outlawed and go underground? The United States can legally implement through Executive Orders that a believer is "an enemy combatant" against the state as the war on Christianity is underway with abandon.

The UN Attack On the Church—Incremental Communism

The encroachment, year after year of socialism/communism with world governments attempting to eradicate Christianity is well organized. It is steady, intrusive and insidious. The United Nations is now going full throttle in its attack on the Catholic Church. Their goal is very simple: eliminate the Christian concept of living and have a new model of total state control—especially where the family is concerned. All of its efforts are escalating in a profound way. Starting primarily with the Cairo Conference on Woman's Reproductive Rights in 1994, the United Nations has been steadily looking to discredit Roman Catholic Dogma and Canon on homosexuality, abortion, pedophilia, and contraception. The Roman Catholic Church remains the final thorn in the side of the globalists keeping them from fully implementing their godless views. The globalists must tear down the authority of the hierarchy and the role of the papacy itself, and render it powerless to do as they choose. It has long been a goal, and the global elite are getting closer to accomplishing total state control.

Animosity and hostility towards the Church has increased over the issue of pedophilia in the priesthood. Government is building public sentiment on that issue. This is the door global policy makers are pushing to enact laws to end the supremacy of any moral authority. In no way is this an apology for the issue of pedophilia and the Catholic Church, but other faiths and denominations and in particular the US government school system are infiltrated with this sin as well, yet they are rarely mentioned alongside the Roman Catholic Church abuses.

The UN has a goal of preventing the Church from having a seat at the table as an authority figure defending parental control of their own children. The goal of the United Nations is universal access to abortion, gender neutrality, homosexuality, parents losing rights to their own children, and removing the Vatican and Catholicism from any influence or position in the United Nations.

In February 2014, the United Nations Committee on the Rights of the Child Report went into direct assault on the Church and families. The Committee Chair on Children's Rights, Kirsten Sandberg from Norway, said the following: "*we urge that the Holy See review its position on abortion which places an obvious risk on the life and health of pregnant girls, and to amend Canon 1398 relating to abortion with a view to identifying circumstances under which access to abortion services can be permitted. The church needs to assess the serious implications of its position on adolescents enjoyment of the highest health standard and overcome all the barriers and taboo's surrounding adolescent sexuality that hinder their access to sexual and reproduction information.*" This statement is open warfare against the Church and its positions on the sacredness of life and marriage.

Sandberg went on speaking about the fact the Church must change its views on homosexuality and other doctrines held sacred by the Magisterium since Peter. Over the last generation the push has been relentless, but in this moral climate that is deteriorating so rapidly, it is easier to foresee this agenda being realized as clergy and laity in the Church capitulate to the State and demands of global elite corporate interests. The goal of the United Nations is to indoctrinate young children about sexual matters and make the killing of the innocent an easy option, and easily accessible in every country of the world. As of this writing there are seventeen countries that legally permit same sex marriage and the list is growing.

According to Human Life International (HLI) located in Front Royal, Virginia, there have been an estimated 1.72 billion abortions in the world over the last forty years. They say the number is growing exponentially due to governments worldwide promoting abortion through state sponsorship and funding. When we factor in sterilization, contraception, Plan B (morning after pill) and other methods of abortion, the numbers just keep getting larger and larger. But this brings up the question of whether we are bringing judgment upon ourselves through our sins, or is it God's wrath? With over 1.7 billion abortions and counting, we can see now why The Warning and The Miracle will be worldwide events.

At Garabandal, Spain, all four visionaries spoke of the world being "communist" at the time of the Warning. Communism is simply socialism with a venomous strain against the things of God. We are galloping in that direction now, and the above public policy being advocated is communist because it removes God from the culture. Communism does not need to be violent to achieve its goals. Today, it is primarily done through government sponsorship and cooperation with tax-payer dollars financing programs like Planned Parenthood. The confluence of evil globally is making this scenario of irreparable harm to children more plausible. It reminds one of what Jesus said, "*Whoever causes one of these little ones who believe in me to sin, it would be better for him if a great millstone were hung round his neck and he be thrown into the sea*" (Mark 9:42).

This heinous plan is the epitome of Satan's agenda to destroy civilization and corrupt the very youngest by brainwashing at the hands of the state imposed by unelected officials with an agenda to dismantle any resemblance of virtue in culture. Billions of dollars are behind the U.N. through member states contributions and other organizations such as the Bill and Melinda Gates Foundation, The Rockefeller Foundation, The United Nations Population Fund, International Planned Parenthood Foundation, CARE International, Save the Children, the World Health Organization, and dozens of other groups promoting a godless agenda—a world without God is their unstated goal. In the present economic and social environment, it is easy to see that with one major event, worldwide public opinion could rule harshly against the Church if states feel threatened for their very survival due to that calamity. When the seers of Garabandal spoke of the world being communist at the time of the Warning, it has in essence already happened through government policies.

Conchita asked why the Miracle was coming. Jesus told her, "*to convert the whole world.*" Conchita asked, "*will Russia be converted.*"

Jesus told her, "*it will also be converted, and so everyone will love Our Hearts.*"

The Blessed Mother at Garabandal asked for Mass, penance, fasting, confession, conversion, making sacrifices, visits to the Blessed Sacrament, and to pray the Rosary every day. To detractors of Our Lady's messages, that doesn't sound like an heretical message.

There is no fear in love, but perfect love casts out fear. For fear has to do with punishment, and he who fears is not perfected in love.

—I John 4:18

JESUS, I TRUST IN YOU

six

The Great Miracle

Peace I leave you; my peace I give to you. Not as the world gives do I give it to you. Do not let your hearts be troubled or afraid.

—John 14:27

The Great Miracle of Garabandal, Spain will be one of the most spectacular supernatural events of all time. Our Lady has promised that a Great Miracle will take place above the grove of the nine pine trees at Garabandal, Spain. Listed below are some facts we know about the Great Miracle.

1. It will occur on a Thursday evening at 8:30 p.m., between the 8th and 16th of either March, April, May, or June.
2. Much of the early literature mentions March, April, or May, but on European television Conchita once said, March, April, May, or June.
3. The Miracle will coincide with an important ecclesial event in the Church.
4. It will happen on the feast day of a young martyr of the Eucharist.
5. Everyone in the village and on the surrounding mountains will see it.
6. All of the sick present will be cured, and the incredulous will believe.
7. Sinners and non-believers will be converted.
8. It will be possible to photograph and televise this event, but not touch it.
9. Russia will be converted after the Miracle.
10. Conchita, who knows the date of the Miracle, is to announce it eight days in advance.

11. Conchita said the reigning Pope will see the Miracle from wherever he is.
12. It will be seen in the sky.
13. It will last about fifteen minutes.
14. It will be the greatest miracle ever performed by Jesus for the world.
15. Saint Padre Pio saw it before he died in 1968.

According to Mari-Loli (deceased April 2009), the Miracle will take place WITHIN ONE YEAR AFTER THE WARNING. The operative word is "*within.*" Mari Loli did not know the date of the Warning, only the year. She said that the Blessed Mother told her: "*A time would come, when it would look like the Church was finished, when priests would have difficulty saying Mass and talking about holy things.*" The Church will pass through a terrible test. When Conchita asked Our Lady how this would happen, Our Lady called it "communism." It must be noted that communism must be thought of more broadly than what we witnessed during the twentieth century in the former Soviet Union or U.S.S.R. A world that submerges into moral relativism where sin does not exist fits a clearer definition of communism. It is a politically secular and acceptable faith that is void of God. We are seeing this prophecy of communism being fulfilled with state control of all social structures on a global basis.

Saint (Padre) Pio's Affirmation

Saint Pio was one of the only priests in the history of the Church to receive the stigmata from Our Lord. Blessed with many spiritual gifts from an early age, Saint Pio believed in the validity of Garabandal. An incident which confirms Saint Pio's belief in Garabandal occurred early in 1966. Conchita, who was only sixteen years old, was visiting Rome with her mother and a priest, and was invited to meet Cardinal Ottaviani, Prefect of the Sacred Congregation for the Doctrine of Faith. During this visit to Italy, Conchita met privately with Saint Pio as well. On this occasion he took Conchita's hand and her crucifix that Our Lady had kissed in Garabandal, and held them both in his own two hands. The crucifix had been passed through the hands of the child Jesus during an apparition on November 13, 1965.

There has been some recent speculation that Padre Pio had doubts about the authenticity of Garabandal and was concerned about one of the four girls receiving visions. In none of the literature from the time of the apparitions to Padre Pio's death in 1968 can anything be found that substantiates this claim. Also, this claim has only surfaced recently. With the constant phrase so commonly voiced today, "*I saw it on the internet,*" may explain a lot for some detractor(s) to perpetuate this story. To think that Padre Pio advised Joey to visit Garabandal, then meet personally with Conchita, and then ask that Conchita receive the veil from his burial garments, Pope Paul VI to voice support, while in fact doubting the authenticity of the apparition, is a contradiction of all literature surrounding Garabandal.

It was also during this visit to Rome that Conchita had a private audience with Pope Paul VI. No report of this papal audience has ever been made public, except the Pope said, "*Conchita, I bless you and with me the whole Church blesses you.*"

On October 16, 1968, Conchita received a telegram requesting that she travel to Lourdes in order to accept a letter from Padre Pio. At Lourdes, she met Father Bernardino Cennamo, who informed her that he had been instructed by Padre Pio to give her a letter and the first veil that would cover his face after death in the old Italian tradition of burial. Conchita asked, "*How is it that the Virgin told me Padre Pio would see the Great Miracle before he died?*" Father Cennamo answered, "*He did see the Miracle before he died. Padre Pio told me so himself.*" The letter from Padre Pio was transcribed by Father Pelligrino, who attended the needs of Padre Pio in his final years. The letter read as follows: "*For Conchita, Padre Pio has said, I pray to the most Holy Virgin to comfort you and guide you always towards sanctity, and I bless you with all of my heart.*" In addition, Blessed Mother Teresa of Calcutta would often visit with the visionaries of Garabandal and believed in them since 1970. Mother Teresa visited with Conchita in New York shortly before her death.

Jesuit Priest Sees the Great Miracle

Father Luis Andreu, a thirty-eight-year-old Jesuit priest, was visiting Garabandal for the second time on August 8, 1961. After an apparition, he was driving home later that night with friends and had a vision. He suddenly cried out "Milagro!" four times. Father Luis then said, "*What a wonderful present the Virgin has given me! How lucky we are to have a mother like that in Heaven! Today is the happiest day of my life!*" Immediately after, he lowered his head and died. Father Andreu died of spiritual ecstasy after seeing the Great Miracle on August 8, 1961. In a later apparition, Our Lady told the Garabandal visionaries that Father Luis had seen her and had also seen the Great Miracle.

Our Lady also revealed to Conchita on September 14, 1965, that Father Luis Andreu's body will be exhumed and found to be incorrupt on the day after the Great Miracle. Father Luis Andreu's body was exhumed when the Jesuits moved all who had died to a new cemetery in 1977. His body was found to be corrupt. As Joey Lomangino's death has caused some confusion, this too is another puzzle—at least for the time being. It is still possible that at the time of the Great Miracle, Father Andreu's body could be found incorrupt. Saint Paul writes about how little we actually know in this life, "*For now we see in a mirror dimly, but then face to face. Now I know in part; then I shall understand fully even as I have been fully understood*" (I Cor. 13:12).

Other Mysterious Phenomena

During the apparitions, the girls were able to detect and recognize priests who came to the village dressed in civilian clothes, trying to conceal their identities. Many times during the ecstatic walks, the visionaries would offer these priests their crucifix to be kissed. During one of Conchita's ecstasies in 1962, two priests were kneeling down in reverence. They were gently encouraged by Conchita to stand up, in order to emphasize the deep respect that Our Lady has for priests. She taught the children to greet the priest before greeting an angel, because a priest is more important, since only a priest can consecrate bread and wine into the Body and Blood of Christ during the Holy Sacrifice of the Mass.

Another remarkable event of Garabandal emphasized the importance of the Eucharist. An angel appeared bearing a golden ciborium. The angel asked the children to think of the One whom they were going to receive. He taught them to recite the Confiteor, after which he gave them Holy Communion. He also taught them to say the Anima Christi in thanksgiving. These direct interventions occurred regularly whenever the priest from the neighboring village of Cosio was unable to come to Garabandal. Many of these "Angelic Communions" were recorded on film, showing the movement of the girl's lips, tongue, and throat. However, since these hosts were only visible to the girls, many skeptics doubted that they were actually receiving Holy Communion. We know the Miracle is Eucharistic, and since Father Andreu died of joy, did he see a precursor to the Eucharistic Miracle like Conchita received by the angel? When questioned about where the Hosts came from, since only a priest could consecrate them, the angel said the Consecrated Hosts were taken from the tabernacle of the church. Therefore, a priest and not an angel had consecrated the Hosts.

Visible Host

On June 22, 1962, Saint Michael told Conchita that God would perform a "*special miracle,*" and that this little miracle will be a preview of the "*Great Miracle.*" Conchita's diary entry for June 30, 1962, stated: "*While I was in the pines I heard a voice which said that the miracle would take place on the 18th of July.*" The angel later instructed her to reveal this message fifteen days in advance. The miracle of the visible Host occurred at 1:40 a.m. on July 19, 1962. Hundreds of witnesses were present. The event was recorded on film by a businessman from Barcelona. This film was later submitted to the Bishop of Santander. Witnesses said that Conchita knelt and put out her tongue to receive the Host. At first, nothing was visible. In a few moments, a white Host, thicker than usual, appeared on her tongue. It remained there for a few moments before being consumed. Conchita refers to this event as the "*little miracle.*" It was chosen to call our attention to the reality of the Real Presence of Our Lord in the Holy Eucharist, and be the precursor of the Great Miracle.

Young Eucharistic Martyr—Blessed Imelda Lambertini

We do know the Garabandal visionaries said that the Great Miracle is to take place on a feast of a young Eucharist martyr of the church. There are several potential saints who may qualify, but none seems to fit the description and circumstances better than little Blessed Imelda Lambertini. Blessed Imelda did not die a martyr in the sense we often think about it: a white rose of dry martyrdom, or a red rose of blood. Her story is most unusual and coincides with the uncommon and unconventional circumstances surrounding Garabandal and the way the Eucharist was received by the young girls.

Wanting to make her First Holy Communion young, Blessed Imelda was denied that privilege before the age of twelve. On the Feast of the Ascension in 1333, a host miraculously appeared in front of her that she then consumed, thus making her first Holy Communion. She then died of spiritual ecstasy. Pope Saint Pius X named her Protectress of First Holy Communicants. All know of Saint Pio's adoration of the Eucharist. He often said, "*It would be easier for the world to live without the sun than the Eucharist.*" After seeing the Great Miracle in a vision, the Jesuit priest Father Andreu died of sheer joy, and his last words before he died was, "*Today is the happiest day of my life.*" We know the Miracle is Eucharistic. We also know Conchita received the Eucharist from St. Michael the same way as Blessed Imelda. Blessed Imelda's feast day is May 13th. This day, May 13th was also known as Our Lady of the Blessed Sacrament, and the messages speak very heavily of the importance of the Eucharist.

Significant Witnesses and Controvery

Two other significant witnesses who were present during some of the apparitions and whose lives were dramatically changed by the events of Garabandal are Joey Lomangino of New York and Father Ramon Andreu, S.J., brother of the previously mentioned Fr. Luis Andreu.

Joey Lomangino was born on October 5, 1930, in Brooklyn, New York. In June 1947, when Joey was sixteen years old, tragedy struck the Lomangino family. Joey was inflating a tire on one of his father's ice trucks when suddenly the tire rim popped out and exploded in his face. The rim struck him between the eyes, severing his olfactory and optic nerves, causing the total loss of his sight and smell. The following years were difficult. However, with much patience and perseverance, Joey completed his education and formed a sanitation business with his three brothers.

While on vacation in Italy in 1961, Joey met Padre Pio. This meeting changed Joey's life dramatically and he recalls that he was not a very religious man at the time. This meeting began the process of conversion in his life.

Joey returned to Italy in 1963 to meet Padre Pio again. It was during this visit that Padre Pio encouraged him to go to confession. Joey states that as he blessed himself to begin his confession, Padre Pio interrupted him and began to list in perfect English all of the sins that Joey had ever committed during his entire life. A few days later, Joey was kneeling and waiting for Saint Pio to begin Mass. As Saint Pio walked by, Joey experienced what he thought to be an explosion in his head. At that moment, Joey instantly regained his sense of smell. He was immediately aware of the scent of roses. Doctors described the miracle as, "*a light bulb suspended in the center of the room, without wires attached, and was still capable of lighting.*" During this visit, Joey asked Padre Pio if Our Lady was appearing at Garabandal. His reply was "*Yes.*" Joey also inquired if he should go there. The answer was "*Yes, why not?*"

On March 19, 1964, Conchita received an interior message from Our Lady at the pines. She was told that Joey Lomangino would regain his eyesight on the day of the Great Miracle. Conchita also was told that Joey would establish a "House of Charity" in New York that would bring great glory to God. Joey traveled throughout the world giving witness to Garabandal.

Joey Lomangino Dies

Joey died at the age of 84 on June 18, 2014 on the fifty-third anniversary when Michael the Archangel first appeared in Garabandal. Joey's death has caused confusion. This is a great disappointment to many people who have been waiting and expecting Joey to receive his sight on the day of the Miracle. As a true prophecy is given, it will happen exactly as it was said, but not necessarily the way we perceive it will happen. It is has been shown over millennia that a prophecy is never completely understood until time passes which will prove it true or false. The only explanation at this point is that we may see a miracle in a way we don't expect it.

On December 6, 1962, Conchita had a ninety-minute ecstasy at 5:30 pm when she mentioned there would be two things that would happen prior to the Miracle. First she said, "*something will happen that will cause many people to stop believing in the apparitions of Garabandal.*" Second, *the doubts and desertions will not be due to the excessive delay in the Miracle happening.*" There is no doubt many people will stop believing in Garabandal now that Joey has died. Whether or not this is an example like Jonah going through Nineveh calling for repentance or the Lord would destroy the city, and then it didn't happen, no one knows. In the time of Jonah the king called for a fast and the people put on sackcloth and the Lord spared the people (Jonah 3). Jonah was so mortified his prophecy did not come true, he went and hid in shame. The prophecy was not as clean and neat as Jonah perceived it—and seldom has it ever been in history. There were conditions and God saved the people because of their mortification and repentance. Will Joey see later in some sort of biblical fashion? Is Joey a part of the larger picture? Only time will tell.

Father Ramon Andreu, S.J.

Father Ramon Andreu also visited Garabandal to investigate what happened to his brother the deceased Father Luis Andreu. The priest who saw the Great Miracle died of joy afterwards. Father Ramon received permission from his superiors to visit Garabandal, and was privileged to have witnessed more than 400 ecstasies. During his visits to the village, he kept a detailed record in his notebooks of everything he saw and heard. These notebooks represent some of the more valuable documentation. The most startling event for Father Ramon was the revelation from the visionaries that they had conversed with his dead brother, Father Luis Andreu. Conchita's diary entries stated the following:

> *"A few days after Father Luis' death, the Blessed Virgin told us that we were going to talk to him. At eight or nine o'clock in the evening, the Blessed Virgin appeared to us smiling, very, very much, as usual. She said to the four of us: 'Father Luis will come now and speak with you.' A moment later, he came and called us one by one. We didn't see him at all but only heard his voice. It was exactly like the one he had on earth. When he had spoken for a while, giving us advice, he told us certain things for his brother, Father Ramon Maria Andreu. He taught us some words in French, German and in English and he also taught us to pray in Greek."*

Father Ramon was told precise details of his brother's funeral and details of his personal life that were unknown to anyone but himself. On another occasion, Father Luis gave a message for his mother: "*Be happy and content for I am in Heaven and I see you every day.*" This was a message of great joy for his mother, who soon after entered the convent, and a remarkable revelation for us all about our loved ones who have gone to Heaven.

The Church's Early Position

Shortly after the apparitions began in 1961, Bishop Doroteo Fernandez, Apostolic Administrator of the diocese of Santander, set up a fact-finding board of inquiry consisting of three priests and two doctors to study the apparitions. Psychiatrist Luis Morales Noriega and Father Francisco Odriozola led the study. This study was not considered a Canonical Commission. Included in the group was Father Juan del Val Gallo, who was later to become the Bishop of Santander. During the four years of apparitions, the members of this group went to the village only on three occasions. They never met as a body nor did they ever issue a common report. Dr. Morales, a leading expert on mental health declared that the events had a natural explanation based on psychological theory. He dismissed the whole affair as "*child's play.*" In 1961, Our Lady told the visionaries: "*A time will come when all four of you will contradict yourselves one with the other, when your families will also contradict themselves about the apparitions; you will even deny that you have seen me or Saint Michael.*" On this occasion witnesses heard the four visionaries while in ecstasy say: "*How is it that one day we will say that we did not see you, since we are seeing you now?*" Our Lady told them: "*Because you are going to pass through the same confusion as the Church.*" These prophetic words did come to pass at the very beginning. The children later did deny receiving apparitions. Thus, the bishop and his successors had cause for serious reservations about the authenticity of the apparitions. Bishop Fernandez and his immediate successor Bishop Eugenio Beitia issued "Notas." These "Notas" advised caution and restricted priests from visiting the village without permission. They stated further that there was no evidence that any supernatural events had taken place.

However, it is significant to note that Bishop Beitia, in his "Notas" of July 8, 1965, stated: "*... We would like to say, however, that we have found no grounds for an ecclesiastical condemnation either in the doctrine or in the spiritual recommendations that have been divulged in the events and addressed to the Christian faithful; furthermore, these recommendations contain exhortations to prayer, sacrifice, devotion to the Holy Eucharist and devotion to the Blessed Virgin under traditional, praiseworthy forms; there are also exhortations to a holy fear of the Lord, offended by our sins...*" Bishop Puchol, who succeeded Bishop Beitia, was not as favorable. He denounced the events throughout the province with a media campaign. Due to Bishop Puchol's untimely death in an automobile accident on May 8, 1967, Enrique Cabo, the Vicar Capitular, headed the diocese until a new bishop could be appoint- ed. The new successor, Bishop Cirarda, similarly discredited the apparitions by sending a letter to all the bishops, through the Church's Secretary of State.

Dr. Luis Morales

A dramatic turning point in the events of Garabandal occurred on May 30, 1983, the eve of the Feast of the Visitation. Dr. Morales, the leading psychiatrist in Santander, delivered an historic address in which he retracted his original negative judgment and defended the reality of the apparitions. This startling reversal of judgment ended the twenty-two years of silence imposed by the Church authorities of Santander. In his opening remarks, Dr. Morales said: "*I am here today to speak to you on the apparitions of Our Lady at Garabandal. It is because she herself has worked this change of attitude in me. Moreover, I am speaking with full permission of the ecclesiastical hierarchy.*" He concluded by saying: "*I will end my conference pleading with the Virgin of Garabandal, that for the rest of my days, she may keep me under her mantle and have mercy on me.*"

New Commission Appointed

On September 14,1965, Conchita said, "*The Virgin Mary likes it very much that we spread the message and she promised to reward everyone, but obedience to the Church must always come first because this will give more honor and glory to God.*"

In 1986, Bishop del Val Gallo appointed a new commission. He announced to the Vatican during his visit to Rome that he was quietly reopening the investigation on the events of Garabandal. One of the prophecies of Garabandal stated that a future bishop of Santander would at first not believe in the apparitions. However, after receiving a sign, he would lift all restrictions that forbade priests to visit Garabandal. In January of 1987, Father Gomez, the pastor of Garabandal, was instructed by the bishop to allow visiting priests to celebrate Mass in the village church. This change in policy lifted the restrictions of 1962. The bishop in a statement carried by the Catholic News Service explained that his decision had no connection with his belief in the apparitions, but was merely out of respect for the priests who arrive with pilgrims.

Another Area Of Confusion—Three More Popes

Conchita said: "*After Pope John XXIII died, Our Lady told me, 'after Pope John, there will be three more Popes, one will reign only a short time, and then it will be "the end of times.*" When Pope Paul VI became Pope, Our Lady mentioned this to me again. She said, '*Now there will be two more Popes and then it will be the end of times, but not the end of the world.*" If this prophesy is true, we are not far away from finding out about the "end times popes." With the election of Pope Benedict XVI in 2005, who stepped down on March 13, 2013 and then the election of Pope Francis, this would put us into an "end time scenario" concerning the papacy. Having two popes still living is out of the norm to say the least.

In other words "*three more popes and then the end of time*" would refer to Pope Benedict XVI as the Vicar of Christ in place as the end times began. Because the meaning of these words is not yet understood, it would be well to point out that when the visionaries speak of the end of times, they refer to the end of an era or epoch of time. Now with Pope Benedict XVI, and Pope Francis, it seems to say that these are the "end times popes." There seems to be no other explanation of what this means. With the extreme dislocation of the world, this is possible.

If one looks at this prophecy at face value, this too is problematic for many people. Our Lady told Conchita after the death of Pope John the XXIII there would be three more popes and then would come "*the end of times.*" After John XXIII came Paul VI, then John Paul I, then John Paul II, then Benedict XV, then Pope Francis. After John Paul I died, Conchita told her mother there would be four more popes, but Our Lady wasn't counting one of them as he would reign only a short time. We know John Paul I died thirty-three days into his pontificate. Conchita's mother forbade her to talk about a pope that in essence "didn't count" as it would be negative to say it. The Blessed Mother said after the third pope, would come the end of times. If that is correct, John Paul II was the second pope, Benedict XV the third, and Pope Francis is the end time pope. Of if the statement of the three more popes is accurate, either way we are in the "popes of the end times."

This is a reasonable scenario as Conchita was only twelve years old when the apparitions began and a mere sixteen years old when the apparitions ended. It is a very young and tender age to be thrust on the world stage and under a spotlight for the world to scrutinize every spoken word, action, and movement. She would have been obedient to her mother to not create scandal. A German journalist by the name of Albrecht Weber spoke to Conchita and her mother about this issue on November 14, 1965, that was later published in the early 1990's in Germany. Are we into a scenario of end times popes? No one can say for sure until the events either fizzle or happen as prophesied. Again, time will tell.

Only after a prophecy takes place do we understand what it means. The word Apocalypse means "*the unveiling.*" Today, we are witnessing the Book of Revelation (Apocalypse) being unveiled for its deeper meanings that have been hidden until now. The Blessed Mother said she is "*opening the sealed book and its secrets*" at this point in history. All prophecy has a veil over it until the actual event(s) occurs. Have we entered New Times in a biblical sense? The following references to "times" are not intended to interpret the meaning of this prophecy, but rather to illustrate other meanings of the expression "times." For example, in the Old Testament, God the Father spoke to us through the prophets (sometimes referred to as the era or times of the Jews). In the New Testament, God the Son spoke to us directly during His public life on earth (known as the time of the gentiles or the era of time that began with Saint Paul). Today, God is speaking to us through Mary, the Mother of God and other prophets. Saint John Paul II called our century "*Marian Times.*" The fourth and final prophecy of Garabandal tells us that the chastisement is conditional on whether we heed the messages of the Blessed Virgin Mary.

The Events In Perspective

The fear of God that is good is the fear that draws souls to God and prompts sinners to amend their lives. This is precisely the purpose that Conchita ascribed to the Warning. It will cause a holy fear of God. Our concern at this moment should be to draw closer to God, cast all sin from our lives, and strive to love and serve Him better. If we do this, we will be ready for the Warning when it comes. To be sure, it will strike fear in our hearts. However, this fear will not kill us. It will bring us closer to God because we fear offending Him as a son fears offending his father who is always good to him. As predicted, there has been confusion and controversy in regard to the spread of the message of Garabandal. Jesus told Conchita on February 13, 1966: "*Don't worry yourself with whether people believe or do not believe... I shall do everything. But I will also give you suffering. I will be with whoever suffers for me... You will have much to suffer for few people will believe you.*" Both the suffering of Conchita, and the lack of belief in the apparitions were foretold by Our Lord.

The Pillar Of Smoke at Garabandal and the Synagogue

Conchita was told by the Blessed Virgin that a sign would remain at the pines and it would remain there forever. It would be possible to photograph and televise it, but not touch it. It would appear as a thing not of this world, but it would originate from God. It would be miraculous, a permanent miracle. It is comparable to a pillar of smoke, but also to rays of sunlight, insofar as it can be seen but not touched. It will be made up of an unknown substance.

All the Hebrews who followed Moses out of Egypt saw the "*pillar of cloud by day and of fire by night*" (Exodus 13:21), that saved them from the Egyptians (Exodus 14:24), accompanied the Torah at Mount Sinai (Exodus 19: 16-18,34-35), remaining present among His people, serving as their guide "*wherever they halted on their journey,*" (Exodus 40:36), "*marking out their encampments*" (Deuteronomy 1:33). It was the Lord who "*appeared to them in this pillar of cloud that rose above them at the tabernacle door*" (Deuteronomy 31:15).

The mysterious cloud invaded the Temple of Solomon (I Kings 8:10). Nehemiah celebrated the Lord "*leading Thy people on their journey, hidden by day in a pillar of cloud, by night in a pillar of fire, to light the path they must tread*" (Nehemiah 9:12, 19). The Psalms mention it five times: as the guide of God's people (Psalms 77:17-21 and 78:14), overcoming the idolaters (Psalms 97:2-7), as protector (Psalms 105:39), as carrying His word: "*His voice came to them from the pillar of cloud; so they heard the decrees, the law He gave them*" (Psalm 99:7). The prophets announced it would come back, "*a cloud and smoke by day, and the shining of a flaming fire by night*" (Isaiah 4:5). "*It shall come to pass that I will pour out my spirit upon everyone all flesh; your sons and your daughters will prophesy, your old men shall dream dreams, and your young men will see visions, and I will show wonders in the heavens and on earth, blood, fire, and pillars of smoke. The sun shall be turned to darkness, and the moon to blood, before the great and terrible day of the Lord comes*" (Joel 2: 28-31).

The luminous cloud has always been a choice subject of rabbinic thought and Christian mystical theology. Most Jewish people know what the pillar meant: a manifestation of God dwelling among His chosen people, tabernacling amidst them, guiding them, shedding light upon them, speaking to them. Other nations also knew this (Numbers 14:14). It is the Shekinah, the most sacred and mysterious sign of the deity. The Shekinah Glory is Heaven itself. It is God's physical presence that was with the Ark of the Covenant in the desert, guiding the Jews to the Promised Land.

Conchita said the permanent sign above the pines will be something like a pillar of smoke. On November 18, 1961, a column of smoke by day and fire by night was seen by a number of people between the nine pines. Ramon Gonzalez, a shepherd about twenty years old, was tending his sheep and noticed a small fire about 50 centimeters in diameter. Again in the fall of 1962, this was seen by a number of people for a period of two or three months, all of whom provided written testimony. It was then seen again on November 25, 1965, by four French witnesses. The column was seen at night, clear and luminous.

The Likely Reaction From the Rabbi's

For faithful Jews and Rabbis, a thorough knowledge of the Scriptures is a large measure of their religious life. In Israel, whatever their beliefs, all citizens have studied the Hebrew Bible as a text of Hebrew classical literature. Whether or not they consider it as divinely inspired, they still know it. They know that it has been prophetically announced that, "*your sons and your daughters will prophesy...* " (Song of Songs 3:6, Joel 2:28 and Acts 2:17-21). Thanks to the media that will cover the event, they will know at once that Catholic women have announced that the Mother of Jesus revealed to them that a pillar of smoke will appear in a Catholic village in Catholic Spain and remain there "*para siempre*" (forever). They will all be interested, especially the Sephardim, the Spanish Jews. Their interest will be extreme and lasting.

Saint Bernard and Saint Thomas Aquinas

Historians consider that the first schism in the history of the people of God was between the Gentiles and the Jews. This schism was caused by the refusal of the Synagogue to accept Jesus of Nazareth as the Messiah. For several centuries, this first schism was not fully effective. In the Roman Basilica of Santa Sabina (early Fifth Century), portentous figures of the Church from the Gentiles and of the Church from the Synagogue stand side by side as true believers. Saint Bernard (1090- 1153) and Saint Thomas Aquinas (1226-1274) wrote that the Church would allow the Synagogue to enter into the fullness of her redemption. Saint Bernard wrote that the Synagogue has not in the eyes of God forsaken her birthright over her sister the Church. The Lord has not revoked His covenant with His people Israel. Saint John Paul II called the Jews "*our elder brothers in the faith.*" Saint Thomas in his commentary on the Song of Songs taught the future reintegration of Israel would usher in the third era of the Church. The Warning and the Great Miracle will be the catalyst for the Jews coming into the faith as the Shekinah Glory is known to all Jews.

Saints and popes alike, including Saint John Paul II, have spoken about the mystery of the Church and the Synagogue. Paul wrote in Romans 11:15, "*Since their (the Jews') rejection meant the reconciliation of the world, do you know what their acceptance will mean? Nothing less than a resurrection from the dead.*" The Second Coming of the Lord and the prelude to it are expanded in 2 Thessalonians 2:7. There will be an "*acceptance*" by that part of Israel which hardened itself (Romans 11: 7-24), and that it will result at least in part from what will happen at Garabandal.

Saint Michael the Archangel

On June 18, 1921, Our Lady appeared to Sister Lucia (Fatima) and said at the end of her message, "*Until San Sebastian.*" Forty years later to the day on June 18, 1961, Saint Michael appeared at San Sebastian de Garabandal, Spain. Also, at Lourdes, France, the Blessed Mother appeared to Bernadette Soubirous eighteen times.

Saint Michael prepared the four young visionaries for the first apparition of Our Lady on July 2, 1961. The first apparitions of Garabandal were of an angel, from June 18 to July 2, 1961. July 2 in the old liturgical calendar is the Feast of the Ark of the Covenant. It is the Blessed Mother who is now the New Ark of the Covenant. A great deal has been written on St. Michael's role at Garabandal. St. Michael is named three times in the Old Testament, each time as a guardian of Israel or as its Prince. Daniel 10:20 reads: "*He ('one in the likeness of the sons of men') said then, 'Do you know why I have come to you? It is to tell you what is written in the Book of Truth. I must go back to fight against the prince of Persia: when I am done with him, the prince of Javan will come next. In all this there is no one to lend me support except Michael your prince.*"

Daniel 12: 1-4 describes Michael again and his role in the latter times:

> *At that time Michael will stand up, the great prince who mounts guard over your people. There is going to be a time of great distress, unparalleled since nations first came into existence. When that time comes, your own people will be spared, all those whose names are found written in the Book. Of those who lie sleeping in the dust of the earth many will awake, some to everlasting life, some to shame and everlasting disgrace. The learned will shine as brightly as the vault of Heaven, and those who have instructed many in virtue, as bright as stars for all eternity. But you, Daniel, must keep your words secret and the book sealed until the time of the end. Many will wander this way and that, and wickedness will go on increasing.*

St. Michael will "*stand up in a time of great trouble,*" and thanks to him "*thy people shall be delivered.*" His power is great as he is "*one of the leading princes.*" Daniel 10:13 writes about the apparition of Michael, "The prince of the kingdom of Persia has been resisting me for twenty-one days, but Michael, one of the leading princes, came to my assistance." Although the Church applies this passage to itself, it is not possible to exclude "*those who are Israelites,*" as they were the first to have Michael as their prince. Romans 9:4-5 speaks about the privileges of Israel. It reads: "*They were adopted as sons, they were given the glory and the covenants; the Law and the ritual were drawn up for them, and the promises were made to them. They are descended from the patriarchs and from their flesh and blood came Christ who is above all, God forever blessed!*"

The Blessed Mother at Garabandal

For the first time in the history of Marian apparitions, as announced by Michael, the Blessed Mother appeared under a title which refers to a biblical holy place—Mount Carmel. The three holy mountains of the ancient people of Israel were Mount Carmel, Mount Sinai or Horeb, and Mount Zion or Jerusalem. Mount Carmel is the mountain made holy by Elijah the prophet. It is the mountain Mary saw from where she lived in Nazareth. Moreover, of all religious orders, the Carmelites are by far the closest to Judaism. Elijah is considered by Carmelite friars and sisters as their founder and model. They celebrate his feast on July 20th of each year.

Conchita described Mary in her diary as a beautiful Jewish woman with dark and wavy hair, a perfect nose, full lips, and a rather dark complexion. Mari-Loli asked her one day if she was Jewish, and her answer was, "*yes, and I am with my people in heaven.*" It was the first time in the history of apparitions that the Blessed Virgin identified herself as such, saying that even in Heaven she belonged to the Jewish people.

The Great Miracle at the Nine Pines

Millions will be able to see the Great Miracle on that day, for Garabandal is perched among hills forming a broad natural amphitheater able to accommodate the vast multitude who will journey there. A great assembly will converge on the village from everywhere, and all who manage to reach its hills will behold the same vision of joy that sent Father Luis to Heaven as he witnessed the miracle.

On June 14, 1979, the Solemnity of Corpus Christi, Father Gobbi, founder of the Marian Movement of Priests, held his only cenacle at Garabandal with the entire published message that he received from Mary devoted to Jesus in the Eucharist. This is important because the primary messages of Garabandal were about the supremacy of the Eucharist and the importance of the priesthood.

On December 8, 1980, the Blessed Mother said to Father Gobbi that when all seems lost in the world, there will be a great manifestation of the Eucharistic Heart of Jesus. Whether or not this is related to the miracle of Garabandal is not known.

The miracle will be ecclesial, that is, it will support the truth that through the Body of Christ which is the Church, all graces come, and all men and women are called not only to follow Jesus personally, but also to enter His Church and to submit to its discipline, teaching, and sacraments. For this reason, the Miracle will happen in connection with an ecclesiastical event.

The World Changes In an Instant

The Miracle is for the conversion of the whole world. This assertion was made by Our Lord Himself to Conchita at Garabandal. The Lord answered her question about Russia's conversion by assuring her that "*the miracle was not only for the conversion of Russia,*" but "*for the conversion of the whole world, thus, all will love Our Hearts*" (the hearts of Jesus and Mary). It seems by His words that somehow the Miracle will show us all how closely the hearts of Jesus and Mary are united, as a symbol of the peace giving love that should unite our hearts. Perhaps the two hearts on the reverse side of the "Miraculous Medal" were a prophecy as well as a lesson, foretelling an age ahead where all hearts will be reconciled as are the hearts of Jesus and Mary. Reconciliation of hearts is what conversion is all about. All the Marian apparitions have this theme.

Those who return from the mountain in Garabandal shall have seen the glory of the Lord and be eager to sound His glory to the world. The glory of Zion, the glory of the New Pentecost prayed for by Saint John XXIII as he opened the Second Vatican Council and again by Pope Paul VI when he drew it to a close, will flow over the whole Church and the entire world. As Jesus revealed to Conchita, "*all will love Our Hearts.*"

There Will Come a Great Sign Which Will Fill the World With Awe

1. Another voice weighing in mystically concerning a worldwide event of great magnitude is Pope Pius IX when he said, *"There will come a great sign which will fill the world with awe. But this will occur only after the triumph of a revolution during which the Church will undergo ordeals that are beyond description."*
2. Father Joseph Brennan, O.C.S., who summarized the prophetic statements made by saints, the blessed and popes, about the coming trials coming to the Church, said: *"they foretell a time of unprecedented and terrible confusion and suffering unlike anything that has ever been experienced in human history. It will affect every area of human life."* When one looks today at the confusion and division surrounding us from every sphere of human endeavor, the global interconnectivity of the world economy, the breakdown of every social structure possible, one would not have to be a visionary to see how things could unravel even more rapidly with a global systemic financial or geopolitical event. Like never before in human history, a large negative event in one country will have profound implications for many other countries.

Saint Faustina

Jesus spoke to Saint Faustina of a cross in the sky in the last days in great detail: "*Before I come as the just judge, I am coming first as the King of Mercy. Before the day of justice arrives, there will be given to people a sign in the heavens of this sort: All light in the heavens will be extinguished, and there will be great darkness over the whole earth. Then the sign of the cross will be seen in the sky, and from the openings where the hands and the feet of the Savior were nailed will come forth great lights which will light up the earth for a period of time. This will take place shortly before the last day*" (Diary 83).

The Chastisement

During July of 1962, Conchita, Mari-Loli, and Jacinta were shown a vision of the impending chastisement. Our Lady told the visionaries that if we do not heed her warnings and mankind does not change after the Warning and Miracle, God will send the chastisement. In a note

Conchita stated: "*The punishment is conditioned upon whether or not mankind heeds the messages of the Blessed Virgin Mary.*" Conchita said in her diary: "*If the world changes, the chastisement can be averted.*" In describing the vision of the chastisement, Mari-Loli said: "*It would be worse than having fire on top of us—fire underneath us and fire all around us.*" She saw people throwing themselves into the sea, but instead of putting the fire out, it seemed to make them burn more.

After the Miracle, a Permanent Sign

A permanent visible supernatural sign will remain at the pines until the end of time. It has been likened to a column of smoke or a ray of sunlight but is not either one. As a result of the Miracle, Russia and other countries will be converted. On the day after the Miracle, the body of Father Luis Andreu will be removed from his grave and found incorrupt.

It will remind us forever of the great miracle, which will center on that very spot. Anyone who wishes will be able to go to Garabandal after the Miracle and see the sign. It will recall to our minds that God summons the world to repentance. Since it will remain there, it will also insist by its presence that the world will indeed one day end, and that Jesus will come again on the "*clouds of Heaven to make all things new, and to judge the living and the dead.*"

The sign will focus our attention on the truth that God has visibly intervened on this mountain, just as He did on Mount Sinai, Mount Carmel, Mount Zion, and Calvary, to call His people to Himself. Patriarchs of old set up altars and monuments to commemorate forever their experience of God at a certain place, which became forever sacred by His coming. At Garabandal the Lord Himself will set His own sign in the pines for a perpetual memorial of His saving act for today's world. It will be the greatest and ultimate act of Divine Mercy in all of history.

Jesus said to her, (to Lazarus's sister Martha before He raised Lazarus from the dead) *did I not tell you that if you would believe you would see the glory of God?*

—John 11:40

JESUS, I TRUST IN YOU

seven

The Path To Growth: Recognizing The Problems And Removing Them

Preserve me, O God, for in thee I take refuge. I say to the Lord, Thou art my Lord, I have no good apart from thee.

—Psalm 16:1

Fear is the greatest reason why a godless agenda has been thrust upon peoples of the world. Satan uses it to disable us. When we feel we know what is righteous and good, but fail out of fear or laziness to be involved in our faith, we are as guilty as the perpetrators of evil. Whether believers or not, if we settle for critiquing the injustices of the world and do nothing, we are lukewarm and culpable for remaining bystanders. Like the political pundit who just talks rather than becoming a part of the solution, the believer who sits by idly watching and observing from a distance is guilty. Satan is the author of fear. Saint Faustina in her Diary (dictated by Jesus to her) in several places says, "***fear is useless, what is necessary is Trust.***" Satan makes us think our voice will not be heard and nothing can be done to alter the scales of injustice and the direction of society. Yet history says the direct opposite. It is the person who takes a stand who changes the culture. Fear is the reason we are where we are. Fear of what others think, fear of the unknown, fear of stumbling, fear of failing, fear of not being loved, fear of falling, is why we fail to start. A good definition of FEAR could be: False Evidence Appearing Real.

Things work better when we all work together for the common good. Saint Paul wrote about this when he addressed the Corinthians. He said, " *...God put all the separate parts of the body on purpose. If all the parts were the same, how could it be a body? As it is, the parts are many but the body is one. The eye cannot say to the hand, 'I do not* *need you', nor can the head say to the feet, 'I do not need you.' What is more, it is precisely the parts of the body that are the weakest which are the indispensable ones; and it is the least honorable parts of the body, that we clothe with the greatest care*" (I Cor. 12:18-23). Every voice and every effort count no matter the profession.

Paul was writing to a church in Corinth that was weak and immature. Paul wrote earlier in the same letter, "*Brothers, I myself was unable to speak to you as people of the Spirit: I treated you as sensual men, still infants in Christ. What I fed you with was milk, not solid food, for you were not ready for it; and indeed, you are still not ready for it since you are still unspiritual. Isn't that obvious from all the jealousy and wrangling that there is among you, from the way you go on behaving like ordinary people*" (I Cor. 3:1-3).

Saint Paul says to this immature church, he can only give them the milk of the gospel rather than the meat because of their weakness of faith. Because they were sensual, they were still infants in Christ. One can tell the maturity of a person by what they choose to argue about. What they choose to divide a relationship over. Rather than find common ground and agree on the essentials, the immature individual will choose to focus instead on minutiae where they can prove a point. We need to rise above the petty differences that divide us. In times of stress, history shows us that inconsequential differences dissipate. There really is no other choice for community to grow. As times get more difficult for many, stress will accelerate.

Stimulation vs. Simplicity

Too much stimulation and outside activity causes us to lose our peace. The more inputs we absorb, without some outlet of silence and reflection, the more difficult it is to hear God's voice. It is the Lord alone who can give us peace, but we have to follow the necessary steps to secure an environment where peace is achievable.

The more an interior life is developed the more people seek silence. It is from this silence that we will find the direction God is asking from us. All of our greatest achievements will come from that silence because our activities will be born from prayer.

On my way home from Orlando several years ago, I was waiting in the airport for my flight home. The flight was delayed, and for several hours I was stuck there waiting. Content sitting in a corner with a book, I noticed kids screaming, yelling, unruly, running around, and a very loud decibel level bordering on chaos for the parents. Time at Disney World had them high as kites. It dawned on me later that what I had been observing is that these kids had nothing but mental and emotional stimulation for days on end at Disney World. They couldn't deal with the constant stimulation they had just experienced. While in the amusement park, it had been a carousel of non-stop activity from morning till night and it had left them in a state of perpetual motion and emotional euphoria they couldn't handle. It was obvious these kids were not in control of themselves, and for that matter the parents weren't in control of them either. This constant activity problem applies to adults as well. If we do not take quiet time for reflection and prayer, we have no chance of peace and hearing what the Lord is asking of us. Quiet, prayer, and reflection are primary ingredients to hear God's voice.

Too many inputs cause our brain to become disoriented and unable to see what is most important in life. The tyranny of the urgent overwhelms us, and it is not long before we will cease to function as we ought, unless we can have more quiet time and eliminate distractions. The more programs we load into our computer, the slower it runs and the more problems it causes for the operating system. It gums up everything when we load program after program, and it is not long before we need a new one. It is the same with us. Pick activities wisely, and it will allow a greater sense of peace in what we do. Saint Francis of Assisi said, "*do few things but do them well.*" We each have a specific purpose that God requires of us, and unless we are able to drown out the noise, we will never know what it is. If there is one gigantic time sapper, it is television and watching an inordinate amount of sports and entertainment. Both have a proper place, and can make life more fun and enjoyable, as well as staying fit and learning from the enjoyment of good television viewing. But, excessive inane viewing is detrimental to what is most important in life. Have you ever noticed how some people use their time well while others just fritter it away? Those who use time wisely get so much more done. Recreation is very important for mental health and is advisable. Mental and physical recreation is necessary for a healthy body and soul. No one would deny variety is the spice of life. But making it our god is another matter. There is time for people to hit the gym hour after hour, watch sports weekend after weekend for decades, but how often in the course of a year is there time for even ONE hour of Eucharistic Adoration for Catholics acquainted with this practice? ONE hour of silent prayer or reading the Scriptures?

Simplicity of lifestyle likewise is an essential element in spiritual growth—not dullness or being dim witted, but maintaining a life of practical simplicity and austerity to the degree possible. Being bothered less by "things" that wastefully occupy our time. Not running madly to and fro all day, all week, all month, year in and year out, but asking the Lord, "*what do you wish from me? What would you like me to do today?*" Saying in prayer, "*Lord, I am here and I am willing to listen.*"

Eliminating the Noise

If we are to hear God we have to eliminate the noise. Everywhere we go, there is noise, and it is impossible to avoid it totally. If we are to be effective in removing the obstacles that create the noise, we need to approach the problem in another way to be successful in conquering it. As a person is serious about dieting and losing weight, they will remove the items from the refrigerator or pantry that are full of sugar or too much sodium. Devise a few short plans to start to eliminate the daily noise. That is one way to start a new plan to create an atmosphere of prayer, less noise and distractions and a general atmosphere of contemplation in the midst of the daily chaos. Between the ever-present social media, there is something always blasting in our ears. To know God is to listen. He speaks with a "*still small voice*" (I Kings 19:12). In that passage of Kings with Elijah, the Lord was not in the great and strong winds of the mountains, the earthquake or the fire, but in the "*still small voice.*" It is in silence where we hear God speak to us, and for this reason a scheduled time of prayer to listen is essential to our spiritual life.

Mother Teresa spoke of the need for silence when she said, "*We need to find God, and He cannot be found in the noise and restlessness. God is the friend of silence. See how nature—trees, flowers, grass— grow in silence. See the stars, the moon and the sun, how they move in silence. We need silence to be able to touch souls.*"

In the future, the noise around us will just continue to increase—and we need to make decisive moves to eliminate it. The political, social, and financial structures will get much more disruptive, and prayer will be the essential element to hold onto, lest we self-destruct. Existing systems that have endured for generations are on the verge of total collapse. If we are to thrive spiritually, Proverbs says, "*above else, guard your heart*" (Proverbs 4:23). We must not let the world's poison into our spirit, but protect it from the world. We need to protect our eyes and mind by what we see. We will need to elevate our thinking, and triage to what is most essential, and eliminate the rest as irrelevant, and no longer worthy of our time. The superfluous will no longer sustain or amuse us in the coming days.

As our relationship with God deepens, some people may gradually move away from us, and we must expect that. Many drug addicts and alcoholics will tell how they had to leave addicted friends if they were to stay clean. Our life will become more of a counter sign from those around us the same way Jesus experienced when He walked the earth. Only those of pure heart stayed the course. The rest faded into irrelevancy. We should not seek the approval of people who are not walking in the light. It will not always be easy, but relationships will not be the same. It is not about shunning people, but we will realize that if we wish to move in a different direction with the Lord as the center of our life, circumstances in relationships will change. Saint Francis de Sales often counseled people on the issue of communication and he said, "*I will not speak until my heart is at rest.*" The Lord will always have the right word for you if you are in prayer.

Speak Lord, Your Servant Is Listening

The story of Samuel and Eli illustrates what it means to listen to God. The young boy Samuel was not accustomed to knowing what it meant to hear the voice of God. It took the older well-trained Eli to instruct Samuel how to listen. Listening is the first step. God gives us instructions what to do when we listen to His voice. The Lord speaks to Samuel:

> *"Now the boy Samuel was ministering to the Lord in the presence of Eli; it was rare for the Lord to speak in those days; visions were uncommon. One day, it happened that Eli*

was lying down in his room. His eyes were beginning to grow dim; he could no longer see. The lamp of God had not yet gone out, and Samuel was lying in the sanctuary of the Lord where the ark of God was, when the Lord called, Samuel, Samuel! He answered, 'here I am!' And ran to Eli and said, 'Here I am for you called me.' But he said, 'I did not call; lie down again…' Once again the Lord called Samuel again, the third time. He got up and went to Eli and said, 'Here I am since you called me.' Eli then understood that it was the Lord who was calling the boy, and he said to Samuel, 'Go and lie down, and if someone calls say, speak the Lord, your servant is listening.' So Samuel went and lay down in his place. Then Samuel lay still until the morning, when he opened the doors of the Lord's temple. He was afraid to tell the vision to Eli, but Eli called him and said, 'Samuel my son. Here I am,' he answered. What message did he give you? Eli asked, do not hide it from me. May God do this to you, and more, if you keep back anything of what he said to you. Samuel then told him everything, keeping nothing back from him. Eli said, "he is the Lord; let him do what He thinks good" (I Samuel 3: 1-4, 7-9, 15-18).

This is a well known story of the ages. The bible is not meant to confuse us, but bring clarity to how God communicates to His people. God is speaking and the untrained ear of young Samuel didn't know what he was hearing. When a person is in prayer they become trained to listen.

A Good Listener

Many years ago there was an evangelical missionary in the Pacific islands by the name of E. Stanley Jones. He had been an itinerant preacher for much of his adult life, and had spent several months in the 1930's and 40's among an indigenous people on a remote island. Jones had been a church planter nourishing people young in their faith. As Saint Paul went to Corinth, Galatia, Ephesus, and other cities, E. Stanley Jones had been a missionary doing similar things hopping to remote areas as he felt called. He spent decades doing this all over the world. He felt that the time had arrived to depart. He was scheduled to leave at an appointed time months in advance as ocean going vessels didn't come around too frequently so he booked passage well in advance. As the time came, the boat showed up on schedule. There was an elaborate ceremony for him in honor of his leaving with festivities, food, drink, and garlands.

Just before departure, Jones said he couldn't get on the boat. He didn't know why, and was embarrassed to tell his hosts that he could not leave. He said he just had a prompting he was not to get on the boat. He didn't know what to say, and there was general confusion about his decision, as months would pass before another boat arrived. Jones decided to stay. Several weeks later the island found out that the boat blew up and sank several days after it left. The explosion and death of everyone on board was news throughout the area. Jones said he had a prompting of the Holy Spirit not to leave, and he was obedient to what he heard in prayer. Jones had two advantages over most believers. One, he was trained as a good listener, and two, he had the courage of his convictions to do as the Holy Spirit instructed him and not be swayed by the opinion of people. There is a lesson in that for all of us today. We too, need the courage to do as the Holy Spirit is asking no matter the embarrassment and awkward circumstances of what appears to be foolish in the eyes of men. The Lord is wanting to communicate with us, but we need to discern His voice. If we do not take time for quiet, we will not hear His voice.

The Entertainment Craze

The formation of faith is more desired in tranquil times than in times of extreme stress. One may grow spiritually while in the fire, but it is not the best place for formation. Spiritual formation requires reading, studying, contemplation, prayer, and times of stress make it more difficult to grow versus just trying to cope. It is better to fix the leak in your roof in July when the weather is fine in a cold climate, rather than on Christmas Eve in the middle of a snowstorm. Being prepared with a solid spiritual foundation is of the utmost value in enduring any trial. Strength of faith is what gives us endurance for the long haul. The Blessed Mother has said at Medjugorje that at some point, "*it will be too late to convert.*" What does she mean by that? One can imagine as prophesied events unfold, the world will be in such a state of turmoil, it will be difficult to find the composure and perspective to place the events in their proper context.

If there hasn't been formation of faith, we will look through the natural eyes of man and not see the supernatural work God is doing in the world. We will be tossed to and fro by the winds if we have not cultivated deep roots. After storms, it is amazing to see massive trees with great girth uprooted. It is the trees without deep roots that are most affected. The tree that has deep roots is able to withstand the wind. One cannot see the wind, but you can see the devastating results it can do. When the rain and winds come, if one has not been rooted in the basic and most enduring aspects of the faith, people will be strewn about like twigs. It is the same with the movement of the Holy Spirit. We can see where the Holy Spirit moves by the peace and tranquility it creates. Likewise, we can see turmoil and sin where the Holy Spirit is not present.

If anyone doubts the U.S. and the world are fixated on the entertainment craze in our midst, they should not be. In 2013, U.S. consumers spent over $20 billion on diet related issues. If one looks at supplements, vitamins, gym membership, the number balloons to ten times that. The average dollar amount spent on entertainment per middle class family is estimated at $2,500 a year. For people making over $250,000 a year, the figure is over $7,000 a year. It is estimated U.S. consumers in 2013 spent over $520 billion on entertainment, and that number may vary greatly depending on what one includes. Presently, there is more activity around the Super Bowl than Easter. Parties weeks in advance and tickets selling for over $100,000 to attend a sporting event. Over 100 million viewers tune into the Super Bowl not including those abroad. The NFL Today programming is on television and cable Eastern Standard Time (EST) from 11:00am to 1:00am east coast time (Pacific coast games occurring later given the three hour time difference) with families congregating around sports all weekend. We will be held accountable for wasted time and grieve during The Warning for our sins of omission as much as those of commission. This is not including the myriad of other sports consuming our lives.

Peace Of Soul In Our Times

Many speak about the sins of capitalism. No financial system or social structure can work without God. Capitalism is flawed like any other system, but this is not the primary issue of the division among men. As man struggles to find an equilibrium within socialism, capitalism or any other "ism," it is destined for failure unless God's spiritual laws are central to its execution. The problem in the world is not capitalism, but *unbridled materialism*. When man becomes frustrated and cannot have all that he desires, an agitation of the spirit will drive him to have a more materialistic view of the world. Over time if there is not a moral check, that man will become frustrated and do things that are increasingly immoral. He may still operate within the law, but nonetheless be immoral. No legal system is able to cover all contingencies of man's behavior. Since true happiness and peaceful contentment elude him, in time he will lose the desire to have the spiritual dimension because it no longer interests him. Until we are able to properly order our priorities in life, a soul will not be at rest.

Our priorities in life are first loving God with our heart, soul, mind, and strength. Second, our spouse if married, third our children, then our neighbor, lastly, our job or career. When this divine order falls into place things go better. When we establish this order, there is greater peace, harmony, and order for everyone—and everything around us. With God's plan for our life, our affections are not disordered. This is where we see the blessings of God.

The Sabbath

How many people have worked sixty hours a week including the Sabbath to see all of the hard work bring destruction to the home? Everything the person worked for produces little fruit because their order was not in line with God's order. Everything they thought important now is a shallow pool of lost financial dreams with a soul wanting God. The person who works on the Sabbath on continued basis will not see the blessings of their labor. Jesus was clear it was permissible to pull the sheep from the pit if it fell in on the Sabbath (Matt. 12:11). The issue is the violation of the day in which God asks us to worship Him. Jesus was clear the Sabbath was made for man, and not man for the Sabbath. It comes down to the order the Lord prescribes for us, and how we should live according to His statutes and commands, not our whims as if He does not exist or is an afterthought.

When we "re-create," we are doing something that was the purpose of the Sabbath—to be re-created in God. The Sabbath was designed by God for man as a day of family worship, rest, and leisure. Sports and TV can be a part of that, but with reason and balance. As the saying goes, "*all things in moderation, but love.*" There are only Ten Commandments, and keeping the Sabbath Holy is one of them. A healthy and vibrant lifestyle is important for us to feel good physically. However, when everything else in life is subordinate to excessive leisure and entertainment, we never hear what God is asking of us. Excessive noise and distractions crowd out all that is meaningful. Jesus emphasized the purpose of the Sabbath was to honor God as the day of rest for man.

Data: Why Church Is Important

The data below from a survey in 2013 illustrates why attending church is important to families.

- If a father does not go to church, only 1 in 50 of the children will attend church in the future.
- If a father regularly or irregularly goes to church, and the mother does not, the children will attend church 66% to 75% of the time.
- If the father does not, and the mother does, the children will attend church only 33% of the time.

The role of the parents and the example they give their children is crucial for their spiritual upbringing and the example they set for the family.

The Internet and Time

In April 2014, the MIT Technology Review reported a correlation between the rise of internet use and the decline of Americans claiming religious affiliation. According to Allen Downey, a computer scientist at the Olin College of Engineering in Massachusetts, the increase in internet usage has a significant inverse correlation with religion. According to the study, in 1990, eight percent said they had no affiliation with religion. In 2010, that figure stood at eighteen percent or 25 million people. Downey analyzed data from the General Social Survey done by the University of Chicago. Downey said the single biggest cause of religious affiliation is upbringing: those who are raised in religious households are much more likely to remain in their family's religion as adults. Since 1990, the number of people raised in religious households has fallen. His analysis concluded that the internet, plus lack of faith in homes, contributes to this enormous decline which is nearly one in five people living in America claiming no religious affiliation.

In an age of relativism and instant gratification, now several generations removed from any theology, philosophy, or Scripture taught in schools, we have a society nearly void of any Godly pursuits. Media, gaming, sports, general entertainment, and the internet govern our waking time.

The Tongue and Complaining

The subject of the inability of people to control their tongue is probably the single greatest reason why people cease to grow and why there is discord in the world. Saint James addresses this issue:

> *"So the tongue is a little member and boasts great things. How great a forest is set ablaze by a small fire!"* (James 3:5).

The problem is not just the tongue, but our heart, because out of the abundance of the heart the mouth speaks. We speak ill of people because our heart is not at rest. A rudder on a boat is very small in comparison to the ship's overall size, but look how the boat can be steered over oceans! That nasty little rudder in between our cheeks can do us, and others enormous damage if our soul is not transformed from our lower nature. For this reason the Lord has said, "*Let what you say be simply 'Yes' or 'No'; anything more than this comes from evil*" (Matt. 5:37). If we are to have harmony in our homes, community and fellowship, the tongue must be tamed to build unity, not division. No one likes to be around negative people as little good comes from them. The tongue can bring betrayal, division, arguments, discord, cynicism, discouragement, rudeness, slander, harshness, deceit, indiscretion, pride, a judgmental spirit, abusive, and more synonyms that are negative. If we took to heart what our mother told us as little children, "*if you don't have anything good to say about anyone, then don't say it.*" If we all lived by this motherly proverb, we would all be the better for it as the words we speak set the course for our life.

As Psalm 34:1 says, "*I will bless the Lord at all times; His praise shall continually be in my mouth.*" Or as the rhyme goes, "*If you complain, you will remain, and if you praise you will be raised.*"

Reasons Why We Are Not At Peace

There are conflicts in the homes and streets of the world because there is no peace in our heart. This is not the final resting place, and heaven is our goal. Saint Augustine said, "*You made our hearts for Yourself O God, and we shall not rest until we rest in Thee!*" The person who does not have a desire to know the things of God, will drift to whatever is fashionable in the world. They will not be able to withstand the storms of life because they will not have the spiritual fortitude to fight the downward slide of the culture. When one believes in nothing, they will believe in anything. When we are alienated from God, we become alienated from ourselves and others. In time, we become alienated from everything but self-pleasure. As the path of self-pleasure progresses, that individual will develop more psychosis and neurosis. The longer one is estranged from God, the more severe the illness. As the mental state continues to deteriorate, physical ailments accumulate, and the negative cycle becomes more severe psychological disorders. At this point the difference between the origin of physical and mental problems become more difficult to discern. The famed psychiatrist Karl Menninger wrote a book on this subject called, *Whatever Became of Sin.* As the founder of the Menninger Clinic in Topeka, Kansas, his conclusion after a lifetime of study and direct observation was most psychological disorders had their roots in sin.

The more we say "yes" to what heaven is asking, the more we become filled with grace. Heaven is searching for people who will do His work. II Chronicles 16:9 says, "*The eyes of the Lord move to and fro throughout the earth, to give strong support to those whose heart is blameless toward Him.*" The Lord is looking for vessels He can use to do His work. His eyes are looking t*o and fro,* searching for the man's heart who is perfect towards Him. The Blessed Mother continues to ask us to cooperate with her plan. To the soul that desires a vibrant faith quickly develops with a confidence the Lord is directing the path of the individual. A holy boldness occurs for this person who will trust, as they know God dwells within them and is ordering their life because they gave it to Him. This self-confidence and assurance is the quality of a person seeking God. To the soul who can say, *God Alone, Nothing Else,* here is true freedom, for the seed of discouragement cannot take root in a grateful heart.

If my people who are called by my name, will humble themselves, and pray and seek My face, and turn from their wicked ways, then I will hear from heaven, and will forgive their sin, and will heal their land.

—II Chron. 7:14

JESUS I TRUST IN YOU

eight

Heal the Family—Heal the Nation

The thief comes only to steal, kill, and destroy. I have come that they may have life, and have it more abundantly.

—John 10:10

There may not be a verse in the Bible that gives a more accurate description of the battle in our midst than the one above—or the true nature of Satan. At the end of Jesus' forty day fast, when He was at His weakest physically, Satan came and said to Him, "*all the Kingdoms in the world are mine to give you*" (Luke 4:6). Satan does dispense power to souls who are willing to work for him. John 10:10, illustrates what's at stake in the battle between Satan's plan to steal, kill, and destroy, and the Kingdom of heaven's gift of life and giving it to the fullest. Grace, love, peace, contentment, virtue, and enjoyment are the fruits Jesus brings. It would logically seem an easy choice, but free will and original sin let Satan enter our lives. The world entices us to taste from Satan's sweet allurements, but in the end that brings nothing but destruction. Sin will often appear to be something we desire or need, and be rationalized as morally defensible, but it brings nothing but grief, isolation, and a broken spirit. Satan entices with the flesh and the spirit of the world that can never satisfy. Man will always want more, but "the more" is only something God can give. Many who appear to have it all, are in reality very unhappy. If worldly riches or sensual satisfaction alone could make us happy, all the wealthy would be happy. For most people, excess money is a portal to vice.

Jesus Christ had a two-fold mission: to preach the gospel, heal the sick and cure the downtrodden. The Lord is about healing of brokenness, healing from division, healing from curses, healing from drugs, healing from divorce, healing from addictions, and healing from everything preventing us from going deeper into the Immaculate and Sacred Hearts. God wants us to be fully alive and fully human. He wants us to have an abundant life worth living and a joyful, spirit filled existence, "*on earth as it is in heaven.*" Saint Ignatius of Loyola said you know something is of God if it is peaceful, calm, and joyful. If it is from Satan, it will be the direct opposite and be preceded by agitation and anxiety.

There is the story of the wise old monk who lived a life of moderation, sacrifice, altruism, austerity, and holiness. He had lived a virtuous life and was on his deathbed awaiting his eternal reward. Half conscious, the devil came before him, and said, "*you have won, you have beaten me.*" The wise old monk opened one eye, and he looked right at the devil, and said, "*not yet.*" The moral of the story is, it's not over until it's over. The devil never sleeps and is on the prowl seeking the ruin of souls. Therefore, we must be vigilant until the end. There is no rest in this life, but there is a promise there will be rest in the next. As the Blessed Mother told a young Bernadette Soubirous at Lourdes, "*I can give you happiness in the next life, but not in this one.*" Life is a test, and it requires never letting down your guard. Knowing the wiles and snares of the evil one is the key to winning the spiritual battle. At the end of his life, Saint Paul confessed this sentiment and his work for the Lord when he said, "*I have fought the good fight, and run the good race, I have kept the faith*" (2 Tim. 4:7).

If there has been a battleground where Satan has wreaked havoc, it is the family. Historians, philosophers, theologians, clergy, parents, teachers, political and civic leaders, law enforcement, sociologists, academics, judges, political pundits, social workers, medical personnel, and others rarely unanimously agree. But all concur that what happens in the family is the basis of what happens in the streets. Strong marriages and families produce healthy balanced children who grow up to become active and constructive citizens. What happens at the dining room table is seen first by the teachers. Russian author Leo Tolstoy once remarked, "*every problem family has a different story, but every happy family has the same story.*" Proverbs provides some insight on why teaching your children the faith is important, "*Train up a child in the way he should go, and when he is old he shall not depart from it*" (22:6).

A litany of horrific data could be provided to illustrate how families have been so harmed by the culture. The focus here is on what it will take to recognize the problem for what it is and provide a solution. The fact is most families have been so overwhelmed by the culture, they really don't know where to start to turn things around. They either lack the will or tools to make changes, or are ignorant of where to look for solutions.

If there is a group at the vanguard of seeing the issue of family instability, it is elementary school teachers. Teachers are the ones who interact daily with the young. In the U.S., it is generally recognized today by most people that our educational system as a whole is in extreme crisis. The best and the brightest from the wide spectrum of society are jumping on board to help find solutions. Financiers, lawyers, investment bankers, and philanthropists are pooling ideas and money to help turn around this downward slide. What is happening in education has now risen to a national security concern as we are falling behind other nations so rapidly. First, public education needs to make radical reforms if it is to survive as intended. However, too much is asked of a teacher to serve as the surrogate parent, disciplinarian, babysitter, counselor, mentor, nursemaid, scheduler, advocate, friend, psychologist, and a dozen other roles that reflect and highlight family dysfunction. When a student walks through the classroom door, many times the setting is not conducive to learning. A student's family dysfunction creates behavioral disruptions for the entire classroom. Despite initially sincere intent and purity of heart on the part of the teacher, they become overwhelmed by "the system" and many quit caring as they feel they are fighting an uphill battle on a daily basis. School room problems originate with family dysfunction.

Often, there are too many other things going on in the child's life which are emotionally disruptive so they are not able to learn with enthusiasm. As a general statement, there are just too many problems in the home for children to perform as expected in the classroom. The reality is family problems trickle through a child's life everyday. When education abandoned God and Faith as the standard of excellence which all children should aspire, our country sealed its fate. Sociological data supports the view that after we kicked God out of the classroom, we have gone steadily downhill ever since in nearly every category of measurement. The metro pages of the newspapers are filled weekly with the dire consequences of our anti-God choices.

Education will not make forward progress under the present system of government that is hostile to faith and religion. It is a mathematical and Biblical certainty we shall end up on the ash heap of history if such hostility by government continues—and there is no reason to believe that is subsiding. It is God who raises nations up and brings nations down. When we abandon fidelity to Him, it is simply a matter of time before we end up in a moral state of depravity. There is no other sensible solution but to bring faith back into the classroom. It will unfortunately, take more blood in the classrooms and streets before God is welcomed back.

Nothing is impossible with God. God's mercy knows no bounds and is endless. No matter the background, restoration is possible as it is the will of the Father that we all be spiritually, physically, and emotionally healthy whole people. Many who have been away from the Lord and the sacraments believe they are unworthy to approach Him. The lie of the devil is that you cannot, or will not be restored and forgiven. The prophet Joel speaks of this when he says, "*I will restore to you the years that the locusts have eaten*" (2:25). No matter what the locusts destroyed in their path, there is a new day that will dawn that will be brighter. No matter the destruction of the past, there is reconciliation and restoration when asked. That is the story of the Lord and His people, and the entire New Testament. Moses killed a man, yet leads God's people out of Egypt. David had Uriah killed, yet became a great King, and God said, "*David was a man after my own heart*" (Acts 13:22). Mary Magdalene (from whom Jesus cast out seven demons) was only one of a few at the foot of the cross during the crucifixion, and the first one that Jesus appeared to in a risen state. Jesus' good friend Peter denied Him, as Jesus had prophesied to him, yet he became the great leader upon whom Jesus built His church. Anyone who came to Jesus with a sincere and repentant heart found solace, forgiveness, peace, healing, and restoration. The mission of Jesus was to restore the sinner to harmony with God.

Generational Sin

We often see the same things occur from one generation to the next within families. Family members into drugs, repeated divorce, children out of wedlock, gambling, child molestation, alcoholism, bad character, and any vice one can think of. Kids in trouble in school, perennially bad students, generally unruly family members, bad marriages, freemasonry in the background, and other issues seem to plague some families. The blessings and promises of the gospel seem to elude some, while others seem to have good fortune is not always easy to discern. How much is of demonic origin with the devil's hand in it, or how much is the result of years of acquired bad habits that over time become psychological? Whether or not we can answer these questions definitively, we can come closer to unloosing the chains by being more knowledgeable. Deuteronomy 5: 8-10 and Exodus 34: 6-7, say, "*the Lord ...visits the iniquity of the fathers on the children and the children's children, to the third and fourth generation.*" This may seem like a harsh thing for God to do when the generation coming up has virtually no control over its own future based upon what some father, grandpa, great grandfather, or great-great grandfather did generations ago. The point is clear, generational sin is slavery that over time becomes family bondage. Leviticus 26:39 goes even further, "*Because of their iniquity, and also because of the iniquities of their fathers they shall rot away like them.*" Why do certain people and families just seem to go from problem to problem and crisis to crisis? Is it bad luck, or is there more happening here than meets the eye? It is disturbing, but there is good news. With the New Covenant, God gave us the means to wipe away this generational sin. We no longer need carry the burden if we actively break the chains of sin with the power and authority God has already given us.

God Blesses

The Bible also says, conversely, "*but showing love to a thousand generations of those who love me and keep my commandments*" (Exodus 20:6). The sins of the father are visited upon three and four generations, but *blessings are visited one thousand!* The requirement is to keep the Commandments. Here again is the unfathomable love of God, no being angelic or otherwise can comprehend. If we conservatively allowed just 20 years for a generation, this would mean the blessings are indeed a very long time!

Seems like an easy choice to make, so long as we know what God has said about it by knowing the Scriptures. Unfortunately, many don't know the Scriptures, and as a result don't seek the blessings God wishes us to receive. Since we are Scripturally illiterate as a society, we will pay the price for ignorance. There is natural law, laws made by man, and there is Divine law. It has been said, "*God always forgives, man sometimes forgives, and nature never forgives.*" No matter the fault, there are repercussions for good and bad decisions. However, there is forgiveness and redemption with God. The devil will use the hurts and mistakes in your life and make you think there is no hope. Jesus thirsts for us and the reason for His death on the cross was for the salvation of sinners.

It's up to us to break the chains that bind us to generational sin: sins and actions that preclude our growth. The gospel message is Jesus came to deliver us from sin. He is the Light of the world. The book of Acts says, "*where ever Jesus went, signs and wonders followed*" (Acts 2:43).

One should expect a healing or restoration when one follows what Jesus promised us. If a lot of water has flowed under the bridge, miracles still are possible, but the healing may follow a different path, as it is not a magic bullet to make everything as it once was. Father Hampsch, a priest who has written on healing for a lifetime, said, "*The problems ahead of us are never as great as the Power behind us.*" No problem exists that cannot be reversed by God. The Lord has given us all the tools in the sacraments, Church teachings, and Scripture for healing. All we have to do is have the courage to apply them. However, there are many mysteries in life, and not everything works out as we think it should. There is suffering, sickness unto death, sickness unto the glory of God, and things we will never fully understand.

One will often ponder in times of difficulty, "*Am I being punished?*" It is a normal human reaction to ask such a question. The question may be, "*Why me all the time, why my family?*" No one can answer that question for you. Even Job, in the midst of extreme misfortune, was confronted by his friends who said he was being punished for his sins. Job's wife was on the verge of cursing God for their misfortune. In the end, Job's blessings multiplied more than he had ever before experienced. The mystery of suffering will never produce a satisfactory answer to the person enduring great trials. The mystery of human suffering is arguably as great as any mystery we have. It ranks along with the Eucharist, the Incarnation, the Virgin Birth, the Resurrection, the Holy Trinity and other mysteries that we will never fully comprehend. It is normal in times of stress and difficulty to ask WHY. Even Jesus on the cross asked why, "*Now from the sixth hour there was darkness over all the land, until the ninth hour. And about the ninth hour Jesus cried out with a loud voice, 'Eli, Eli, la ma sabach-tha ni!' that is, 'My God, my God, why hast thou forsaken Me*'" (Matt. 27:45-46).

The following bullets and framework are from the work of Father Hampsch and Father Ssemakula. In the past I have attended several seminars that address these issues that have far reaching implications in our daily lives. We all need to pay attention, especially youth, as many mistakes in life are avoidable. I have personally seen many breakthroughs in family bondages when people are obedient to the fundamentals of the faith addressed in this book. What is outlined is not an immediate panacea for all that is wrong in a family with results coming overnight. It will take time, and if one person in a family begins to apply the principles, it can ripple throughout the entire family tree and the healing process can begin. Applying the principles day by day will help families to begin healing. We can expect to see better days ahead emotionally and spiritually, but sin and dysfunction are often passed from generation to generation. In time we can see results, but they are not always immediate. Often so much water has flowed under the bridge that it can take a long time to see restoration, but there has to be a starting point to reverse the course of negative events that caused the problems. If we turn to the Lord, He will enter our families. Day by day, month by month, and year by year, we will see positive results if we remain faithful to God's promises. The key is to believe and trust it will happen no matter the circumstances. God works miracles.

There is much we can do to greatly minimize the negative events coming our way in life through spiritual obedience, and awareness of evil and their snares. So how can we best go into combat and defeat the enemy whose sole agenda is to devour souls? The longer we don't pay attention to Satan's wiles, the more susceptible we become to negative events impacting us. There are toeholds, footholds, and strongholds that must be discerned to break these bondages as soon as they are spotted as being troublesome. To know the wiles of Satan is to defeat him.

The Five Cardinal Points Of Knowing How the Devil Works

1. We are physical and spiritual beings.
2. We are created attached to other people.
3. We do not have total control of the choices in our life. Many are made by others.
4. What we say has enormous impact.
5. There is tremendous power in the name of Jesus.

These are the starting blocks to identify how the enemy seeks to steal, kill, and destroy. Obviously, we have more control over some of these than others.

1. It is obvious that we are spiritual as well as physical beings. It is God who has created us in His image and likeness. No matter how we argue the point, we are spiritual beings designed by our Creator, to know, love and serve Him. The longer we deny that, the more pain we endure until we submit to His will. When we walk into a home we can feel its spirit. Its occupants exude either positive or negative spirits. We can sense a spirit of acceptance and love, in the same way we sense a spirit of rejection or evil. Some environments are so negative we can feel evil spirits. Sometimes there is a spirit of anger, hostility, sarcasm, violence, discord, strife, disorder, and other negative emotions. On the other hand, other homes convey love, tranquility, harmony, peace, and enjoyment where you feel relaxed. The more someone is not moving with the Holy Spirit, the less you will feel the virtues of God in that venue. Saint Paul says, "*we wrestle not against flesh and blood but against principalities and*

spiritual wickedness in high places" (Eph. 6:12). There is a hierarchy of good, and a hierarchy of evil.

We are also physical beings. We are flesh and blood. We have free will that can make good choices, and sometimes not so good choices. It is often our spirit that initiates things that affect our body. Our thought life can affect our physical life. It may be the thought life that has more control over how we feel in our body. The science of positive thinking shows an enormous connection between what we think and how we feel, and vice versa. Take a soldier who loses a limb in battle. That injury immediately affects the soldier's spirit often creating depression or despair. The spirit and the flesh function in unison. The same applies to something as small as the common cold. A minor illness can sap the life from our spirit. Satan can get a stronghold if we are not cognizant of the interconnectivity of the spirit and the physical world.

2. We are created attached to each other. We are all created from the union of others. After creating the heavens and the earth, the Lord said about the creation of man, "*it was very good*" (Genesis 1). Then on the seventh day He rested. God in His Almighty wisdom as the Creator of the universe decided to bring children into a family unit, of father, mother, brothers and sisters. It is simply His design. In our age of godlessness, it is being challenged like never before in all of history. A unique historical phenomenon showing just how perverse we have become as a nation, and as a world, is the widespread acceptance of homosexuality. It is bringing down God's wrath and judgment upon us. Historically, we have seen people turn their face from God in small and even large numbers, but nothing like today. We are born into a family that is designed to be a domestic church. The embodiment of "*on earth as it is in heaven*" is the intent of God for families. But not all hold this truth to be self evident, and problems start from the outset. Drinking, drugs, gambling, workaholic behavior, divorce, infidelity, and a host of other social ills cause destruction for the entire family. No one comes away unscathed from the vices affecting families. Due to the familial connection, all are impacted. The process of healing needs to take place if the home and family is to become tranquil and be released from evil. Due to this negative impact, decisions are made consciously and unconsciously by family members that often perpetuate vice. Like it or not, you are connected to them and share the same DNA.

Have you ever noticed how children of alcoholics often become alcoholics, and then marry children of alcoholics, and then the kids start drinking young—and they become alcoholics? The same with divorce. The sin then becomes a generational continuation until someone has the will to break the connection to the past sins of the family. What is seen in the household is considered normal because it is what the children saw growing up. The cord of connection needs to be broken if there is a negative pattern. There are ways to do that just by renouncing it with a strong prayer from the heart, but it will take an alteration in habits, which is where the physical side of the equation comes into play with strong will and desire for God's best in our lives. There are prayers that should be said to renounce our past life of sin.

3. The most important decisions are made for us by our parents when we are young. Where we go to school, the food we eat, what sports we were introduced to, the church we go to, what type of social activities and so forth are the culture of a family. The very young do not make decisions for themselves. Sometimes it is healthy, and sometimes not. What we are introduced to very young, we have no choice in those decisions. Only with advancing years, do options appear, sometimes they have to be fought for, and other times emerge without our acceptance. These early choices and decisions by parental authorities or guardians have a lasting affect in our lives. Again, the influence can be positive or negative, and when a person gets older, decisions have to be made that can be difficult and require maturity. Our thought patterns and habits are so ingrained in us it is hard to break out of the routines if we come from a negative environment. We tend to become what we are used to.

If a child is brought up in the projects or in a crack house, unless there is a positive experience in the child's life through a friend or mentor, the cycle is hard to break. Prisons are filled with men and women who have not had positive role models. There is the story where a prison warden gave every man in the prison a Father's Day card with a stamp on it. The inmate only had to come and get the card and it would be sent out. The warden said not one man came to get the card. If a young child does have the desire to break out of a downward spiral, he can see the influence of a kid like him in the neighborhood now getting rich by selling drugs. It is only normal for many of these kids to start dealing, and the rest is history. Sooner or later they get caught, and the cycle begins again for another generation of dereliction. Who we associate with is an area of the devil's interest.

4. The power is in the mind. Matthew 12:34, says, "*out of the abundance of the heart the mouth speaks.*" What we think about is what we talk about and then the way we act. What we speak in joy or frustration counts. The people who change the world see the reality of the world and operate with joy in it. Can you think of many things the atheist has brought to the world? Have they contributed to virtue in man? Do you like being around them? Are you inspired by them? Here is an area where we have complete control if we choose to exercise it. It is not always easy as the lower nature of man comes into play to see the negative. Have you ever noticed how someone who says they are sick, is always sick? No one likes to see him or herself as a hypochondriac, but that is what they are. The battle is in the mind. Is there sickness, yes! Can it be valid, absolutely. The point is how we give Satan room to take control in our life as it concerns faith if you doubt God's graces. The discussion here is about your thought life and your tongue and always expressing negativity and doubt. Doubt is the opposite of faith. When we speak the Word of God, we are expressing faith. It is why Scripture memory is so important. When we speak faith, good things happen. This is an area that should be read, researched, and studied at length.

When we speak we release one of two energies, doubt or faith. Belief or unbelief. Doubt is of Satan, faith is of God. We reap what we sow, and reap what we speak. We then reap a new destiny based on trusting in God. It is why we must associate with people of faith and not doubters or skeptics as they do not elevate our spirits. All of the great men and women of God have been people of faith. Not a faith based on false promises, but faith that God will move in our lives. Trust. In Christ all things are possible. Good things happen when we are obedient to God in humility and faith. This is where God goes into action and hears our cries. This area should be greatly studied to obtain the promises of God. Reading and studying on family bondage to discern your particular problem is something that one should do to break the bondage.

The Bible is a book about many great men and women of faith. No matter where we look we find them. One particular story about extraordinary faith is the story of the Shunammite woman in 2 Kings 4. The Shunammite woman and her husband wanted a child. As Elisha the prophet and his servant Gehazi traveled through their area, the Shunammite woman and her husband perceived they were "Holy Men," and they offered them hospitality and lodging on the top of the roof of their home. The wife was barren, and she asked Elisha to intercede to God for a child, and the request was granted. However, shortly afterwards the child died. Heartbroken, she then traveled to meet Elisha to "heal" her son as she was not accepting death. She had been promised a child and now it was taken away, and she did not accept it. She went to find Elisha. Traveling some distance, she was met by Elisha's servant Gehazi, as Elisha had sent him out to greet the woman. Gehazi asked, "*are you well, is your husband well, is your child well?*" She answered, "*Yes*" (4:26). Upon meeting Elisha the story grows and the child is resurrected from the dead. It was faith and the power of the spoken word that her son would be healed. When asked how the child was doing she said, "*Yes, my child is well.*" The power of faith was in her tongue because she expected great things from God and had been promised a son. Yes, the spoken word matters. Faith enables God to work. Jesus was not able to perform miracles in certain places because He said there was no faith. Lack of faith constricted Jesus in being able to heal as He wanted to.

5. There is power in the name of Jesus. The devil has to flee when he hears the name of Jesus. Have you ever noticed that people all over the world curse in the name of Jesus? Have you noticed when people need deliverance, they seek a Catholic priest? Have you noticed anyone curses saying,"*Oh Buddha?*" A Muslim curse saying, "*Oh Muhammad?*" No, the world curses in anger using the name of Jesus Christ. Muslims and all faiths curse using that name. Why? Because there is power in the name of Jesus. Jesus was the only person who came into the world to die. He was the only person in history who prophesied He would die, and rise in three days. He was the only person in history to have a tomb guarded for fear of His rising. He alone is God, and in that name is power. Demons are cast out in the name of Jesus.

The Access Points and How the Devil Can Take Control

There are many different levels of the devil being involved in a person's life. The book *Heart of Darkness* by Joseph Conrad is about the progressive nature of evil. It is a short story about a man by the name of Charles Marlow, based on Joseph Conrad's trip as a young man. The story is about an ivory merchant sailing down the Congo River in Africa encountering horrors the further he goes. The movie *Apocalypse Now*, directed by Francis Ford Coppola, is based on the book. The book starts with a steamer jaunting down the river in what is supposed to be a normal trip. But each day Marlow encounters the pagan barbaric savagery of man, versus the civility of man he has known. Towards the end of the trip more things are seen which show the reprobate nature of man. Ultimately, what starts out as an innocuous journey ends in death. In the end, sin brings horror and an ultimately ugly death.

There are primarily four access points where evil is given reign in a person's life if not checked, and stopped in its tracks early. Sin is often generational and passed onto the children as discussed earlier. Sin must be stopped to prevent it from being passed onto the next generation and we can take full control of that through our self-will and by asking the Holy Spirit for enlightenment—and wanting to be free. Sometimes the spirits are strong, sometimes not as strong, depending on how much room we have given them to take control.

The four areas are:

1. Unforgiveness and Childhood Trauma
2. Unhealthy Relationships with People
3. Involvement with the Occult
4. Family Bondages

Unforgiveness and Childhood Trauma

Nothing gives the devil a greater playground than the root of unforgiveness in a person's life. Unforgiveness is the single greatest reason we never get God's best and eliminate the shackles of bad repetitive behavior and unhealthy habits which bind our growth—short, medium, and long term. Forgiveness is the essential requirement for growth. It is why confession is so necessary to cleanse our soul, start fresh and move on. Volumes can be written about this and how important it is to forgive.

In the entire New Testament, the Lord only taught the apostles one prayer—*The Lord's Prayer* or *The Our Father*. In the body of that prayer it covers a multitude of infractions we commit or people commit against us. It says, "*forgive us... as we forgive those who trespass against us.*" Here is the Lord teaching His new shepherds of the church only one prayer and forgiveness is central. How often have we said that prayer and not forgiven someone who has hurt us? Lack of forgiveness is a primary reason why we harbor bitterness and resentment and cease to grow and receive graces. Not forgiving is the road to perdition that we choose for ourselves. In that decision we become the property of Satan, and in the process we become the ultimate loser. From the act of not forgiving, we have different forms of arrested development, stunted growth, and in most cases—we become bitter people. Choosing not to congregate around people who are negative or trouble and someone who has wronged us is a different issue than not forgiving them.

When we don't forgive, we become the loser by giving another dominion over us. I have often wondered how a person goes to church for 5, 10, 20, 30, 40, 50, or 60 years, and remains unchanged. If you strike up a conversation with that person on an intimate basis and talk long enough, you usually will find a deep hurt that never was forgiven. It is inevitable. Lack of forgiveness precludes growth. Without it people remain stunted doing and saying the same things for a lifetime with little or no fruit. They are often bitter sad people and lack joy. Everyone gets hurt and needs to forgive. Grudges only hurt the grudge holder. The soul that is open to God forgives. The first healing of the human heart and soul begins with confession. Confession is the single door to unlock all of the others. It is God's great meeting place of mercy.

Little needs to be said about childhood trauma to a discerning or rational adult. The sins are carried forward if they are not healed. We carry forward all the guilt, the trauma, the hurts, the molestations, the drugs, physical, emotional, sexual abuse, the anger, the alcohol, the fights, the discord, the sin, and the general spirit of the trauma into our jobs, marriages and relationships, often for the rest of our lives. These issues cast a negative spell around us, and for the most part we don't even know it. It is not meant to be that way. After losing a parent young, the death of a spouse or loved one, or something else deemed too unfair in the form of a personal trial, people often blame God and stay away from the Sacraments and Church for a lifetime. In anger they may stay away from God to get even with God due to the perceived unfairness of the personal trial. They then stay away from God out of spite, as odd as that sounds. The conversation inside the head goes something like this, "*if You were a good merciful God, You would never have let this happen to me when I was a poor defenseless child.*" After a lifetime away from God, and all the hurts it can bring, it is they who have not received the blessings God wanted for them. They have chosen to stay away from God, yet God is still awaiting their return.

At Rue du Bac, Paris, the Blessed Mother came to Sister Catherine Laboure' (now saint), then a twenty four year old novice sister, and gave the world the *Miraculous Medal*. Her title there was Queen of the World, as she stood on top of the world, and on her fingers were rays of light going forth to the world. She said the rays were unasked for graces that she wanted to give to those who asked for them.

Our Lady makes it clear to her that the prayer and the Miraculous Medal originates with the Mother of God. Sister Catherine writes about the experience, "*Her feet rested on a white globe... I saw rings on her fingers... Each ring was set with gems... the larger gems emitted greater rays and the smaller gems, smaller rays... I could not express... what I saw, the beauty and the brilliance of the dazzling rays.*" Sister Catherine heard an interior voice say, "*These rays symbolize the graces I shed upon those who ask for them. The gems from which rays do not fall are the graces for which souls forget to ask.*" An oval frame formed around the Blessed Virgin, and within it in letters of gold Catherine read the words: "*O Mary conceived without sin, pray for us who have recourse to you.*" The voice spoke again: "*Have a medal struck after this model. All who wear it will receive great graces; they should wear it around the neck. Graces will abound for persons who wear it with confidence.*"

The Church has given us tools to be better people with the gifts the Lord has given us, all we have to do is have the humility to ask. The graces are for everyone, but not everyone asks either due to pride, or lack of knowledge. The issues that can happen in childhood are too numerous to enumerate, so heaven gives us the tools necessary for the ascent to the Lord. Why bad things happen to good people is a mystery, but we all have to climb out of some hurt to know God.

Unhealthy Relationships with People

Here is an area where self-will has much more to do with our choices, than something we have virtually no control over like childhood trauma. People often take the easy route, which leads to a life of sin and difficulty. When the devil calls with what looks like the easy road versus the straight and narrow road of God, we must say no. Think of a person who is behind on a payment of some kind and has befriended someone who makes money illicitly, such as a drug dealer. If the person then asks the dealer for money on a short-term basis with a plan to pay it back, and then can't, the dealer can then take control of that person's life as they are now in bondage to that person. It is only a matter of time before any borrower is doing illegal things to try and pay a lender back. If they can't, the downward spiral begins. The same thing applies to the young person hanging around sexually promiscuous friends. It is not long before their guard is let down, and if alcohol is present, a fascination develops and they can easily fall into temptation. It then takes root and a habit forms. They then reap a destiny that appeared to be something innocuous at first, and just grew to something way beyond what they can control. There are a lot of unplanned pregnancies and drug habits that result from that type of behavior. If there is an unhealthy relationship, it needs to be cut off immediately.

Young adults should know the difference between missionary dating, just being a friend, versus hanging around with someone as a good buddy where bad habits rub off. If a person doesn't share the same values as another, it is only a matter of time before the person of faith can be dragged down to the level of the unbeliever. Many parents know this, but often they don't watch closely enough. British priest and exorcist Father Jeremy Davies of England speaks of the necessity of healthy relationships: "*Promiscuity, whether heterosexual or homosexual, and New Age practices can lead to demonic possession, and sexual perversions as well as trendy New Age practices can open the door to demonic spirits. Among the causes of homosexuality is a contagious demonic factor, explaining the explosion of homosexuality in recent years.*" Father Davies, an Oxford graduate and medical doctor, shows a progression that moves from "*extreme secular humanism or atheistic scientism to rational Satanism.*"

Christian fellowship is important for not just the young, but everyone. Jesus sent the apostles out two by two to hold each other up so they would not morally fall. Two or more people walking the same road provide safety. Community is important as it helps the person who is following Christ to know that they are not alone and that others think as they do, supporting them emotionally and morally.

Involvement In the Occult

What starts out as a game and fascination, like a new toy, evolves to something much more sinister and diabolical. The devil entices and snares his victims. He is pure evil masquerading as something intellectual, fun, and innocuous. He does not masquerade around dressed like he's in a Halloween costume with a funny pitchfork. He is incarnate evil out to kill and destroy. His greatest accomplishment is making us think he doesn't even exist. All people instinctively know there is good and evil as God plants that knowledge in the human soul. When one dabbles in the occult, there is a desire to go deeper as people then see that there is some kind of real power there. The majority of the time, dabbling in the occult is a free choice of a person who has reached the age of reason.

The genesis of the occult starts as all other vices, exposure and then a fascination, then a habit, then a lifestyle. It may start with a Ouija Board, and then move onto more diabolical things where Satan is at work. If the mind is not filled up with the things of God, it will find other avenues of thinking and action. There is the old saying, "*an idle mind is the devil's work shop.*" Also, I believe, "*a tired boy is a good boy.*" One thing in life leads to another, and before long, kids are hooked, and the parents see strange behavior around the house. Over time, you have a real problem on your hands at the dinner table—if they even show up for dinner at all. So what starts as the innocent word "dabble," ends up in death of mind, body, and soul if not stopped cold in its tracks on behalf of the undiscerning mind. Parents must be attentive and know what their kids are watching and doing.

We Are All In Process

There is a Latin phrase "*in fieri.*" It translates in English to—*In Process*. We are all "*In Process.*" No one has it all together, nor is anyone perfect. Where you are strong, another is weak, and vice versa. We all need each other's support for something. We are all a work in process, and in progress. Saint Paul said, "*all things work together for the good of those who love God*" (Romans 8:28). No circumstances are beyond the reach of heaven to touch our lives, as we all have our failings.

God is a jealous God who wants no idol before Him. He alone is to be worshipped. There are only Ten Commandments that the Lord gave Moses, and the very first three commandments deal directly with this issue. They are from Exodus 20:3-6:

1. *You shall have no other gods before Me. Thou shall not make to thyself a graven thing, nor the likeness of anything that is in heaven above, or in the earth beneath, nor of those things that are in the waters under the earth. Thou shalt not adore them, nor serve them: I am the Lord thy God, mighty, jealous, visiting the iniquity of the fathers upon the children, unto the third and fourth generation of them that hate Me: and showing mercy unto thousands to them that love Me, and keep My commandments.*
2. *"You shall not take the name of the Lord your God in vain."*
3. *Keep holy the Sabbath day.*

It should be noted the first three commandments are vertical: man's relationship to God alone. The remaining seven are horizontal, or man's relationship to each other. The promulgation of the social justice gospel badly distorts this and minimizes the first three commandments, concentrating on the remaining seven inordinately to the detriment of what God ordained from the very beginning of time. The social gospel group feels the Sermon on the Mount is the modern day version of the Ten Commandments, which they say has replaced the Ten Commandments. There are religious orders in the Church that have focused so heavily on this social gospel, they have become a blur with no salt to believers. Vocations are drying up in those orders. Their theology has no black and white—no absolute truths. The social gospel of service is very important and should be an outgrowth of the changes taking place in our heart as a result of conversion. Often when the social gospel is introduced, all doctrinal structures take a back seat as do the sacraments, to a "feel good meeting" where anything goes. Often the social gospel proponents are pro-homosexual marriage and pro-abortion, and generally have a liberal agenda. There is a direct correlation to the disconnect we see in society to this principle, as it has caused enormous unbelief and confusion in the pews. Saint Paul said, "*thinking themselves wise, they became foolish*" (Romans 1:22).

Family Bondage

This is an area where the individual can take control if he/she is:

- **a.** Trained in Scripture to know they can unchain the shackles of the past.
- **b.** Have a friend who can help them become free.
- **c.** Recognize the situation for what it is and they know in their spirit they need help and seek a solution.
- **d.** Have the presence of mind from the Holy Spirit and want to be released of all things blocking who they can be in Christ Jesus.

The Scriptures are clear there are things in the past or present that put a person in bondage. However, if we are in the mud, we can get out—we don't have to stay there. In the West and the USA in particular, it is somewhat rare for a person to know much of their ancestral past due to excessive mobility available to the U.S. However, in Africa and Asia, people will know substantial amounts of information about previous generations, as most family history has been passed down orally, often up to 150 years or more. Also, the family has not moved as much as they do in the West. They know if a curse (placing a bondage on someone) has ever been broken or if it has mutated, and they see the ramifications of a family curse. If multiple family members suffer from the same sinful ways, it could be the result of a curse. Unless a curse is driven out of the family, and one surrenders to break it, it is perpetuated into the next generation, and the next. The healing of families is about breaking bondages.

The Mystery Of Suffering

Suffering is not God's will for us. Whether it be poverty, illness, famine, crime, or sickness, it is not God's desire. Suffering to a great degree is a mystery. In the gospel we see Lazarus suffering and being entombed for four days. This was a suffering unto the glory of God. There is also redemptive suffering where one accepts or takes on suffering willingly for the good of another. The Lord often allows suffering for our own good to purge away vice and sin. It is only when we surrender our will to the Lord, do we only then begin to grasp its mystery. Until a person is broken, God can't use him/her to the fullest extent. Man's pride and self will need to be purged first. It was only when Moses was molded by God, he could do God's work. In that suffering which can keep us humble, we can learn valuable lessons. If we try to escape suffering and the cross, we often will be given a heavier cross to carry. Job 5:17 delivers a mystery as deep as life itself when the Lord says to Job, "*Blessed is the one whom God reproves, therefore despise not the discipline of the Almighty.*" If we accept the cross given to us in the Divine Plan for our life, we will not only endure it, but spiritually prosper from it. Nothing lasts forever, and after the trial we will be stronger (II Cor. 4:17-18). If we accept the trial with joy and see God's plan, we will be a new person in Christ at the end. The trial will bring a new joy of God's fidelity to us, and in that joy will bring a new freedom. A freedom we know in our heart and soul originates in God. The operative word in difficult times is Trust.

Examples Of Grace and Bondage

I know a man who is a Catholic priest. If one were to write a book on his life, it could be categorized in mental health, fiction, inspirational, horror, or religion. His youth was a horror show chained to beds, harshness, cruelty, deprived of affection and love, then enlistment in the Navy, went AWOL, time in the brig, discharged, into drugs, a thirteen year heroin habit, models, sex, fast cars, body building, boats, and attempted suicide. On an attempt of suicide, he cried out to God for relief. The Lord heard his cry. Over the next several years, the Lord began to transform him because he was open and wanted help. Few ever go through this kind of horrendous ordeal. A saving grace was in his reading books on faith as there was no formal education past high school. He started to develop a serious prayer life, and had a renewal to Sunday Mass that developed into daily Mass over time. He grew like a bean sprout. He saw life through the eyes of God and never looked back. He had been to hell and never wanted to go there again. He visited old drug friends and fell early on, and knew he had to sever all ties with them. He did. He traveled in his spare time to pilgrimage sites all over the world. Lourdes, Fatima, Medjugorje, Rome, Assisi, Florence, San Giovanni Rotondo (Saint Padre Pio), Monte Sant'Angelo, LaSalette, Rue du Bac, and the Holy Land several times. Over time, he developed a unique love for Eucharistic Adoration, where he said his healing took place. He did these things and acts of service for many years before entering the seminary.

While applying to be a priest he had to go through a battery of psychiatric evaluations, and he came up normal. No one could understand it, but he was normal! Having known him well now for nearly 25 years, I can attest he is normal because he applied the principles specifically in this chapter and generally in this book as it concerns faith and abundant living. He made the right decisions, with the right people around him, and doing the right things on a daily basis, where he made the Mass the center of his life. Today he is an active priest having an enormous impact on people with addictions and other afflictions. Several years ago he got cancer and the diagnosis was there was no cure other than chemotherapy. He gave it over to God while maintaining a peace about him, and today he is cancer free after not going through chemo. He has turned into a scholar with a great sense of humor, who understands the times in which we live, and has a joy about him. His growth can be attributed to being open to the Holy Spirit and whatever that brings in his life. He will not be swayed by false doctrine as it got him nowhere in life taking the easy way out and fooling himself while young. He has stayed the course now for over 25 plus years. If you met him you would know he is a man of God.

Rather than get into the complete history of family and personal bondages, the above story illustrates that God heals and restores the years the locust destroyed. There is a way to reverse the negative behavior and habits. We are not lost and the Lord never abandons us if we ask for help with a sincere heart—and are willing to amend what we do.

Another common area of family bondage is divorce and adultery. I know a woman who has had a history of adultery and divorce throughout her entire family. Her uncles, father, and relatives have all divorced and married several times. Her father had divorced and married a woman thirty years younger than him. After sexual issues in the marriage, his son who had been married for about thirty years had to leave a town in California due to a restraining order by the court because of associating with a minor. In her early fifties, she herself became involved with a man twenty-five years younger than her. This is the family bondage that needs to be broken. After professing Christianity her whole adult life, she can't seem to overcome the bondage of family and generational sin. The question is why can't she break it while others can? Principally, she has accepted she has to live that way, and is not educated to know that she can break the bondage.

It has been asked many times, does the Massachusetts political family, the Kennedy's, have family bondage, or a family curse? The patriarch Joseph P. Kennedy suffered the death of his son Joe during World War II flying a secret bombing mission, a plane accident killed his daughter Kathleen over the French Alps, his daughter Rosemary had a lobotomy after years of mental difficulty, President John F. Kennedy was shot in Dallas, Senator Bobby Kennedy while running for president of the United States was shot in the head during the California primaries at the Ambassador Hotel, Teddy Kennedy's wife Joan suffered from alcoholism, and Mary Jo Kopechne, a twenty-eight year old companion in Teddy Kennedy's car drowned in 1969 in the car on Chappaquiddick Island, in Martha's Vineyard, Cape Cod. We haven't' even addressed the offspring, and "the cousins" who have had all sorts of problems.

The continuation of problems for this generation has plagued the family. Now, the question must be asked, did Joseph P. Kennedy bring this on his children through his open adultery and philandering? Importing liquor into the United States, having adulterous affairs with Hollywood starlets, bootlegging, and as one of the ten wealthiest people in the Unites States doing pretty much as he pleased. What sort of back room deals were consummated? What has never been brought to the light of day? Were the agreements with the Mafia and vote fixing with the Chicago unions an ingredient in the Kennedy curse? Why do some families exhibit a sense of virtue, peace, and tranquility, while others just seem to go from one problem or crisis to the next? No one can say for sure, but is there a Kennedy curse? Is the behavior simply a pattern from one generation to the next because it is observed and followed, or is there more to it?

The chains of bondage and curses must be severed if spiritual health is to be achieved. Verbally and through prayer, a curse must be renounced as having any authority in the life of a family. Does divorce, abuse, and addiction run in families? The answer is yes. If there is a pattern of problems, there is the starting point to dig deeper. Bad behavior can be broken. In no way is the information provided here meant to be easy or definitive. There are problems in everyone's lives which are sometimes difficult to overcome, and to pinpoint the exact place of entry must be discerned with trained people. But, with prayer, fasting, confession, and the Sacraments, problems can be overcome. If there is a will, a family can be restored to wholeness.

Likewise there are spirits that continue in holy families. If you look at many canonized saints and holy families, you will see the continuation of Godly children. Therese of Lisieux, Pope Pius X, Saint (Padre) Pio and many others were brought up in holy families. An atmosphere of love was nurtured in the home that continued into their formative years and into their adult lives, and they lived the expression of their faith which had an impact on those around them. Holy men and women of God change culture. The Lord blesses into thousands of generations (Exodus 20:6).

The new testament of the Bible is virtually full of Jesus healing and setting the captives free. Nothing is impossible with God. This is a complex subject and takes great discernment. There is the diabolical and there is the psychological. Get good books and start being active and finding solutions. You are not meant to live in a hopeless situation or one of despair. Saint Faustina said, "***discouragement and an over exaggerated sense of anxiety is of the devil.***" Don't give an overemphasis to the problems you face. Change the circumstances you are in and plead with God for help. The Blessed Mother said very early on in the apparitions at Medjugorje, "*I have a great plan for the salvation of mankind, and I come to tell you God exists.*"

There are Sacraments in Roman Catholicism, and Satan has his sacraments. When a person votes for abortion, they are pledging fidelity to the god of Baal and Asherah—the gods of death and abortion. When a person pledges fidelity to homosexuality, they are pledging fidelity and belief to sodomy, and thus become a Sodomite, not often even aware of it due to ignorance and widespread cultural acceptance. Satan is an imitator and always has an alternative to God's ways. Those looking for pleasure in evil are looking to the demons to keep them happy. The Hebrew word for pleasure is "Eden." It was the *Garden of Pleasure* that God gave us as originally ordained. That too became twisted and a false way of living.

Due to such strong negative circumstances around us because of curses of the tongue and otherwise, we need to be constantly blessing those around us: doctors blessing patients, parents blessing their children, teachers blessing their students, and spouses blessing each other as they walk out the door. We are speaking faith by doing so. We see this all over Scripture as Rebecca knowing how important it is by telling Jacob to get his father's blessing (Isaac) before he dies. Also, we see this concept with Moses.

"The Lord said to Moses,

> *"Say to Aaron and his sons, "Thus you shall bless the people, of Israel: you shall say to them, The Lord bless you and keep you:*
>
> *The Lord make His face shine upon you, and be gracious to you:*
>
> *The Lord lift up His countenance upon you, and give you peace.*
>
> *So shall they put my name upon the people of Israel, and I will bless them"*
>
> (Numbers 6: 22-27).

This concept of blessing comes from speaking it into existence. When we speak faith, we are speaking God's laws into our lives. We can give life or death by the power of the tongue. It is our choice. But, unless we know how God works, we don't activate His ways.

Read all you can, pray all you can, and ask God for deliverance for all that ails you. If you do your part with a sincere heart, the Lord will do His part.

Greater is He that is in you, than he that is in the world.
—I John 4:

JESUS, I TRUST IN YOU

nine

Pray, Trust—And Don't Worry

The righteous flourish like the palm tree, and grow like a cedar in Lebanon. They are planted in the house of the Lord, and flourish in the courts of God.

—Psalm 92:12-13

For those who are older and knew the "good old times" of the previous generations, it is hard to watch the rapid disintegration of morals in the USA. Saint (Padre) Pio often said, "*Pray, Hope, and Don't Worry.*" That advice is still appropriate for today. The great question is, *How do we incorporate that into our daily routines and still maintain peace of soul?*

In the book of Jeremiah, the Lord instructs the Hebrew people how to maintain their culture and faith in a pagan and foreign environment. The Jewish people were in captivity, and the Lord gave them a prescription how to survive while enduring hardship. He did not say take up arms, He did not say stage a revolt, He did not say return to where you came from, and He did not say be submissive to Babylon and their foreign idols. He did say maintain your identity by doing as I tell you and you will endure the hardship. This advice was critical for the survival of the Jews. This has great relevance for believers today, struggling with the demise of our culture and how we are to maintain our identity and faith in an increasing hostile environment. Our circumstances today present the same dilemma the Jews have faced for millennia.

Believers are increasingly becoming isolated as freedoms are whittled away due to governmental tyranny. This isolation requires those who wish to maintain fidelity to time tested truths of the Magisterium, and Christian values that have endured for 2000 years to seek alternatives in lifestyle. The present crisis is as great as any in Church history, and the Lord gave His people a way to deal with adversity that we may want to take a serious look at.

The Lord allowed the Jews to be subjected to captivity because of their sin. If the Jews had taken the advice of Jeremiah to repent, they would have been spared the ordeal. The Lord's prescription via the great prophet Jeremiah is profoundly appropriate for today. The Lord Himself gave His people these instructions for enduring hardship while in captivity. As the culture becomes more oppressive and decadent, we will need to build a community with like-minded people. Here is where we will find support for our families, and maintain our faith in the process. As believers are increasing outside the mainstream power elite in control of society legislating godless laws, this is a form of white martyrdom. The Lord below instructs a code of conduct to endure the trial.

In Jeremiah chapter 29, he writes a letter to the exiles in Babylon. The Hebrews many times disobeyed God's laws and in essence received a "*Divine Pruning*" like we see in Isaiah 6:9-13, and throughout Scripture. Disobedience cost them dearly. Jeremiah says,

> *"These are the words of the letter which Jeremiah the prophet sent from Jerusalem to the elders of the exiles, and to the priests, the prophets, and all the people whom Nebuchadnezzar had taken into exile from Jerusalem to Babylon" (1). "Thus says the Lord of hosts, the God of Israel, to all the exiles whom I have sent into exile from Jerusalem to Babylon. Build houses and live in them, plant gardens and eat their produce. Take wives and have sons and daughters; take wives for your sons, and give your daughters in marriage, that they may bear sons and daughters; multiply there, and do not decrease. But seek the welfare of the city where I have sent you into exile, and pray to the Lord on its behalf, for in its welfare you will find your welfare. For thus says the Lord of hosts, the God of Israel: Do not let your prophets and your diviners who are among you deceive you, and do not listen to the dreams which they dream, for it is a lie which they are prophesying to you in my name; I did not send them, says the Lord. For thus says the Lord, when seventy years are completed for Babylon, I will visit you, and I*

> *will fulfill to you my promise and bring you back to this place. For I know the plans I have for you, says the Lord, plans for welfare and not for evil, to give you a future and a hope. Then you will call upon me and pray to me, and I will hear you. You will seek me and find me; when you seek me with all your heart, I will be found by you, says the Lord, and I will restore your fortunes and gather you from all the nations, and all the places I have driven you, says the Lord, and I will bring you back to the place, from which I sent you into exile"* (29:4-14).

This is a prescription by God for the prosperity and survival of the Hebrew people in exile. In times of great stress, a formula by God Himself is given for the continuation of the Covenant with His chosen people. The Lord is saying, go on living, have families, give your sons and daughters away in marriage, plant, harvest, raise your families in captivity, conduct commerce where you are, I will hear you where you are: seek and you will find Me, and instruct your children in the faith. Stay the course with My doctrine and not the doctrine of those who will tickle your ears with false idols. The Lord had a great plan for His people and they needed to be faithful at this difficult time that was caused by their sin. We need to take the words of the Lord to heart today. We are now in a strange and foreign land with unjust, ungodly, and heinous pagan laws. Abiding by them is becoming increasingly difficult, and people are struggling.

As the Lord gave the prescription to His people on how to live, we too can use the same principles today. There is a faithful remnant that can see through the confusion and the fog of the world and understand what the Lord is doing. The Lord will be faithful as He has been throughout history. We must trust because it is the hallmark of the saints. There will be hardship to endure by all, as it rains on the just and the unjust, and the innocent often suffer with the guilty.

The world is no longer a single small tightly located community like the ancient Jews living in isolated locations. All people will be affected by whatever is coming to the world. In Jeremiah 29:15-22, the story continues where the Lord curses all of those who are not listening to His prophets and obeying His commands. They live a life of absolute misery as a result of sin.

Accepting Our Emotions and Sticking To the Fundamentals

The events that are prophesied to come our way will prompt a wide range of emotions that are normal for everyone who hear them. Canonized saints felt loneliness in the midst of "*the dark night of the soul.*" When we encounter harsh events and face the reality that God's ways are not our ways, and that His plan for the salvation of mankind is very foreign to our natural way of thinking, we can expect a clash of nerves. With the death of a loved one, we have at some point to get back to normalcy, even if it is a new and painful normal. At the death of Blessed Mother Teresa, it was revealed by a priest who was very close to her that she felt abandoned and lonely, and questioning if God was really there in the last years of her life. Her humility was so deep, she tried to conceal it from those close to her. Saint John Vianney, the Cure' d'Ars, on three occasions attempted to flee his parish, but was brought back to his rectory in the dead of night by parishioners. Out of the millions of parish priests throughout history, he is the patron saint of parish priests and model of one who transformed his community through the confessional, principally through a regimen of prayer and fasting.

In sports, business, and family, sticking to the fundamentals is what matters most. Whenever you hear a Super Bowl, World Cup, World Series, Stanley Cup, or major champion winner, in the locker room or on television, you often hear the exact same phrase year after year. Someone on the team being showered with champagne says, "*We stuck to the fundamentals all year, day in and day out.*" In that same locker room is a friendliness that is contagious and an "esprit d'corps" the players speak of, and how much fun they have in the battle. The team has little rituals, traditions, playfulness, and they play off-season sports together, and congregate as friends and families. They simply enjoy each other's company. It is unity that has built a championship and they all know it—and they relish in it. It is no different for a family or a church. Satan is the author of disunity and it is his primary attribute. It is not to say there will not be some disagreement, but it is worked out to not cause problems for the good of everyone. A divisive spirit breaks unity and causes an infection. Emphasize the fundamentals and unity, and you have a potent formula for success anywhere.

As Marie said to the young Von Trapp family in the Sound of Music, "*let us start at the very beginning, it's a very good place to start.*" Nothing replaces the fundamentals in life and sticking to them. Grace builds on nature as a result of mastering the fundamentals. And as many a great athlete has said, "*the more I practice, the luckier I get.*" The same applies to our faith. We don't need to go out and seek the things that are superfluous, but sticking to the most rudimentary and basic tenets of our faith is what will sustain us when we need it most. This reserve capacity of faith is what we need to be building by sticking to the fundamentals daily. As Saint Francis said, "*keep your eyes to the ground, and your heart towards heaven.*"

Why Gideon's Army Matters Today

The stories in the Bible are consistently about the few battling the many. Whether it be Lot and his family leaving Sodom, Noah against the world with his warnings about the impending flood, or Saint Paul traveling and promoting the gospel to a hostile world. We see that God is faithful to those who believe and trust. It is people of great faith and courage who speak the truth when it is not popular to do so. Jesus brought a new paradigm to all mankind that few understood, and this ultimately cost Him His life. The entire history of the bible up to modern day saints is about the few looking to impact the many through personal sacrifices for the sake of the greater good. That is the history of the Hebrew fathers and Christianity. The salvation of the many depends on the work of the few. It is that way because those following Jesus yesterday and today are called the remnant. The Lord works through minorities for the salvation of the multitudes. It is simply how He works.

With the story of Gideon and his little army, we see how the Lord uses the few to win His battles. The story begins in the book of Judges chapter 6. The Lord has chosen Gideon, a young man whose name means Mighty Warrior, to rid the land of idols. This is something we see time and again in the Old Testament. It is a recurring theme how Israel turns away from the Lord in prosperous times and resorts to idols. Their riches bred arrogance, thinking they didn't need God in times of affluence—the same today for most people of the world. Gideon not only asks for one sign of God's involvement but two (verse 36-40) by requesting for direct signs of water on a fleece. Gideon asks the fleece be wet and then he asks that it be dry. The Lord complies with Gideon's request in abundance, so Gideon will have no doubt. Gideon is asked to go into battle against the Midianites and Amalekites, but the Lord tells Gideon he has too many men, as Gideon will think that he was the victor, and not God. Gideon started with 32,000 men that the Lord first reduces to 10,000. The Lord then says that those 22,000 can go home with honorable discharges if they choose not to fight. Now Gideon only has 10,000 remaining and is far outnumbered. But the Lord is not done yet. The Lord then instructs Gideon to send the men down to the river to drink. Most kneel to drink while only a few lapped the water like dogs. Those that lapped the water like dogs are now the 300 men the Lord wants for battle. The Lord says to Gideon, "*that is your new army.*" So from 32,000 to 300 the Lord has whittled away Gideon's army. Gideon has seen his army culled by the Lord of 99% of its original strength. The Lord has crafted insurmountable odds against Gideon to teach His Hebrew people a lesson of trust. Gideon now can have no doubt that it was not he who won the battle; the victory is to be God's alone.

"The Lord said to Gideon, "*I will deliver you with the 300 men who lapped and will give you the Midianites into your hands: so let all the people go, each man to his home*" (Judges 7:7). The remainder of the story should be read as it illustrates how the Lord orchestrated Gideon's victory. The Lord is clearly telling Gideon that, if he does exactly as He tells him, Gideon will be the victor. Gideon trusted, and Israel removed the idols from its altars and peace was restored to Israel. The Lord made it indisputably clear that Gideon was not to be the victor, but merely a least apt instrument, nonetheless chosen by God to win on the Lord's terms, not on the basis of Gideon's rational thinking. The lesson here is not a metaphor or an allegory. It is a real story that the Lord used to teach His people another lesson in obedience in the face of astronomical odds. It will be the same for us today.

Today, the remnant is far out-numbered and weak as was Gideon. The barbarians are inside and outside the gates. But Heaven and its cohort will be the victor. We don't know how, but we are told the victory will be won by the Immaculate and Sacred Hearts. We have to stand on that promise when there are times of doubt—that God has a magnificent plan. The Blessed Mother has said to the Marian Movement of Priests, "*right when it appears Satan is the victor, victory will be snatched away in a trice*" (29g). The word trice means quickly. In times of stress or doubt, we must remember the Lord is faithful and merciful. We are on the winning side of history. There will be bruises and bumps for everyone along the way.

The Lord Will Fight Your Battles—Trust and Praise

There a similar story in II Chronicles 20 where The Lord tells King Jehoshaphat of Israel how He will win a battle as He has similarly told Gideon and Moses," (Exodus 14:14- Moses). *Do not be afraid, do not be daunted by this vast horde: this battle is not yours but God's." ...Take up your position, stand firm, and see what salvation the Lord has in store for you. ..Be fearless, be dauntless; march out against them tomorrow and the Lord will be with you* (II Chron. 20:16-17). Then the Israelites did something that warms and changes the heart of God—Praise and Worship. "*Jehoshaphat bent his head, his face to the ground, and all Judah with those who lived in Jerusalem fell down before the Lord, worshipping Him. Then the Levites—Kohathites and Korahites—began praising the Lord God of Israel at the top of their voices*" (18-19). Then the Lord said, "*Have faith in the Lord your God and you will be secure; have faith in His prophets and you will be secure"* (20). *Then, having held a conference with the people, he set the cantors of the Lord in sacred vestments, at the head of the army, to sing praises to Him. 'Give praise to the Lord' they sang 'for His love is everlasting.' As they began to sing their joy and their praise, the Lord laid an ambush for the Ammonites and Moab...*" (21-22).

It is clearly a time of great stress for the people of Israel against great odds, and the Lord told them where their security lies if they do as He asks. We see this in Church history at the Battle of Lepanto (1571) and the Battle/Siege of Vienna (1683) against the Muslim Empire where all Europe was at stake. Prayer and praise changed the circumstances there as well. Also, when Joan of Arc was preparing for battle, she required all of her men to go to confession first, and then sing songs of praise as they entered the battle. The battles she won defy all reason when one looks at the facts of why she should NOT have been victorious.

It is obedience, trust, praise, and love the Lord desires. If you look at the early life of Jesus, He didn't join the academic, social, political, or power circles of the day to prepare for His ministry. He lived in anonymity and obscurity in a workshop as a carpenter, and as the son of a carpenter. He did not occupy the great halls of learning, but chose a solitary life of learning in a humble and devout home-schooled environment with His mother and foster father. Again, as always, the path that Jesus takes is different from that of the world. His purpose in coming is to redeem man and by going to the cross to set the captives free.

Peace of Soul is found by living in God's Divine Will. Until we are at peace with God, we will not be at peace with ourselves. **Being submissive to God's will is peace of soul.** Not my will, but Yours be done. We are created in the image and likeness of God, and His nature is found in us.

The prophet Jeremiah addressed the issue of obedience and fidelity to God. The Lord makes it clear He sends prophets as advocates to guide them.

> *But this command I gave them, 'Obey My voice and I will be your God, and you shall be My people; and walk in all the way I command you that it may be well with you.' But they did not obey or incline their ear, but walked in their own counsels, and the stubbornness of their evil hearts, and went backward and not forward. From the day that your fathers came out of the land of Egypt, to this day, I have persistently sent all My servants the prophets to them, day by day, yet they did not listen to Me, or incline their ear, but stiffened their neck. They did worse than their fathers. So you shall speak all these words to them, but they will not listen to you. You shall call to them, but they will not answer you. And you shall say to them, this is the nation that did not obey the voice of the Lord their God and did not accept discipline; truth has perished; it is cut off from their lips* (Jeremiah 7:23-28).

Parable of the Bridesmaids

All through Scripture we are asked to be vigilant. There is no letting our guard down at any time. The passage of the bridesmaids is very appropriate for the uncertain day in which we live.

> *"Then the kingdom of heaven will be like this: Ten bridesmaids took their lamps and went to meet the bridegroom. Five of them were foolish and five were sensible: the foolish ones did take their lamps, but they brought no oil, whereas the sensible ones took flasks of oil as well as their lamps. The bridegroom was late, and they all grew drowsy and fell asleep. But at midnight there was a cry, 'The bridegroom is here! Go out and meet him.' At this, all the bridesmaids woke up and trimmed their lamps, and the foolish ones said to the sensible ones, 'Give us some of your oil: Our lamps are going out.' But they replied, 'There may not be enough for us and for you; you had better go to those who sell it and buy some for yourselves.' They had gone off to buy it when the bridegroom arrived. Those who were ready went in with him to the wedding hall and the door was closed. The other bridesmaids arrived later. 'Lord, Lord they said, open the door for us." But he replied, "I tell you solemnly, I do not know you.' So stay awake, because you do not know either the day or the hour."* Matt. 25:1-13

Several things are clear from the above. First, there is great mystery in life. In Scripture there are absolute truths, metaphors, allegories and other literary methods of communicating. We must have the Holy Spirit living in us. When Jesus tells someone "*if your eye causes you to sin, pluck it out; it is better for you to enter the Kingdom of God with one eye than with two eyes to be thrown into hell*" (Mark 9:47), He is clearly talking about the devastation sin causes. It is clear the meaning of the bridesmaids parable is, "*stay awake because you do not know either the day or the hour.*" We can take nothing for granted in life.

The Normalcy Factor

In the age of technology we have become accustomed to the instantaneous and easy. Fast food, prepackaged items and convenient technology are just a click of a mouse away from the request. Presto, the appearance of whatever we wish! Movies arrive from a world away via satellite, and just about instant everything to the living room easy chair. It would not take much of an event to disrupt the supply chain of goods. If there were a serious disruption, in several hours grocery store shelves would go empty. We have grown accustomed to a trait called "*normalcy.*" We all think that things will be as normal tomorrow as they are today. The last several generations have allowed us to become accustomed to excessive creature comforts. At some point in the not too distant future the comfort of normalcy will no longer be as it is today. On the surface, things look fine, but it will only take one event to alter our worldview and lifestyle.

We can either live a life of optimism or pessimism, realism, delusion or fatalism. Living in God's plan and promises is peace and where we will find joy. If we needed to make to many decisions everyday we couldn't handle it. In time we would have a break down if we had to live like that. As a result of the "*normalcy factor*" we have failed to recognize what the Lord is doing. Change is coming at us at a ferocious pace and people lack hope and peace. The new normal in society is instability. Adjusting to find peace of soul will require that God has a plan and we need to go along with it in a turbulent future. Heaven will move with or without us and once we come to the realization that things will be difficult in the future, common sense tells us to make an amendment of habits. Insanity is often described as doing the same thing everyday and expecting a different result. It is for this reason alone we need to make an adjustment in our daily living to not be caught up in the chaos. Heaven moves at its own pace and timetable.

There were a group of people who recognized Jesus for who he was when He walked among them, and those who did not. It is the same today. It requires courage and a realistic view of the world and the societal data points to the fact change is here. It is this "normalcy factor" that has precluded so many from seeing His plan unfold before our eyes. As Jesus didn't have the majority of the population on His side, nor should we expect it. The Lord works His miracles with small numbers to show His might.

Life can change in the blink of an eye with a fast moving and interconnected world.

Bilderberger and founding member of the Trilateral Commission David Rockefeller addressed this very issue when he said, "*We are on the verge of a global transformation. All we need is the right major crisis and the nations will accept the New World Order.*" Prince Phillip of England has said, "*nothing like a good virus to cull the species.*" It appears we are close to this point. Where or when the event is coming, no one knows, but there are ample signs it is not far off. The parable of the Ten Virgins is apropos, "*stay awake;*" and be vigilant in your faith.

The New Springtime

Speaking to the world on the Jubilee of the Year 2000 Saint John Paul II went a little further than normal into this subject and raised it to a new level. He said, "*We are approaching a New Springtime of the Church, a New Pentecost, a new descent of the Holy Spirit.*" This is a profound thing for the Vicar of Christ to say. The topic is something the hierarchy of the Church dismisses, as only a small minority, are willing to confront its reality.

What exactly did Saint John Paul II mean by "*A New Springtime?*" There are two camps in the Church on this subject: those who believe the messages of the Blessed Mother, and those who disregard such language as nonsense or the musings of lunacy and hysterical thinking. For some in the hierarchy, it is too controversial, so they shun the issue as a whole. Saint (Padre) Pio often said, "*the hierarchy in heaven is different than that on earth.*" Most in the hierarchy prefer to leave sensitive issues alone as emotions run high on what the Church should or should not do on releasing the messages of the Blessed Mother at apparition sites. When the Blessed Mother appears in a diocese of the world, the Bishop doesn't get a moment of peace until she leaves or he leaves. Unfortunately, it doesn't need to be like that as the mission of heaven is always for the betterment of mankind.

Saint John Paul II gives a guideline on how the believer should conduct their life when he said on February 23, 1980, "*It began with Peter. At the moment of Christ's arrest at Gethsemane, Peter had drawn his sword. It had been a natural reaction. Whoever is attacked unjustly has the right to defend himself. And he also has the right to defend another innocent person. However, Christ said to Peter: 'Put your sword back into its place; for all who take the sword will perish by the sword.' And Peter understood. He understood up to his last breath that neither he nor his brothers could fight with the sword; because the kingdom to which he had been called had to be won with the power of love, and with the power of truth, and only in this way...*

I think, dear brothers and sisters, that precisely at this moment, we are on this very path.

Medjugorje, Bosnia

Medjugorje has been a place of great inspiration and fascination since the inception of the Blessed Mother's appearances began in 1981. There are a total of six visionaries. She told them there will be a maximum of ten secrets released to each person. Three visionaries as of this writing have nine secrets, while the three others have all ten. What we do know is the 1st secret deals specifically with *Medjugorje*. The 2nd deals with a *regional* issue, which is a very broad statement. The 3rd deals specifically with a *Permanent Sign* to be left at Medjugorje, which is one and the same after the Miracle to be seen at the site of her appearance at Garabandal, Spain. Secrets 4, 5, and 6 are unknown. Secret 7 we have been told involved a chastisement that was mitigated in the mid to late 1980's. Number 8, 9, and 10 deal with *the world in general* and they are inevitable. They will not change.

There has been heavy speculation that one secret speaks of "*an overthrow of a region of the world.*" If one were to look at the Near and Middle East, and see what has happened with the Arab Spring and violence in Tunisia, Libya, Egypt, Syria, Iraq, Afghanistan and Iran, and the movement of the Islamic State (IS), that would constitute a region of the world. With the emergence of a new Caliphate, there is an emergence of a new order in the entire Middle East. Christianity has been in the Middle East since the Apostle Saint Thomas brought it there, and it is now being virtually wiped out in many Islamic countries.

Over the years more has come to light as Medjugorje has been going on for so long and there have been so many interviews. French Mariologist Father Rene Laurentin was present when the 9th Secret was given the children and it was obvious it was something terrible as the visionaries were visibly distraught upon hearing it. The Blessed Mother told the visionaries that after the Permanent Sign appears, the events prophesied by her, will happen rapidly. Mirjana Dragicevic is the only visionary who is supposed to disclose the secrets, as no one else is under any obligation to do so. She has a parchment that she alone can read as of now. When it is time for the secrets to be released, the priest doing so will be able to read it as well.

It should be noted the word secret means secret and they are not to be revealed. Is there an overlap of the secrets from one apparition site to another? No one knows for sure. Do the visionaries speak of them to each other? However, since 1981, no specific secrets have been leaked, but a general description has been given by the visionaries on the general subject matter. For instance, Marija Pavlovic (now Lunetti) has said after all the secrets come to pass, we will be living as in biblical times. We will know every breath we take will be from God, and nothing we do will be done without His help. It will be that extraordinarily different. On December 12, 2012 at a prayer meeting in the Grand Theater in Canazei, Italy, Marija said, "*What do we have to fear? The prophets, hurricanes, or that the end of the world is coming? The end can come any day. But it seems that our life depends on the horoscope of the day, but we must learn from those in the past who trusted God. I do not know what will happen to us, but God teaches us that without Him there is definitely no future for us. What is a hundred years if there is no eternal life? We are too busy with evil television and computers, how much time do we devote to God. The important thing is to have your heart free from anxiety, fear, pain, and live through every test of your lives, remaining steadfast in prayer and love. So many times we do not believe in miracles, but they are there. My testimony is intended to be a sign of God's love for you. We are nobody, I am nobody, but we are here as a sign that Our Lady intercedes for us.*"

All those affiliated with the visionaries of Medjugorje have seen a remarkable consistency over the years in how they speak. They all downplay the secrets, but always speak of living in the present moment, the centrality of Holy Mass, the emphasis on confession and weekly fasting for our healing, and adhering to the most basic elements of the faith necessary for personal growth. Medjugorje is about hope for the future. The Medjugorje seers have emphasized all these years focusing on Christ and nothing else—our sole goal being holiness. Multiple thousands of messages over the years speak of changing ourselves first, and the rest will follow. A total commitment and amendment of life should be our sole goal. That is what is being asked by heaven. The Blessed Mother gives a simple prescription that is an antidote to what ails the world, and the remedy for the culture.

To date, there are an estimated 21,000 men who have become priests due to the apparitions at Medjugorje. Tens of millions have journeyed there and found something they were looking for in their hearts. The ripple effects of what has taken place there are incalculable. As the Blessed Mother said there very early on, "*I will go to every home if necessary to bring my message.*" There is a very large mosaic that heaven is piecing together, that no one can completely understand. Only when the mosaic is complete can we see how all the little pieces fit in and make sense. Only when we step back can we gain perspective. We all have our views of the realities around us, but it is beyond us to fully grasp it all. We need to place ourselves at the foot of the Cross in humility, intense prayer, self denial, silence, and faith to understand and be open to what heaven's plan is at this point in time—and then be courageous enough to embrace it. We need to be gathered as friends and believers in spiritual community to uphold one another with pure hearts and pure intentions, simplicity, and holiness.

Great Men and Women Of the Bible

All of the "*greats*" in spiritual history have been people of faith. Queen Esther interceded with her king to save the Jewish people through fasting, a holy boldness and a quick wit. Ruth had the faith and courage to travel to a new land, and her descendants included King David and Jesus. Pick any prophet and you will see supernatural intervention and guidance from heaven. Hebrews 11, which I call the *Hebrews Hall of Fame,* illustrates just how faith is the basis of spirituality and obedience. "*Now Faith is the substance of things hoped for, on the evidence of things unseen*" (Heb. 11:1). Listed below is a small sample of what great men and women "saints" of the Bible, accomplished through belief.

— *It was because of his faith that Enoch was taken up and did not have to experience death* (11:5).

— *It was through his faith that Noah, when he had been warned by God of something that had never been seen before felt a holy fear and built an ark to save his family. By his faith the world was convicted, and he was able to claim the righteousness which is the reward of faith* (11:7).

— *It was by faith that Abraham obeyed the call to set out for a country that was the inheritance given to him and his descendants, and that he set out without knowing where he was going. By faith he arrived as a foreigner, in the Promised Land...* (11:8-9).

— *It was equally by faith that Sarah, in spite of her being past the age, was made able to conceive, because she believed that He Who made the promise would be faithful to it. Because of this, there came from one man, and one who was already as dead himself, more descendants than could be counted, as many as the stars of heaven, or the grains of sand on the seashore* (11:11-12).

— *It was by faith that Abraham, when put to the test, offered up Isaac* (11:17).

— *It was by faith this same Isaac gave his blessing to Jacob and Esau for the still distant future* (11:20).

— *It was by faith that Moses, when he was born, was hidden by his parents, for three months; they defied the royal edict when they saw he was such a fine child* (11:23).

— *It was through faith that the walls of Jericho fell down when the people had encircled them for seven days* (11:30).

— *Is there need to say more? There is not time for me to give an account of Gideon, Barak, Samson, Jephithah or David, Samuel and the prophets. These were men who through faith conquered Kingdoms, enforced justice, received promises, stopped the mouths of lions, quenched raging fire, escaped the edge of the sword, won strength out of weakness, became mighty in war, put foreign armies to flight* (11:32-34).

Since the early Fathers of the Church, we have had great men and women of God who have moved mountains and altered history through heroic faith and deeds while they pursued the Kingdom of Heaven. We have been told that the days we now live are extraordinarily unique. Why should we believe it? Not because flesh and blood is saying it, but the Queen of Heaven and Earth has said it repeatedly at the major apparition sites where she has appeared and is still appearing today. The visionaries themselves are important as mouthpieces conveying the message, but the messages far outweigh the role of the messenger and the cult of personality that often attaches to an apparition.

To see where we are going in this time of Transition or Transformation phase is critical if we are to join in and be an active participant in what heaven is doing. It is now our appointed hour to be Apostles of the Last Times, seeing the world through the eyes of faith and joy. The men and women of history who preceded us had their time, and it is now our time. We have all been placed in the world at this precise time in history for such a time as this. The Lord has His reasons. We will hear the voice of God if we start with prayer.

Noah and the Flood—It's Not the End, It's A New Beginning

In many respects, today is like the time of Noah. People are eating, drinking, divorcing, marrying, and making merry. The circumstances of Noah are very similar to those of today. The story begins in Genesis 6 where people were living like there was no tomorrow. Depravity and wickedness had permeated the land. The story of the flood is a fascinating one that has no equal in history. It was an epic time when the Lord destroyed the world due to sin. A few key verses:

> Genesis 6:5, *The Lord saw how great the wickedness of the human race had become, and that every inclination of the thoughts of the human heart was only evil all the time.*
>
> Genesis 6:9, *Noah was a righteous man, blameless among the people of his time, and he walked faithfully with God.*
>
> Genesis 6:11, *Now the earth was corrupt in God's sight, and was full of violence.*
>
> Genesis 6:22, *Noah did everything as God commanded.*

It was a time of depravity the world had never known before. The story of Noah and the flood is only three chapters long, but a strong point is made by the Lord because of sin in the world. In just three chapters God is mentioned twenty times, and Lord is mentioned nine times. Noah's family was a part of a tiny remnant that the Lord chose to save because of Noah's faithfulness. Scripture tells us Noah and his family were the only righteous people on earth. Only eight people made it into the ark—Noah and his wife, their three sons, and their wives. Eight is the mystical number for God the Father. That's the sum total of all that were righteous before God and without blame. The remnant can get very tiny indeed. Noah was considered the local fool when he began to build a boat. Not just a boat—a very large one. People would have jeered at him, mocked him publicly, humiliated his family, and thought him the local fool—until it started to rain. And rain it did. So the moral of the story here is that there was great sin in the world, and the number of people staying in fidelity was extremely small. But most of all, Noah did everything God commanded. He trusted when all the odds were against him. The Blessed Mother said to the Marian Movement of Priests (#507), "*the times in which we are living are 1,000 times worse than at the time of the flood and no other time in history have we had the immoral behavior of man so decadent...and so very possessed by evil spirits.*" Think of what is being said, the times today are one thousand times worse than at the time of Noah! One would have to be foolish or very caught up not to see the signs of the times all around us.

We Bring Judgment On Ourselves

We all have trials in life. Everyone is dealing with something. There is no getting around that. We are asked to bear trials. There is birth, death, sickness, and other physical infirmities that will surely come our way at different times. Everything has a season. Saint James is clear that there is an end to the trial if we remain faithful to the statutes and commands of God. Nothing is permanent. Everything in life comes from God and there is not a hair on our head that is not counted. We are asked to trust. Saint James writes,

> *"Blessed is the man who endures trial, for when he has stood the test he will receive the crown of life which God has promised to those who love Him. Let no one say when he is tempted; I am tempted by God, for God cannot be tempted with evil and He Himself tempts no one; but each person is tempted when he is lured and enticed by his own desire. Then desire when it has conceived gives birth to sin; and sin when it is full-grown brings forth death. Do not be deceived, my beloved brethren. Every good endowment and every perfect gift is from above, coming down from the Father of lights with whom there is no variation or shadow due to change. Of His own will he brought us forth by the word of truth that we should be a kind of first fruits, that we should be His creatures"* (James 1:12-18).

Elijah and the 7,000 Faithful Israelites

"*Elijah was a man with a like nature with ourselves and he prayed fervently that it might not rain, and for three years and six months it did not rain on the earth. Then he prayed again and the heavens gave rain; and the earth brought forth its fruit*" (James 5:17-18). The Bible says Elijah was a human being like ourselves and had a range of emotions much like us when confronted with the living God. He performed some of the greatest miracles in all of Scripture. Elijah struggled and tried to hide his face from God, because he had difficulty doing what God asked in light of public opinion. He was like any other man with human emotions. Elijah never died after being carried away in a fiery chariot. When people saw John the Baptist they thought he was the incarnation of Elijah, because Elijah had a similar strength of personality and spirit as the Baptist. Elijah struggled regarding how he should act and what he should say. He was humiliated and marginalized in front of people, often ostracized, and lacked food and lodging on his travels. Elijah confronted corrupt King Ahab and he addressed the king's sinful ways. John the Baptist similarly spoke to King Herod, and said to him "*you are sleeping with your brother's wife*" (Mark 6:18). Elijah and John the Baptist both spoke truth to power. Truth to power—something we are called to do if asked. To fear God rather than man is what makes all the difference in the world and can reverse the destiny of a nation.

Saint Paul writes of the story of Elijah how he felt isolated and alone in the midst of being an outspoken prophet in ancient Israel. Saint Paul tells the story of the emotional swings of Elijah when he says, "*Do you not know what the Scripture says of Elijah, how he pleads with God against Israel? Lord, they have killed thy prophets, they have demolished thy altars, and I alone am left, and they seek my life. But what is God's reply to him? 'I have kept myself seven thousand men who have not bowed the knee to Baal. So too at the present time there is a remnant, chosen by grace. But if it is by grace, it is no longer on the basis of works; otherwise grace would no longer be grace*' (Romans 11: 2-6). Saint Paul is telling the story based upon the narrative in I Kings 19: 13-18 where Elijah is lamenting he is the only righteous person in Israel and is left alone to speak the word of God. Elijah runs away a day's journey and complains of his condition and hides under a furze bush. Elijah is lamenting he is the *only one left* in fidelity to God as he is being chased by King Ahab and Queen Jezebel (I Kings 19:10-11). Yet, the Lord tells Elijah that a total of 7,000 men have not bowed to idols.

The bible is about God communicating to His people to protect them, give them laws, guidelines to abide by, precepts, statues, exhortations, and commands. He does this through men and women called prophets. The Lord says, "*Surely the Lord does nothing, without revealing His secret to His servants the prophets*" (Amos 3:7). Nowhere is this more evident than in I and II Kings where it is clearly stated that Elijah and Elisha were members of a group of men called "*the company or brotherhood of prophets*" (I Kings 20:35, II Kings 4:38 and throughout the stories of Kings). King Ahab and wicked Queen Jezebel on several occasions were out to find the prophets and kill "the brotherhood of prophets." As a result they were hidden in caves and secret places by the faithful to protect the integrity of their mission by the faithful. Provisions were even provided to the point where the Lord commanded ravens to feed Elijah *bread in the morning and meat in the evening* while in the wilderness (I Kings 17:5-6). On another occasion an angel awakens Elijah and told him there were scones and water "*there at his head*" (I Kings 19:5-7). It is clear that God provides, and is faithful in the most unique circumstances.

There is no break in the lineage of prophets to this very day as God continues to use men and women to convey His word. The voice of God is contrary to the spirit of the world, and for this reason alone prophets who proclaim the word of God with strength will always be spurned and marginalized. A prophet does not have to predict the future (some may) as many might think, but a prophet is one who speaks the truth of the gospel. Prophets walk among us and it makes good sense to listen.

The Lord says there are many other people like Elijah, and Saint Paul equates this to the remnant, which always was, and always will be—to speak the truth for God. Elijah showed his humanity as did Peter during a trial and ran away. To feel alone in the midst of the grave sin in our midst is normal for those following the Lord. Many people today are feeling emotionally distraught for the exact same reasons as

Elijah and want to retreat from the battle. But, the Lord rebukes even the great Elijah to get back doing as asked, as there are many other good people around him who have not bowed their knee to Baal.

The Prophets—Battling Their Human Nature

The Scriptures are full of great men and women of God who faltered in their steps. Jacob deceived his father (his Hebrew name means deceiver), yet he became Israel. Abraham (initially named Abram) lived in fear of being robbed so he denied Sarah was his wife (then named Sara). Jeremiah ran away from God, not initially accepting the task God wanted to give him, and Isaiah felt inadequate to speak. Moses murdered an Egyptian and was banished to the desert for a greater work God had in mind. Elijah went and hid rather than deal with dissent. Peter walked with Jesus for three years every day and saw all that Jesus said and did, and then denied him three times in His hour of need. Thomas doubted God. Only one apostle, John, was found at the foot of the Cross, while all the rest ran off in fear.

If you read the Scriptures carefully, these stories are more the norm than just the exemplary tales of the saints. God's servants in the past at some time all struggled in their flesh. It is normal and natural. Today, it is no different for us. The great women and men of Scripture and throughout history had their struggles and we have ours. There were heresies that they struggled with in their time, hardship, provisions, unbelief, persecutions, and doubt at nearly every point in Church history. No age or person is immune from it. People who speak and write of the great men and women of God, many times romanticize saints who overcame great obstacles. They often fail to give adequate space to the extreme difficulties, doubt, and sufferings they endured along the way to sanctification.

One thing must be understood by believers today. Those who are in the spiritual fight today are no different from those of the past. We suffer the same doubts, foibles, inadequacies, and failures as every believer from the past. The apostles had their doubts and squabbles for a variety of reasons, and we have ours. Differences of opinion are natural in relationships. However, the early apostles worked together as Paul respected Peter's primacy even though they disagreed on some issues, and the gospel was promoted.

It is unbelief that brings us to discouragement and despair. During this time of Transition and Transformation, events will take place that will be difficult for the world. A birthing process is taking place. As we see in Revelation 11:18-19, "*the nations were seething with rage and now the time has come for your own anger, and for the dead to be judged, and for your servants the prophets, for the saints and for all who worship you, small or great, to be rewarded. The time has come to destroy those who are destroying the earth. Then the sanctuary of God in heaven opened and the ark of the covenant could be seen inside it. Then came flashes of lightning, peals of thunder and an earthquake, and violent hail.*"

THEN—immediately following this disruption and violent time, we move to Revelation 12:1-2,

> *"Now a great sign appeared in heaven: a woman clothed with the sun, standing on the moon, and with the twelve stars on her head for a crown. She was pregnant, and in labor, crying aloud in the pangs of childbirth."*

Before a birth there is pain and travail. Then after the ordeal, there is a new birth. It is the Blessed Mother as the Woman Clothed with the Sun, with the moon under her feet wearing a crown of twelve stars as the prophetess of our age, and the ark of the New Covenant tasked by the Holy Trinity to usher in the New Age. Again, and again the message from heaven is—TRUST. A definition of TRUST may be: True Resolve Under Severe Testing.

We are asked to believe. Hebrews says,

> *"The Holy Spirit says: If only you would listen to him today; do not harden your hearts, as happened in the Rebellion, on the day of Temptation in the wilderness, when your ancestors challenged me and tested me, though they could see what I could do for forty years. That is why I was angry with that generation and said: How unreliable these people who refuse to grasp my ways! And so in anger, I swore that not one would reach the place, of rest I had for them"* (3:7-11).

The book of Hebrews explains why the Israelites didn't make it to the promised land. "*And those who made God angry for forty years were the ones who sinned and whose dead bodies were left lying in the wilderness. Those that He swore would never reach the place of rest He had for them were those who had been disobedient. We see then, that it was because they were unfaithful that they were not able to reach it*" (Heb. 3:17-19).

The Feeding Of the Five Thousand

The parable of the feeding of the five thousand is in the sixth chapter of the Gospel of John. Saint John writes about the event when he says, "*Lifting up His eyes, then, and seeing that a multitude was coming to Him, Jesus said to Philip, 'How are we to buy bread that these people may eat?' This He said to test him, for He Himself knew what He would do*" (John 6:5). There are very few if any funny scenes in the entire New Testament, as that was not the mission of Jesus. But, here is God (Jesus) saying to Philip tongue in cheek, Philip, how are we going to feed all these people? We don't have any money to do this, nor enough bread or fish. Jesus says to Philip, "*There is a lad here who has only five barley loaves and two fish; but what are they among so many*" (6:9). The intent of Jesus was to test the apostles to trust in God's providence. Jesus is about to teach all of those in attendance a lesson how God provides for those who have faith.

You can imagine the setting if you have ever cooked for thirty people at Thanksgiving or a large picnic. Food is quickly eaten and disappears with a lot of hungry people. Here are 5,000 people to feed with only five loaves of bread and two fish! The apostles and disciples of Jesus didn't have any resources to feed people, no supplier of bread, no distribution channels, and nowhere to turn for help.

The gospel of Matthew (14:13-21) also provides narrative on the feeding of the five thousand but in verse 21 Matthew specifically mentions, "*and those who ate were about five thousand men, besides women and children.*" It is very possible there were upwards of 20,000 people being fed as it says *5,000 men*, and "*they took up twelve baskets of the broken pieces left over*" (20).

The five loaves and two fish are God's provision for His people against impossible odds. It defies all reason, and is in the miracle category. Jesus was introducing a new paradigm of spiritual food that nourishes the soul. Nothing is as important as the spiritual food that Jesus brings in the form of the daily bread—The Eucharist. It is the source and summit of the

Catholic faith. The story in John 6 is the most crucial test of our faith, the one that differentiates believers from another. It is the chapter where the Gospel of John speaks specifically about the Eucharist—The Bread of Life. The parable of the Bread of Life takes a more serious turn that it is not just physical bread that sustains us for only a day. Jesus moves the conversation to something that can sustain us for a lifetime, something that can bring us eternal life. Several times Jesus refers to Himself as the *Bread of Life* (6:35-51), leaving no doubt in distinguishing between physical bread and Himself as the sustaining Eucharist—the Body and Blood of Jesus. Jesus said, "*Truly, truly, I say to you, it was not Moses who gave you the bread from heaven; my Father gives you the true bread from heaven. For the bread of God is that which comes down from heaven, and gives life to the world*" (32-33).

Jesus then delivers arguably the strongest message of the New Testament on who He is when He says, "*Truly, truly, I say to you, unless you eat the flesh of the Son of Man and drink His blood, you have no life in you; he who eats My flesh and drinks My blood has eternal life, and I will raise him up on the last day. For My flesh is food indeed, and My blood is drink indeed. He who eats My flesh and drinks My blood abides in Me, and I in him. As the living Father sent Me, and I live because of the Father, so he who eats Me, will live because, of Me. This is the bread which came down from heaven, not such as the fathers ate and died; he who eats this bread will live forever"* (John 6: 53-58). The language is clear here for all to read; however, the followers of Jesus said, *"this is a hard saying*" (John 6: 60). After the discourse it says, "*After this many of His disciples drew back and no longer went about with Him*" (John 6: 66). The truth of this doctrine was so critical to Jesus' ministry that He was willing to stake everything on it. Not only would He let the disciples leave, He then challenged His apostles as to whether they too would leave Him as well. Peter's act of faith response reveals how they all knew He meant it as He asked them if they too would leave, without at all having understood it: "*Lord, to whom shall we go? You have the words of eternal life; and we have believed, and have come to know, that You are the Holy One of God*" (John 6: 68-69).

A line is drawn in the sand where the doctrine was too difficult for many to believe, and hard to comprehend. John Chapter 6 cannot be casually dismissed. This is the discourse in the Gospels on the Eucharistic Real Presence. The language is clear that this doctrine was just too difficult for Jesus' followers at the time He said it. It took an act of faith to accept it.

Just as Jesus, Mary, and Joseph walked the earth and knew times of stress and hardship, heaven knows our circumstances. At one point Joseph was told in a dream to flee for the safety of his family. Being obedient, he left in the middle of the night with the Holy Family and they lived as refugees in Egypt. Here is a lesson for believers today who are struggling. If we follow the gospel message and believe, there will be heavenly directions for provision of physical and spiritual nourishment. The story of the entire bible from Genesis to Revelation is a God of miracles. In Deuteronomy 7 Moses says, "*You may say to yourselves these nations are stronger than we are. How can we drive them out? But do not be afraid of them; remember well what the Lord your God did to Pharaoh and to all Egypt* (Deut. 7: 17-18). *Do not be terrified by them, for the Lord your God, who is among you, is a great and awesome God*" (Deut. 7:21).

The fruit of silence is prayer.
The fruit of prayer is faith.
The fruit of faith is love.
The fruit of love is service.
The fruit of service is peace.
—Blessed Mother Teresa

Can any of you, for all his worrying, add one single cubit to his span of life? And why worry about clothing? Think of the flowers growing in the fields, they never have to work or spin; yet I assure you that not even Solomon in all his regalia was robed like one of these.

—Matt. 6:27-29

JESUS, I TRUST IN YOU

ten

Finding Peace Of Soul

Thus says the Lord: If you remove from your midst oppression, false accusations and malicious speech; if you bestow your bread on the hungry and satisfy the afflicted; then light shall rise for you in the darkness, and the gloom shall become for you like midday; then the Lord will guide you always and give you plenty on the parched land. He will renew your strength, and you shall be like a watered garden, like a spring whose water never fails. The ancient ruins shall be rebuilt for your sake, and the foundations from ages past you shall raise up; "Repairer of the breach," they shall call you, "Restorer of ruined homesteads.

If you hold back your foot on the Sabbath from following your own pursuits on My holy day; if you call the Sabbath a delight, and the Lord's holy day honorable; if you honor it by not following your ways, seeking your own interests, or speaking with malice—then you shall delight in the Lord, and I will make you ride on the heights of the earth; I will nourish you with the heritage of Jacob, your father, for the mouth of the Lord has spoken.

—Isaiah 58: 9-14

The Roman Catholic Church and its Magisterium have given us all the tools necessary for knowing God in an intimate and personal way. The resources heaven has bestowed are enormous. Not least, the Scriptures, the Catechism, the Sacraments, papal encyclicals, the Mass (Eucharist), Adoration, Confession, Consecration or Entrustment, the Blessed Mother's apparitions all over the world, the lineage and the writings of great men and women of God who have provided examples of holy living and inspiration over the centuries, to name only a few. All of the things necessary for anyone to achieve sanctity are available if one is willing to search them out. The list we will provide here is by no means a definitive one. If one were to take to heart and begin a regimen of spiritual activity, lives would be changed. As the culture declines and the winds of change accelerate, leaning on the essential elements of the faith will provide a safe refuge for our families. Without God, the odds are very high that keeping one's head above water will become nearly impossible. There are time-tested elements of the faith given to us by the Lord for maintaining peace no matter the circumstances around us. Several are below.

Eucharistic Adoration

He who kneels before God will stand before all men.

The strength to continue the mission of truth can be found in the Eucharist. Whether one be a priest, professed religious, or lay person, holiness will be found in front of the Eucharist. Answers to our problems will be found in front of the Monstrance or Tabernacle asking for God's guidance. A priest who spends time in Adoration over time will become holy, and that holiness will sanctify the faithful in his parish, who in turn will sanctify others. Those who adore Jesus in front of the Eucharist will be able to accept the teachings of Jesus with littleness and humility, and fulfill the mission God has for them to the fullest—with the greatest of fruit. Sanctity will come in the solitary hours with no one knowing and watching but the choirs of angels, and grace will come in superabundance that we alone will know is directed by Jesus Himself. His goal is for us is to be alone with Him in the Real Presence. He is there and He is alive. He is the Real Presence of the Eucharist and we must receive Him worthily. We need to become holy as He is holy. Through the centuries there has been consistent thinking and action from all the saints and church fathers that the Eucharist is the Real Presence of God on earth. The Eucharist is a gift from heaven to gain strength and solace in a fallen world. The manifestation of God made flesh and blood in our modern day. Eucharistic Adoration is a source of strength where God channels grace freely to those who ask for it.

To believers and non-believers, here is some math that should cause all to take an inventory on how we value our spirituality. Listed below is how much time we have over days, weeks, months and years. It is based on a thirty-day month not factoring in leap years, or months with 31 days versus 30. Here is a general breakdown in time:

— 24 hours in a day
— 168 hours in a week
— 720 hours in a month
— 8,766 hours in a year
— 43,830 hours in 5 years
— 87,660 hours in 10 years
— 175,320 hours in 20 years
— 262,980 hours in 30 years
— 350,640 hours in 40 years
— 438,300 hours in 50 years

How many people do you know who are in Eucharistic Adoration on a yearly basis for one hour? Adoration has the ability to reverse natural law, but many people are just "too busy" to spend one hour in deep prayer in front of the Lord. One hour over a lifetime, yet hundreds of thousands of waking hours are frittered away in meaningless activity. When Jesus was praying in the Garden of Gethsemane the night before His death, He said to the apostles,

> *"'My soul is sorrowful to the point of death, wait here and keep awake with Me.' And going on a little further, He fell on his face and prayed. 'My Father He said, 'if it is possible let this cup pass Me by. Nevertheless, let it be as you, not I, would have it.' He came back to the disciples and found them sleeping, and He said to Peter, 'So you had not the strength to keep awake with me one hour? You should be awake, and praying not to be put to the test. Be on guard, and pray that you may undergo the test"'* (Matt. 26:38-41).

Saint Faustina describes her long silent time in adoration where she "*talked*" to the Lord.

> *"Silence is so powerful a language that it reaches the throne of the living God. Silence is His language, though secret, yet living and powerful"* (Diary 888).

> *"In silence I tell you everything, Lord, because the language of love is without words"* (Diary 1489).

There seems to be time for everything else in life today, except the spiritual. Mother Teresa often said that the Missionaries of Charity didn't really experience growth until they started Eucharistic Adoration as an order. We talk a lot, but we don't pray. We may even talk a lot about praying, without doing it commensurately. The Blessed Mother said to a gathering of English and Irish priests of the Marian Movement of Priests in October 1984 (#296), "***more is obtained through one day of intense prayer than through years of continuous discussions.***" Think how profound this statement is in releasing the power of God to solve our problems. When addressing a group of Italian priests in August 1987, Our Lady further pleaded with the entire Church to return to adoration and reparation before the tabernacle "*O Church, ...you must understand that the center of your life, the fount of your grace, the source of your light, the beginning of your apostolic action is found only here in the tabernacle where Jesus is truly kept. And Jesus is present to teach you how to grow, to help you to walk, to strengthen you in giving witness, to give you courage in evangelizing, to be a support for all your sufferings...* " (Message # 360). To all those with a burden they wish lifted, Adoration is something that can reverse the course of events. We are conflicted because we have not placed God at the center of our life and made it the most important element.

The second book of Timothy addresses the issues of a life and gospel with no substance, "*The time is sure to come when, far from being content with sound teaching, people will be avid for the latest novelty and collect themselves as a whole series of teachers according to their own tastes; and then, instead of listening to the truth, they will turn to myths.*" In other versions of the bible, it speaks of "doctrine that tickles the ears" (2 Tim. 4:3). Regular time before the Blessed Sacrament can help us form proper priorities and remain rooted in the faith.

Fasting

Jesus was very clear about the power of fasting and why it was necessary. Just prior to His public ministry He fasted for forty days, and forty nights. Fasting alone in the desert for forty days! Most of us get irritable after missing a single meal. Jesus had a mission to fulfill and He knew He needed to be fortified to do as the Father was asking. Jesus knew He was entering battle, and therefore He fasted. Dealing with the demonic and difficult cases, He said, "*This kind cannot be driven out by anything but by prayer and fasting*" (Mark 9:29). Prayer and fasting reinforce one another.

At the height of Jesus' physical weakness during the fast, Satan appeared to Him and tempted Him with the enticements of the flesh, "*all of the Kingdoms in the world are mine to give you if you bow down and worship me*" (Luke 4:6). Jesus, then responded, "*You shall worship the Lord your God, and Him only shall you serve.*" Fasting prepares the believer for spiritual combat. Jesus was laying down some ground rules for difficult cases by showing the need to fast. Prayer is necessary, but fasting is required for combating the devil in many instances. Jesus was saying that fasting can set us free, and set spirits in general free in places where our own prayers may need fasting behind them.

With fasting should come deeper prayer, because when we deny sustenance to the flesh, we free and elevate our spirit to see and hear things we don't normally hear when our flesh is satisfied. When we deny the flesh, we become a more receptive vessel to hear God. With prayer and fasting come spiritual power. Together they are the twin elements to go into spiritual combat. The denial of the senses in fasting requires an additional level of commitment, and denies Satan the channels through which he habitually works. Freed of those constraints, and empowered through the greater commitment, prayer is more effective.

Whether you fast or not will depend on your worldview. Whom do you serve? People may juice, eat less, or not eat at all for cosmetic and dieting reasons, but it is the believer who fasts with the intent to improve themselves spiritually and be ready for battle. Motives for fasting count. If we live in a world obsessed with pleasuring the flesh, why fast? We fast because the Lord says, this is where hard battles can be fought and won.

Why We Fast

We live in a world, especially in the West where we have cool rooms in the summer, and heat in the winter. We satisfy every urge with pleasures in countries where income is greatest. Every need can be met with little to no discomfort if there is disposable income. However, Jesus is saying to deny the flesh voluntarily for our own good to fight our corrosive lower human nature is necessary. The great Patriarchs like David, Jonah, Daniel, and others fasted. Fasting is similar to dying and we do it to love more and move mountains through faith. We deny ourselves so something or someone else will be better. It is a sacrifice because we love, because love is doing something for someone else's interest. When there is a serious obstacle it will take fasting to break down that wall of resistance where Satan may have a stronghold. We live in a culture that is poisoned by a virus than can only be defeated in the spiritual realm.

Everything with Jesus is the opposite of man. He came to die so that we may life. He chose poverty over riches. He served rather than be served, and so forth. We live in a world where there is an inherent conflict of body and soul. Our body in the morning says, "*I am hungry,*" and we feed it. At noon and dinner it says the same thing. Later in the evening it says, "*I am tired.*" So we go to sleep. The fight in life is with our flesh demanding we feed it, contrary to our spirits that say deny the flesh for the betterment of the spirit. When we try not eating at any of the allotted three times a day, we see it takes willpower with a higher purpose and greater goal in mind to deny the flesh.

We fast to battle the Seven Capital Sins. They are:

1. Gluttony
2. Lust
3. Avarice (or Greed)
4. Sloth
5. Anger
6. Envy
7. Pride

Since this section is about fasting and not the Seven Deadly Sins, we'll stop at gluttony. The list has gluttony first because that sin leads to so many other vices where we don't control desires of the flesh. If we can control gluttony, we have a better chance of having spiritual progress and denying the flesh its voracious appetites. Fasting starts not necessarily just with food, but with other appetites. We can fast from television, how we speak, sweets, things we like or crave, and many other things to mortify our flesh and heighten our spirit. There is the story of Saint Francis of Assisi throwing himself into a thorn bush. He said when he was in pain he wasn't able to think about satisfying the flesh and pleasures. Saint Francis was trying to control his flesh from doing things he didn't want to do. It is also why he called his body Brother Ass as he knew man is in constant battle to control the flesh.

Saint Thomas Aquinas gave three principal reasons why we need to fast.

1. Overcoming concupiscence or lust,
2. Preparing the soul for higher things,
3. Atoning for sin.

Each sin in the list above is another good reason to fast, because each sin makes the next sinful trap easier to fall into. Fasting helps make the future what we desire it to be. For those wishing to start fasting, begin with achievable goals, such as missing one meal a week, then maybe two meals a week, and so forth. If fasting from food is a problem (many get headaches), we can always give up something we crave. Think in terms of how an athlete trains. Implementing a regimen of discipline and planning.

Saint Matthew provides some guidelines about fasting, "*When you fast, do not look gloomy like the hypocrites. They neglect their appearance, so they may appear to others to be fasting. Amen, I say to you, they have received their reward. But when you fast, anoint your head and wash your face, so that you may not appear to be fasting, except to your father who is hidden. And your Father who sees what is hidden will repay you*" (Matt. 6:16-18).

Saint Augustine tells us, "*Fasting purifies the soul. It lifts up the mind, and brings the body into subjection to the spirit. It makes the heart contrite and humble, scatters the clouds of desire, puts out the flames of lust, and enkindles the true light of chastity.*" In intensely challenging times such as ours, fasting is more valuable and important than ever.

The Celebration Of Mass, the Most Powerful Weapon Against Evil: Jesus Speaks To Saint Faustina

> *"Today, from early morning, divine absorption penetrates my soul. During Mass, I thought I would see the little Jesus, as I often do; however, today during Holy Mass I saw the Crucified Jesus. Jesus was nailed to the cross and was in*

> *great agony. His suffering pierced me, soul and body, in a manner which was invincible, but nevertheless most painful"* (Diary 914).
>
> *"Oh, what awesome mysteries take place during Mass! A great mystery takes place during Mass. With what great devotion should we listen to and take part in this death of Jesus. One day we will know what God is doing for us in each Mass, and what sort of gift He is preparing in it for us. Only His divine love could permit that such a gift could be provided for us. O Jesus, my Jesus, with what great pain is my soul pierced when I see this fountain of life gushing forth with such sweetness and power for each soul, while at the same time I see souls withering away and drying up through their own fault. O Jesus, grant that the power of mercy embrace these souls"* (915).

There are literally hundreds of authentically documented and scientifically verified miracles of the Eucharistic Host changing into human flesh and/or bleeding. Saint Faustina, whose full name was Maria Faustina of the Blessed Sacrament, and whom Jesus chose to be the secretary of His Divine Mercy, was once ill in the infirmary for thirteen days. Because of her great love for Him in the Eucharist, Jesus commissioned an angel to go to the Tabernacle on each of the thirteen days and bring Faustina His precious Body and Blood. Jesus told Saint Faustina that the tabernacle is the throne of His Divine Mercy.

Eucharist Miracles In Akita, Japan

The Church-approved apparitions and messages of Akita, Japan in the 1970's began with a spectacular Eucharistic miracle around the tabernacle in the chapel of the sisters of the Handmaids of the Eucharist. Then the Blessed Virgin Mary appeared to Sister Agnes as "*Mother of the Eucharist*" and added the word *Truly* to Bishop Ito's (Bishop Ito approved Akita) prayer where the inclusion begins, "*Most Sacred Heart of Jesus "Truly" present in the most Holy Eucharist...*" It's also noteworthy that when Our Lady of the Rosary appeared as the Queen of Peace in Fatima in 1917, the first apparition occurred on May 13th, which was at that time celebrated as the Feast of Our Lady of the Blessed Sacrament.

In the encyclical *Mystici Corporis Christi* (The Church as the Mystical Body of Christ), written on June 29, 1943 at the height of World War II and the worst time in the history of the world, Pope Pius XII begged people to go to Mass and receive Jesus every single day if possible. Pope Pius saw the only way to end the war was increased Mass attendance. There are 200,000 "*Daily Miracles*" of celebration of the Holy Sacrifice of the Mass every week in the USA, and almost 2,000,000, every week throughout the world. St. Pio (Padre) once said, "*the sun never sets on the Holy Sacrifice of the Mass.*"

Sacraments

The destructive power of sin grows and unless stopped perpetuates in a persons life. Sin disables a life because the protective shield of grace is removed. We are a Sacramental Church. The Lord in His gracious and infinite mercy has given us the Sacraments as a tool to go deeper into relationship with Him in a more intimate and personal way. Confession and the Eucharist are gifts from heaven to seek God and His kingdom first. Confession is the portal that opens graces.

The Seven Sacraments are:

1. Baptism
2. The Eucharist
3. Reconciliation/Confession
4. Confirmation
5. Marriage
6. Holy Orders
7. Anointing the Sick

Mortal and Venial Sin

There are varying degrees of severity of sin. Reconciliation or confession is where heaven has given us the ability to come back to grace, and it is for this reason it is so important. Jesus told Saint Faustina about the graces from confession when He said, "*The Tabernacle is the throne of My Divine Mercy, and the confessional is the Tribunal of My divine Mercy. I am there with the priest waiting for you.*"

The Catechism of the Catholic Church speaks of Mortal and Venial Sin.

It says, "*Mortal sin destroys charity in the heart of man by a grave violation of God's law; it turns man away from God...by preferring an inferior good to Him. Venial sin allows charity to subsist, though it offends and wounds it*" (1855).

"*Mortal sin results in the privation of sanctifying grace, that is, the state of grace. If it is not redeemed by repentance of God's forgiveness, it causes exclusion from Christ's kingdom and the eternal death of hell*" (1861).

"*One commits venial sin when in a less serious matter, he does not observe the standard prescribed by the moral law, or when he disobeys the moral law in a grave matter, but without full knowledge or complete consent*" (1862).

"*Venial sin weakens charity...and...merits temporal punishment. Deliberate and unrepentant venial sin disposes us little by little to commit mortal sin. However, venial sin does not break the covenant with God*" (1863).

I John 5:16-18, says, "*if anyone sees his brother committing a sin that is not deadly sin, he will ask, and God will give him life for those whose sin is not deadly. There is sin which is deadly; and I do not say one is to pray for that. All wrongdoing is sin, but there is sin which is not deadly. We know that anyone born of God does not sin, but He who is born of God keeps him, and the evil one does not touch him.*"

The Blessed Mother has said at Medjugorje there are five essentials of our faith. She said, "*I give you the weapons against your Goliath. Here are your little stones:*"

1. Prayer with the Heart
2. Eucharist
3. Holy Bible
4. Fasting
5. Monthly Confession

In all simplicity and truth there is the prescription given to mankind from the mother of Jesus to fight the culture. These are the Five Pillars of Sanctity given by heaven as tools and weapons. If another stone were to be added it would be the necessity for fellowship or community to strengthen one another.

Humility

Saint Anthony of Padua had a vision one day where he saw the whole world covered with the nets and snares of Satan. They were spread out to catch the souls of men. Saint Anthony said, "*who can ever hope to escape all these snares, for they are everywhere?" Saint Anthony then heard a voice that said, "The man who is humble.*" Saint Vincent de Paul said about humility, "*it is the most powerful weapon with which to overcome the devil, because, not knowing how to use it, he does not even know how to defend himself from it.*"

Prayer

Man needs prayer as a dying man needs oxygen. Prayer enables a person to endure the daily trials of life more easily. No matter what the trial, with prayer we will see the divine plan that is happening amidst the negative circumstances, as we will be better prepared to weather a crisis in a spirit of confident faith.

Rosary

Saints, popes, and scholars agree on the immense value of the Rosary and attest to its power over Satan. The Blessed Mother said to the Marian Movement of Priests the Rosary is as powerful as a nuclear weapon and, "*At this time above all, I am asking you to pray with fervor and joy by means of the Holy Rosary. It is the weapon which is to be used by you today in fighting and winning this bloody battle; it is the golden chain that binds you to my heart; it is the lightning rod that will keep far from you, and from those that are dear to you, the fire of the chastisement; it is the sure means of having me always close to you*" (Message 264h).

Throughout history, praying the Rosary has always been stressed by the Blessed Mother as a weapon against Satan.

The Fifteen Promises Granted To Those Who Recite the Rosary

These are the promises given to Saint Dominic, founder of the Dominican Order, and to Blessed Alan de la Roche in the 13th Century for those who pray the Rosary.

1. Whoever shall faithfully serve me by the recitation of the Rosary shall receive signal graces.

2. I promise my special protection and the greatest graces to all those who shall recite the Rosary.
3. The Rosary shall be a powerful armor against hell; it will destroy vice, decrease sin, and defeat heresies.
4. The Rosary will cause virtue and good works to flourish; it will obtain for souls the abundant mercy of God; it will withdraw the hearts of men from the love of the world and its vanities, and will lift them to the desire for eternal things. Oh, that souls would sanctify themselves by this means.
5. The soul which recommends itself to me by the recitation of the Rosary, shall not perish.
6. Whoever shall recite the Rosary devoutly, applying himself to the consideration of its sacred mysteries shall never be conquered by misfortune. God will not chastise him in His justice, he shall not perish by an unprovided death; if he be just he shall remain in the grace of God, and become worthy of eternal life.
7. Whoever shall have a true devotion for the Rosary shall not die without the sacraments of the Church.
8. Those who are faithful to recite the Rosary shall have during their life and at their death the light of God and the plenitude of His graces; at the moment of death they shall participate in the merits of the saints in paradise.
9. I shall deliver from Purgatory those who have been devoted to the Rosary.
10. The faithful children of the Rosary shall merit a high degree of glory in Heaven.
11. You shall obtain all you ask of me by the recitation of the Rosary.
12. All those who propagate the Holy Rosary shall be aided by me in their necessities.
13. I have obtained from my Divine Son that all the advocates of the Rosary shall have for intercessors the entire celestial court during their life and at the hour of death.
14. All who recite the Rosary are my sons and daughters, and brothers and sisters of my only Son Jesus Christ.
15. Devotion to my Rosary is a great sign of predestination.

In message #336 to the Marian Movement of Priests, titled The Rosary Brings You Peace, Our Lady says, "*Pray, above all with the prayer of the holy rosary. Let the rosary be, for everyone, the powerful weapon to be made use of in these times. The rosary brings you peace. With this prayer, you are able to obtain from the Lord the great grace of a change of hearts, of the conversion of souls, and of the return of all humanity to God, along the road of repentance, of love, of divine grace and of holiness.*"

Our Lady of Fatima is Our Lady of The Rosary, and her message was, "*Pray The Rosary Every Day For Peace in The World.*" Our Lady showed the children of Fatima souls falling into hell like snowflakes especially because of sexual sins. Our Lady of Fatima added the following prayer at the end of each decade of the Rosary, "*O my Jesus, forgive us our sins, save us from the fires of hell, and lead all souls to heaven, especially those most in need of Thy Mercy.*"

In the first half of the 13th century, while Saint Dominic, St. Francis and St. Angelus were together in Rome, the Blessed Mother appeared to them holding up the Rosary in her right hand, and the Scapular in her left hand and said, "*One Day Through The Rosary And The Scapular I Will Save The World.*"

The Sun Stands Still

All of nature is subordinate to the Lord. All laws are suspended whether they are man made or natural, when faith is active with an individual within His Divine Will. See the story in the Book of Joshua when Joshua commanded the sun to stand still: "*Then spoke Joshua to the Lord in the day when the Lord gave the Amorites over to the men of Israel; and he said in the sight of Israel, 'Sun, stand thou still at Gibeon, and thou moon in the valley of Ai'Jalon.' And the sun stood still, and the moon stayed, until the nation took vengeance on their enemies. Is this not written in the Book of Jashar? The sun stayed in the midst of heaven, and did not hasten to go down for about a whole day. There has been no day like it before or since, when the Lord hearkened to the voice of man; for the Lord fought for Israel*" (Joshua 10:12-14).

Joshua was going to battle against five kings of the Amorites and the Lord told him, "*do not fear them for I have given them into your hands; there shall not a man of them stand before you*" (10:8). The Lord had told Joshua as He had told Moses in the desert, *The Lord will fight for you, and you have only to be still* (Exodus 14:14). Joshua would have to do just as he was commanded to have favorable circumstances for battle. What is fascinating for so many intellectual skeptics of the authenticity and veracity of Scripture is that the Chinese calendar records the sun not setting on this day. The simple fact is that in a time of great need, God granted a profound miracle because a man of great faith like Joshua asked for it.

Evil

The more evil increases, the greater we will see Divine manifestations of God's grace to endure and conquer in unprecedented ways. In the coming years, due to the virulent and vile nature of sin that is rampant in the world, we will see more of God's miracles on a scale no one today is used to witnessing. The apostasy will increase and become darker. If you do not have your faith with you when you travel, you may not find faith somewhere when you arrive. We are now at a point in many places faith will be hard to find unless you bring it there.

In message #449 titled, The Pope of My Secret (1991), Our Lady says to the Marian Movement of Priests, "*My Church today is wounded by a deep division; it is threatened with the loss of the true faith; it is pervaded with an infidelity which is becoming greater and greater. When this Pope will have completed the task which Jesus has entrusted to him and I will come down from heaven to receive his sacrifice, all of you will be cloaked in a dense darkness of apostasy, which will then become general.*

There will remain faithful that little remnant which, in these years, by accepting my motherly invitation, has let itself be enfolded in the secure refuge of my Immaculate Heart. And it will be this little faithful remnant, prepared and formed by me, that will have the task of receiving Christ, who will return to you in glory, bringing about in this way the beginning of the new era which awaits you."

There is a lot being said in the above and the direction of the Church. Saint John Paul II died on the vigil of Divine Mercy Sunday April 2, 2005. Since his death we have seen the Church become progressively darker. The general theme of this book is the Lord is in control, and we are to have peace of soul during this loss of faith, because heaven has told us it will be so. Our Lady is saying the Church is cloaked in a dense darkness of apostasy, which will become generalized. This is precisely what we are seeing today. The word "dense" is a very strong word here.

The coming Warning and Great Miracle will be of biblical proportions and will redirect the momentum of how we live.

Forgiveness

If there is a (or the) primary reason why people don't grow spiritually, it would be from a lack of forgiveness in their life. Think of a person holding an umbrella on a rainy day. Envision the sun or rain as rays of graces looking to penetrate our soul. The graces cost us nothing to receive if we say "*yes*" to them. It is our choice to say yes or no. If a soul is in a state of mortal sin, the graces are blocked from that soul as the umbrella is functioning to do as designed. Graces are rebuffed as the umbrella shields the graces from penetrating our heart and soul. It is the same with forgiveness. If there is no forgiveness, we constrain ourselves from growing because we are emotionally and spiritually shackled—unless we forgive. Until we forgive, we block graces God wants to give us.

Once there is bitterness in a relationship, other problems begin to happen. Once a person retreats emotionally due to bitterness, varying degrees of isolation happen where they remove themselves from interacting with people. In that isolation, God's grace is stunted and a person ceases to reach the potential the Lord desires. The act of self-will of not forgiving is the single greatest inhibitor to spiritual growth for anyone. God wants us to be full of joy, and to be people who transfer the Holy Spirit to others. By not making the willful act to forgive, we stunt that process. Father Joseph Ssemakula, author of *The Healing of Families,* tells the story of once going by a church where the sign read, "*Unforgiveness is like drinking poison, and expecting the other one to die.*" Not forgiving someone is like drinking poison. In one big gulp it kills you quickly, and if taken in small doses day after day, month after month, it just kills you slowly. Once we say in our heart we want to forgive, the Lord will do the rest. One single act of love can make the soul return to live. Then the rays of the sun will warm our heart and soul and we grow into our potential.

Prayer and Faith = Forgiveness

Prayer and faith have a significant impact on our health and healing. Over the last twenty years there has been a great deal of science that empirically shows the positive impact of peace of soul on our health. There has also been a great deal of research on those who harbor bitterness and have poor health. There has been significant data supported by the American Medical Association (AMA) that a positive mental attitude of prayer and faith has a healthy impact on our general well being.

None can deny that there are hurts for many of us that run deep, from small infractions to heinous sins that affect us where many things have not been our fault, but in which we became victims. Things that have happened to us through no fault of our own continue to plague us when we choose (perhaps without realizing it) to carry the negative baggage. Voluntary resentment, bitterness and not forgiving are the primary blockages to the Holy Spirit. By telling the Lord we wish to be free, we have started the healing process. This healing process begins with an act of the will. It may not be immediate, but just by asking the Lord to free us from carrying poison around, we have begun the process of healing.

Our brain acts as a memory bank. Painful memories can consume us over time and we will often see an individual having a general negative spirit about them. When we do our part, the Lord will do His part. That is where the element of grace enters. Grace becomes operative when we can no longer do something on our own, but want what God promises for our life. Sister Faustina says in her Diary, "*Even if sins be as scarlet, let that person draw near to Him*" (Diary 699). See The Diary of Saint Faustina 327, 1520, 1182, and 1602 on God's Mercy to the soul who Trusts Him in time of need. No soul is beyond God's mercy. When a person asks to be released from the bondage of bitterness for the healing of memories, the Lord will begin to free that person.

He has showed you, O man, what is good; and what does the Lord require of you but to do justice, and to love kindness, and to walk humbly with your God.

—Micah 6:8

JESUS, I TRUST IN YOU

eleven

The Hope—The Gift Of Divine Mercy

But they constrained Him saying, "stay with us for it is toward evening, and the day is now far spent." So He went into stay with them. When He was at table with them, He took the bread and blessed, and broke it, and gave it to them. And their eyes were opened and they recognized Him; and He vanished out of their sight. They said to each other, "Did not our hears burn within us while He talked to us on the road, while He opened to us the Scriptures?

—Luke 24: 29-32

Of all that can be said about Hope, nothing can be more majestic, true, and inspirational than the messages Jesus gave to a young woman in Poland during the 1930's by the name of Helen Kowalska. Now known in the Catholic Church as St. Maria Faustina Kowalska, or simply Saint Faustina. If a person internalizes these messages, nothing else is necessary to understand the mercy and love of God. Nothing is more hopeful than the messages of Divine Mercy. The messages are one of a kind in the history of the Roman Catholic Church where God communicates love and mercy to His people. Jesus told Sister Faustina they are specifically for our times, and she would be His secretary to write down the messages He wanted to give the world.

Standing in the Divine Mercy Basilica in Krakow Poland in 2002, Saint John Paul II quoted from the diary of St. Faustina and said, "*From here (Poland) must go forth the 'spark' which will prepare the world for (Jesus') final coming*" (1732). This spark came by the grace of God for our troubled times. This fire of mercy needs to be passed onto the world. The spark Saint John Paul II spoke of were the messages of Divine Mercy.

The book called *Divine Mercy in My Soul,* (Diary) speaks of God's constant and everlasting love for His people. It provides a road map for the future for all humanity. If one truly understands what is being said, we would wait in joyful hope for the future and not be fearful. In the Introduction to the Diary it says, *To this simple, uneducated, but courageous woman religious, who trusted Him without limit, Our Lord Jesus consigned the great mission to proclaim His message of mercy directed to the whole world: 'Today I am sending you with My mercy to the people of the whole world. I do not want to punish aching mankind, but I desire to heal it, pressing it to My merciful heart* (1588). *You are the secretary of My mercy; I have chosen you for that office in this and the next life* (1605). *...to make known to souls the great mercy I have for them, and to exhort them to trust in the bottomless depths of My mercy* (1567).

We will let the messages below speak to you and see the great hope the Lord has for the future of mankind if people trust in His mercy. The hope for mankind is living and internalizing what Jesus tells Saint Faustina.

Jesus tells Saint Faustina:

> *Today bring Me the souls who especially venerate and glorify My mercy, and immerse them in My mercy. These souls sorrowed most over My Passion and entered most deeply into My Spirit. They are living images of My Compassionate Heart. These souls will shine with a special brightness in the next life. Not one of them will go into the fire of hell. I shall particularly defend each one of them at the hour of death* (1224).
>
> *Most Merciful Jesus, whose Heart is Love Itself, receive into the abode of Your Most Compassionate Heart the souls of those who particularly extol and venerate the greatness of Your mercy. These souls are mighty with the very power of God Himself. In the midst of all afflictions and adversities they go forward, confident in Your mercy. These souls are united to Jesus and carry all mankind on their shoulders. These souls will not be judged severely, but Your mercy will embrace them as they depart from this life.*

A soul who praises the goodness of her Lord
Is especially loved by Him
She is always close to the living fountain
And draws graces from Mercy Divine.

Eternal Father, turn Your merciful gaze upon the souls who glorify and venerate Your greatest attribute, that of Your fathomless mercy, and who are enclosed in the Most Compassionate Heart of Jesus. These souls are a living Gospel; their hands are full of deeds of mercy, and their spirit, overflowing with joy, sings a canticle of mercy to You, O Most High! I beg You O God: Show them Your mercy according to the hope and trust they have placed in You. Let there be accomplished in them the promise of Jesus, who said to them, I Myself will defend as My own glory, during their lifetime, and especially at the hour of their death, those souls who will venerate my fathomless mercy (1225).

There is faith, and there is Trust. We can think of trust as faith in action or faith's execution. If a person has weak ankles and wants to accomplish the task of running, the natural tendency is to first strengthen the ankles. Faith, being different from the natural realm, says start your project on weak ankles, trust in the Lord, and He will see you through the task because without Him we can do nothing. In faith and trust, we will strengthen our ankles as we walk on them. That is faith in action. We activate trust by stepping out in faith when we can't see the future.

"*Fear nothing; I am always with you* (586). *And if this person responds with a sincere heart, **Jesus, I Trust in You,** he will find comfort in all his anxieties and fears...* "

See some consoling messages below from the Diary of Saint Faustina reassuring us that the Lord keeps a watchful eye over us.

The greater the sinner, the greater the right he has to My mercy (Diary 723).

1. *Because this people honors Me with their lips, but their hearts are far from Me* (Is 29:13).
2. *Blessed are the merciful, for they shall obtain mercy* (Matt 5:7).

The Image, the Feast, and the Promise

Paint an image according to the pattern you see, with the signature: Jesus I Trust in You. I desire that this image be venerated, first in your chapel, and (then) throughout the world (47). *My image is already in your soul. I desire that their be a Feast of Mercy. I want this image, which you will paint with a brush, to be solemnly blessed on the First Sunday after Easter; that Sunday is to be the Feast of Mercy* (49). *The soul that will go to Confession and receive Holy Communion* (On Divine Mercy Sunday-the Sunday after Easter) *will obtain complete forgiveness of sins and punishment* (699). *...I am giving mankind the last hope of salvation; that is, recourse to My mercy. My heart rejoices in this feast* (998).

...Whoever approaches the Fount of Life on this day will be granted complete remission of sins and punishment. Mankind will not have peace until it turns with trust to My mercy (300). ***Let no soul fear to draw near to Me, even though its sin be as scarlet*** (699).

The above are arguably the greatest promises in the Diary. The profound promise is unlike any other for the wayward or devout soul. "*Complete remission of sins...*" The person who does the Novena as asked finishing on Divine Mercy Sunday, has all sins washed away even if their sins are as scarlet—through true repentance their soul becomes white as snow. The Lord also says, there will be no peace in the world until it turns with trust to His mercy.

Proclaim that mercy is the greatest attribute of God. All the works of My hands are crowned with mercy (301).

I am offering people a vessel with which they are to keep coming for graces to the fountain of mercy. That vessel is this image with the signature: "Jesus, I Trust in You" (327).

My Heart overflows with great mercy for souls, and especially for poor sinners... it is for them that the Blood and Water flowed from My Heart as from a fount overflowing with mercy (367).

Jesus explains to Sister Faustina the meaning of His Divine Mercy and their promises. Jesus makes it clear to Faustina that He is everywhere and she cannot escape Him, and that with Him she can do all things.

You will prepare the world for My final coming. *Faustina then says, these words moved me deeply, and although I pretended not to hear* *them, I understood them very well and had no doubt about them. Once, being tired out from this battle of love with God, and making constant excuses on the grounds that I was unable to carry out this task, I wanted to leave the chapel, but some force held me back, and I found myself powerless. Then I heard these words, You intend to leave the chapel, but you shall not get away from Me, for I am everywhere.* **You cannot do anything, of yourself, but with Me you can do all things** (429).

Beg for mercy for the whole world (570).

Oh, what great graces I will grant those souls who say this chaplet; the very depths of My tender mercy are stirred for the sake of those who say the chaplet. Write down these words, My daughter. Speak to the world about My mercy. **It is a sign for the end times; after it will come the day of justice.** *While there is still time, let them have recourse to the fount of My mercy; let them profit from the Blood and the Water which gushed forth for them* (848).

Jesus speaks of praying the chaplet: *The souls that say this chaplet will be embraced by My mercy during their lifetime and especially at the hour of their death* (754). *By saying the chaplet you are bringing mankind close to me.* (929).

Let the greatest sinners place their trust in My mercy. They have the right before others to trust in the abyss of My mercy. My daughter, write about My mercy, towards tormented souls. Souls that make an appeal to My mercy delight Me. To such souls I grant even more graces than they ask. I cannot punish even the greatest sinner if he makes an appeal to My compassion, but on the contrary, I justify him in My unfathomable and inscrutable mercy. Write: before I come as a just Judge, I first open wide the door of My mercy. He who refuses to pass through the doors of My mercy must pass through the doors of My justice... (1146).

Saint Faustina echoes the prophet Jeremiah in reminding us that God is faithful, God is everywhere, and He never abandons His people. God sees all and knows all.

I demand from you deeds of mercy which are to arise out of love for Me. You are to show mercy to your neighbors always and everywhere.

You must not shrink from this or try to excuse yourself from it... Even the strongest faith is of no avail without works (742).

External God, in whom mercy is endless, and the treasury of compassion inexhaustible, look kindly upon us, and increase Your mercy in us, that in difficult moments, we might not despair, nor become despondent, but with great confidence, submit ourselves to Your holy will, which is Love and Mercy itself. Amen (950).

I am Love and Mercy itself (1074).

Souls who spread the honor of My mercy I shield through their entire life as a tender mother her infant, and at the hour of death I will not be a Judge for them, but the Merciful Savior (1075).

I want to grant a complete pardon to the souls that will go to Confession and receive Holy Communion on the Feast of My mercy (1109).

Proclaim to the whole world My unfathomable mercy...My daughter, be diligent in writing down every sentence I tell you concerning My mercy, because this is meant for a great number of souls who will profit from it (1142).

On the cross, the fountain of My mercy was opened wide by the lance for all souls—no one have I excluded! (1182).

If a soul does not exercise mercy in some way, it will not obtain My mercy on the day of judgment (1317).

You expired, Jesus, but the source of life gushed forth for souls, and the ocean of mercy opened up for the whole world. O Fount of Life, unfathomable Divine Mercy, envelop the whole world and empty Yourself out upon us (1319).

My great delight is to unite Myself with souls... When I come to a human heart in Holy Communion, My hands are full of all kinds of graces which I want to give to the soul. But souls do not even pay any attention to Me; they leave Me to Myself and busy themselves with other things. Oh, how sad I am that souls do not recognize Love! They treat Me as a dead object (1385; also see 1288, 1447).

In the Tribunal of Mercy (the Sacrament of Reconciliation) ...the greatest miracles take place and are incessantly repeated (1448).

Come with faith to the feet of My representative (1448).

Were a soul like a decaying corpse, so that from a human standpoint, there would be no hope of restoration and everything would already be lost, it is not so with God. The miracle of Divine Mercy restores that soul in full. Oh how miserable are those who do not take advantage of the miracle of God's mercy! (1448).

I never reject a contrite heart (1485).

My mercy is greater than your sins, and those of the entire world. I let my Sacred Heart be pierced with a lance, thus opening wide the source of mercy for you. Come then with trust to draw graces from this fountain (1485).

I have opened My Heart as a living fountain of mercy. Let all souls draw life from it. Let them approach this sea of mercy with great trust (1520).

No soul that has called upon My mercy has ever been disappointed (1541).

The Hour Of Mercy and Promises

...that as often as you hear the clock strike the third hour, immerse yourself completely in My mercy, adoring and glorifying it; invoke its omnipotence for the whole world, and particularly for poor sinners; for t that moment mercy was opened wide for every (145) *soul. In this hour you can obtain everything for yourself and for others for the asking; it was the hour of grace for the whole world—mercy triumphed over justice* (1572).

The graces of My mercy are drawn by means of one vessel only, and that is—trust. The more a soul trusts, the more it will receive (1578).

Here the misery of the soul meets the God of mercy (1602).

When you go to confession, to this fountain of mercy, the Blood and Water which came forth from My Heart always flows down upon your soul (1602).

I Myself am waiting there for you. I am only hidden by the priest...I Myself act in your soul (1602).

Make your confession before Me. The person of the priest is, for Me, only a screen. Never analyze what sort of a priest it is that I am making use of; open your soul in confession as you would to Me, and I will fill it with My light (1725).

Promises Of the Chaplet For the Dying

The souls that say this chaplet will be embraced by My mercy during their lifetime and especially at the hour of their death (754). *At the hour of their death, I defend as My own glory every soul that will say this chaplet; or when others say it for a dying person, the indulgence is the same. When* (205) *this chaplet is said by the bedside of a dying person, God's anger is placated, unfathomable mercy envelops the soul, and the very depths of My tender mercy are moved for the sake of the sorrowful Passion of My Son* (811). *My daughter, those words of your heart are pleasing to Me, and by saying the chaplet you are bringing humankind closer to Me* (929).

External God, in whom mercy is endless, and the treasury of compassion inexhaustible, look kindly upon us, and increase Your mercy in us, that in difficult moments, we might not despair, nor become despondent, but with great confidence, submit ourselves to Your holy will, which is Love and Mercy itself. Amen (950).

Encourage souls to say the Chaplet which I have given you... Whoever will recite it will receive great mercy at the hour of death... When they say this chaplet in the presence of the dying, I will stand between My Father and the dying person, not as the just Judge but as the Merciful Savior... Priests will recommend it to sinners as their last hope of salvation. Even if there were a sinner most hardened, if he were to recite this chaplet only once, he would receive grace from My infinite mercy. I desire to grant unimaginable graces to those souls who trust in My mercy...through the Chaplet you will obtain everything, if what you ask for is compatible with My will (687, 1541, 1731).

Sooner would heaven and earth turn into nothingness than would My mercy not embrace a trusting soul (1777).

In message 316 the Blessed Mother speaks to the Marian Movement of Priests with similar themes when Our Lady says she is the Mother of Hope and Trust, "*I am the Mother of Hope and of Trust. Live with me through these times of your second advent. As I was the virginal Mother of the first coming of Jesus, so also today I am the glorious Mother of His second coming.*"

Mercy—Your Sins Are As Scarlet— Manasseh

We see in the Old Testament a similar story of the Lord's great mercy when there is sincere contrition and then the Lord grants complete forgiveness. There are not many places in Scripture where we see the love and mercy of God as great as the story of Manasseh in II Chronicles 33. Manasseh was twelve years old when he came to the throne of Israel and reigned for fifty-five years. His father King Hezekiah had been one of the great kings of Judah, restoring the worship to the Temple in Jerusalem after destroying all the false gods and deities of Baal. But his son Manasseh was proud and arrogant.

"He did what was displeasing to the Lord, copying the shameful practices of the nations whom the Lord had dispossessed for the sons of Israel. He rebuilt the high places that his father Hezekiah had demolished, he set up altars to Baal and made sacred poles, he worshipped the whole array of heaven and served it...He practiced soothsaying, magic and witchcraft, and introduced necromancers and wizards...He did very many more things displeasing to God, thus provoking His anger...placing images of idols in the temple" (33:2-8).

So all the good his father had done, Manasseh, undid during his reign. The power of a boy elevated to king had gone to his head. His abuses went on for fifty-five years! He had become hard of heart, callous, and arrogant with his authority. In the past the Lord had severely had chastised Judah for lesser sins than Manasseh was now committing, but the king paid no attention to the Lord (9-10).

The Lord is so displeased with Manasseh He sends the generals from Assyria to capture him with hooks, and put him in chains and lead him away to Babylon (11). As a prisoner in a moment of great distress he seeks to appease the Lord his God, humbling himself deeply. He prayed to the Lord, *"and God relented at his prayer, hearing his plea and bringing him back to Jerusalem and his kingdom. Manasseh then realized that the Lord is God"* (13-14).

Here is a man who willfully in a time of power and authority rejected every responsibility before man and God possible. He had enjoyed every privilege as a king, and was drunk with power, committing sin and grievous abominations. However, the Lord hears his cry of shame and sin, and forgives him. The key here is he cried out for forgiveness.

This story is about the infinite mercy and love of God as are the messages God gives to Saint Faustina. It is incomprehensible in the human realm to grasp this type of mercy, especially if one had been on the receiving end of Manasseh's brutal behavior. This type of mercy is foreign to our natural way of thinking, but the point is clear: there is no sin too great if there is true repentance.

Manasseh did not sin greatly for a year or two, or three, or four, or five, or even ten. He was away from grace for fifty-five years and had a tyrannical reign as king. Manasseh was the recipient of an ocean of mercy. God's mercy and love in times of repentance is unfathomable. It is not to be understood by mortal men, but there can be restoration of the wasted years if God ordains it. Manasseh then restored the temples that had been desecrated, removed all altars to foreign gods, and they then resumed sacrifice only to the Lord their God (17). So the kingdom of Israel was preserved due to Manasseh's repentance.

We see a similar story again when the Lord tells Ezekiel He forgets the sins of those who repent. Here is the Lord saying He "*doesn't remember*" the sins because they are washed away. Here is great hope and trust for anyone to come to the Lord no matter their background. Mercy is available for the asking. Ezekiel writes, "*But if a wicked man turns away from all his sins he has committed and keeps all My statutes and does what is lawful and right, he shall surely live; he shall not die. None of the transgressions which he has committed, shall be remembered against him; for the righteousness which he has done he shall live*" (Ezekiel 18: 21-22).

The extension of this principle is what Jesus told Saint Faustina: that if there is true repentance, a person's past can become as white as snow even though one's sins have been red as scarlet. Life can then begin as a newborn babe. That is Mercy man can never understand.

The Lord knows the days of the blameless, and their heritage will abide forever; They are not put to shame in evil times, in the days of famine they have abundance.

—Psalm 37:18-19

JESUS, I TRUST IN YOU

twelve

Consecration: The Surest and Safest Way

For with God nothing will be impossible. And Mary said, "Behold, I am the handmaid of the Lord; let it be to me according to your word." And the angel departed from her. ...and Elizabeth was filled with the Holy Spirit and she exclaimed with a loud cry, "Blessed are you among women and blessed is the fruit of your womb... And blessed is she who believed that there would be a fulfillment of what was spoken to her from the Lord." And Mary said, "My soul magnifies the Lord, and my spirit rejoices in God my Savior, for He has regarded the low estate of His handmaiden. For behold, henceforth all generations will call me blessed; for He who is mighty has done great things for me, and holy is His name. And His mercy is on those who fear Him from generation to generation. He has shown strength with His arm, He has scattered the proud in the imagination of their hearts, He has put down the mighty from their thrones, and exalted those of low degree, He has filled the hungry with good things, and the rich He has sent empty away. He has helped His servant Israel, in remembrance of His mercy, as He spoke to our fathers, and to Abraham and to His posterity forever."

—Luke 1: 37-38, 41-45

There are many things that are very advantageous to the spiritual and devout life, but there is no surer and safer way to the Heart of Jesus than via the Consecration to the Heart of the Blessed Mother. Saint Anthony Claret said, "*Those who burn with the fire of Divine Love are children of the Immaculate. Wherever they go they enkindle that flame. Nothing distresses them. They rejoice in poverty. They laugh off false accusations. And they even rejoice in anguish.*" St. Albert the Great said, "*Mary is the divine page on which the Father wrote His Eternal Word.*"

Saints, mystics, popes, and the faithful have known of this as "*the sure way.*" If there is a spiritual shortcut to the Heart of God, Consecration to the Blessed Mother is just that. The Consecration by Saint Louis de Montfort outlines how the Blessed Mother intercedes for mankind to the throne of heaven—Because Jesus can refuse her nothing. Consecration is to be experienced, not simply read. The mystical event of giving oneself over to the Blessed Mother is not an understanding entirely of the intellect. Through the intellect only so much wisdom can be transferred to a person. When the Consecration or Entrustment is done, words cannot convey the mystical union heaven has given to that soul.

Consecration is where a person or place is "*set aside,*" or separated for a particular purpose or mission. It is a movement of the heart and soul, not only the head or intellect. It is something that comes from our deepest spirit, and then heaven will take over in our littleness and humility. Only when we surrender to the heart of God, and ask for the Blessed Mother's intercession, do we begin to understand its mysteries. Then, the miracles begin to happen—one by one—in God's good time. Along the way, we become transformed. In that transformation is a new life where we do all for God, not man. Consecration is when we dedicate our life to be used totally for Our Lady's plan, which is always God's plan. It is a place where we no longer care about the opinions of man, but God alone. We become new in the process and heaven takes over in a profound mystical way. Not our will, but His be done. If there is a single solution to what is wrong with us as individuals and society, it would be the Consecration. Over the years it has been called a Consecration, but Saint John Paul II felt the word Entrustment was a more accurate word describing the experience.

In February of 1990, while in Poland, I made a trip to the Nazi death camp of Auschwitz, and learned about the spirituality and life of Saint Maximilian Kolbe. It was a cold, raw, wet day which only reinforced in my mind the harshness of the conditions of the imprisoned, and what it must have been like for the millions of people who endured hardship for their religious and political beliefs during World War II. Kolbe is often referred to as the Saint of Auschwitz as he gave up his life during World War II for a man he didn't even know. Until 1990,

I had only known Kolbe's name, but little of his life. Over the next several years I read about his life and began to understand that the roots of his spirituality were in the mysteries of the Blessed Mother, whom he called *The Immaculata.* I asked myself, how was he able to give his life for another? How did he write with such reverence, insight and understanding? What prompted him to start the *Militia Immaculata?* Where did his strength and courage come from? What was the origin of his writings illuminating the deepest mysteries of life—and unlocking them? St. Maximilian was given the wisdom to enable him to have one of the largest friaries in the world (nearly 800 inhabitants) at that time in Poland with printing presses, works of mercy, and evangelism, while sending missionaries throughout the world. This massive evangelization effort was incredible at that time.

Kolbe saw the world heading to a crisis, and found a solution. The great men and women of history, many of whom become saints, not only articulate the problem, but find lasting spiritual solutions that endure for ages. The great men and women of spirituality change lives, and thus alter the destiny of nations.

As a young boy Kolbe wondered what he would do for his life's work. One day entering a church he asked that question. He later recalled what followed.

> *"Then the Virgin Mother appeared to me holding in her hands two crowns, one white and one red. She looked at me with love and asked me if I would like to have them. The white meant that I would remain pure, and red I would be a martyr. I answered yes, I wanted them. Then the Virgin looked at me tenderly and disappeared."*

From the outset he said he would be a white (dry) and red (wet) martyr. The red rose stood for martyrdom of bloodshed; the white rose stands for purity, which can be a martyrdom of the heart. In just a few seconds he knew the future in a general sense, but not specifics. Kolbe earned a doctorate in philosophy in 1915, and another doctorate in theology in 1919 from the Pontifical University of Saint Bonaventure in Rome. It was during this time in Rome that he saw Freemasons marching in Vatican Square saying they would destroy the Church of Rome. It was this event that prompted him to form the Militia Immaculata (MI). On August 14, 1941, on the vigil of the Feast of the Assumption (15th), Kolbe the prisoner was injected at Auschwitz with carbolic acid in a cell that in February when I visited was littered with fresh red and white roses. His body was incinerated on August 15.

Kolbe was fascinated with the title that heaven gave Our Blessed Mother when she came to Lourdes, France. She said, "*I am the Immaculate Conception.*" It was not until the end of Kolbe's life that he really understood what it meant.

The Spark Will Come From Poland—Divine Mercy

In the Twentieth Century Poland produced three great saints with a common thread and interconnectivity: Saint Faustina (Helena Kowalska), Saint Maximilian Kolbe, and Saint John Paul II. It was a young Polish Archbishop by the name of Karol Wojtyla from Krakow, Poland who started vigorously the investigative process under the auspices of the Holy Office into the life of Helena Kowalska. On April 18, 1993, Sister Faustina was beatified, and on April 30, 2000, Sister Faustina became the first saint of the new millennium under the watchful eye of Pope John Paul II. As the event came to its conclusion that day, Saint John Paul II said, "*this is the happiest day of my life.*" It had been a goal of his to see Divine Mercy as a Feast Day, and to institute Divine Mercy Sunday on the Church calendar. Today it is celebrated on the First Sunday after Easter.

Saint John Paul II knew we were living in the age of Divine Mercy, as he mystically knew the future impact Faustina's writings would have on the Church. The writings of Saint Faustina are about God's unfathomable Mercy. Faustina records in her Diary Jesus' words to her, "*I myself will defend as My own glory, during their lifetime, and especially at the hour of their death, those souls, who will venerate My fathomless Mercy*" (1225).

As a young man, Karol Wojtyla endured privations and hardships like few others his age. His mother had died when he was eight, his sister died (before he was born), his older brother Edmund of thirteen years died of scarlet fever, and in 1941 his father died of a heart attack. The young Karol said, "*at twenty I had lost all the people I loved.*" Now an orphan, he immersed himself in the theater and studies. As a quiet studious man, he enjoyed languages and theater, and in matters of faith he excelled.

When he received his call to become a priest, he intensely studied three books in his spiritual and intellectual formative years. They were the *Bible, Das Kapital* by Karl Marx, and *The True Devotion to Mary* by Saint Louis Marie de Montfort. Each had a purpose. To understand Communism after World War II, Russia had Poland in a vise lock, and he felt he had to understand Communist Marxist ideology. He wanted to understand the Soviet ideology to combat it. Wojtyla said reading *True Devotion to the Immaculate Heart of Mary* was the defining event of his life. It was here, one's mind, heart, and soul become supernaturally illumined in a way no human can put words to the experience. It was here under the influence of Montfort, that Wojtyla the priest, the Bishop, and the Pope signed many letters and writings in his lifetime, *Totus Tuus* (Totally Yours), referring to his dedication to the Blessed Mother. Saint John Paul II understood what Louis de Montfort said, "*It would be easier to separate light from the sun than to separate Mary from Jesus.*"

When one reads the prayers, the method, and the meditations the Immaculata proposes, only then does one understand the profound impact it has on one's spirituality. You become immersed in her wisdom and grace, with the secrets of the universe in your grasp. Wojtyla and Kolbe both knew that Consecration was the solution to all the problems in the world. If people would only follow the path to the Immaculata as Montfort, Kolbe, and as others had done, the world would have greater peace. Kolbe realized the quickest and surest way for the world to change was for people to do a Consecration, and he worked tirelessly towards that goal. Since Wojtyla had been a young man, and until he was elected Pope in 1978, he had lived under oppressive German and Russian occupation. It was said that Saint John Paul II did the Entrustment often as a young man and continued it into the final years of his life. His mysticism was enhanced by the writings of Saint Teresa of Avila and Saint John of the Cross, which had such an impact on his early life as a young man, that he nearly became a Carmelite.

Saint Maximilian Kolbe and Saint Faustina

It was Saint John Paul's mysticism and charisms that enabled him to carry out the mission he was given that stretched across the globe. He said it was the Blessed Mother who guided the bullet when he was shot point blank in Vatican Square on May 13, 1981. He said, "*one hand fired the bullet, another guided it.*" Doctors were amazed at the bizarre path the bullet took inside his body, as it missed all his vital organs. On a trip to Fatima, he placed the bullet that came from inside his body into the crown of the statue of the Blessed Mother that now sits atop the church, in thanksgiving for saving his life. It was the Blessed Mother's fingerprint on his soul that he became heaven's handpicked Vicar of Christ to lead the Church in the troubled twentieth century. Pope John Paul II was canonized on April 27, 2014.

It was Saint John Paul II who early in his pontificate that proclaimed Maximilian Kolbe a saint on October 10, 1982. Kolbe's spirituality had taken root in the young Polish priest from Krakow, Karol Wojtyla, and it had left an indelible imprint upon him as had the writings of Faustina, the Apostle of Divine Mercy. Kolbe, Faustina, Saint John Paul II and others, found a secret few probe, and even fewer accept. A veritable treasure chest of graces was available for the asking. When one consecrates their life to Jesus and Mary, they become a vessel of graces released by heaven. The Blessed Mother never desires adulation or seeks attention herself, but always leads us to the Son, and is always magnifying God.

It is in the heart of the mother we find peace of soul in troubled times. When all is lost with seemingly no way out, children run to their mother. The world is fast approaching this moment in time as godless man-made structures are collapsing around us. Soon, the world will run to the Immaculate Heart. As a young man Karol Wojtyla was orphaned, worked as a day laborer in a stone quarry, and studied in an underground seminary. He had to deal with a brutal, cruel German occupation, then a Russian system equally as harsh, and then rose to the heights of personal greatness as a man handpicked by the Blessed Mother for our troubled time.

The Church has given us the necessary resources including the Sacraments to find our way and to prosper spiritually: tools for combat, tools for prayer, and tools for living a virtuous life. *True Devotion* is one of those special tools to go deeper into the heart of God's mercy and love. It is a grace to have these instruments at our disposal.

It is not by coincidence that in our age of such widespread sin, more people are finding out about True Devotion and Entrustment, because "*where sin abounds, grace abounds all the more*" (Rom. 5:20). God's mercy has provided this tool for us today as our age is so evil.

The Entrustment/Consecration

The Consecration or Entrustment is an exercise that takes 33 days according to the way it was designed by Saint Louis Marie de Montfort. As part of this devotion there are prayers, litanies, devotions, Scripture readings, and mediations. This devotion is about a change in the way we view life. Who do you work for? What do you value? How do you spend your time? It is a process where one realizes their life is not their own. It is a meditation of the heart and not the head. It is not some rote formula, but a plan for change. When one views it as such, the results are dramatically different than just going through some procedural readings to say you "*did it.*" When the Consecration is comprehended there is a change in your heart and soul. Kolbe said, "*The Spirit of the Militia Immaculata is to be an instrument in the Immaculate's hands. Begging her to direct us. Doing as much as we can as quickly as we can. Proclaiming the gospel with the greatest efficacy and to ever widening circles. Letting her preach through us and in us. Letting her make our life her own.*"

If one were to take a picture of the Matterhorn Mountain in Switzerland, or the Grand Canyon in Arizona, the picture would not convey to another what the photographer felt when taking the photo viewing all their beauty. The emotion doesn't come across on film. It is the same here. The Entrustment is an interior conversion one only knows through experience. It is about a deep felt interior desire to know and understand spirituality more intimately. It allows us to plead and beg God for His graces so we can better serve Him. The participant alone will know they have entered a new chamber, a new room, and new mansion. One will begin to gain greater understanding and spiritual insight into life you never had before. Grace descends. In your heart you know you are different. This is not to say all difficulties and crosses will disappear. However, after doing an Entrustment, you will be given the graces to deal with adversity in a new way.

No matter the academic pedigree, upbringing, domestic situation, ethnicity, stage in life, male or female, young or old, it is a spiritual (mystical) event that will alter one's life like nothing else. People who do the Consecration seem to have an instinctive awareness of others who have done it. In other words, heaven is placing a spiritual mantle over you as you have now pledged fidelity to a state of *Totus Tuus*. We become a more useful instrument to be used for His greater purpose, giving everything to the Blessed Mother to distribute graces for us. A less cumbersome process for figuring out what we think we need versus what heaven knows in advance. Graces pour mystically from the decision to have an Entrusted Life.

The problems in the world are no longer able to be solved with the wisdom of men. It is heaven's hand to play now, and people all over the world feel helpless as never before. The great mystics of our day are in agreement on this issue. That is precisely why *The Warning and The Great Miracle* are soon to come. The world will implode without it. This one specific thing can be done; costs nothing other than the price of a book, and will take about thirty minutes a day for 33 days. Doing the Entrustment will put your life on a different path. That is the fruit of the Entrustment. As Satan's time nears an end, he continually attempts to destroy the things of God. It will take putting all of the tools available to us to resist the temptations and wiles of the devil. Nothing will yield more fruit than doing what the great saints have done before us. We need the protection of the Blessed Mother's mantle if we are to do heaven's work. As Jesus told Peter, he would be "*sifted like wheat*" (Luke 22:31) if the Holy Spirit were not protecting him.

A family can do an Entrustment together. Those who do it as a family receive heavenly graces scented with the fragrance of perfume. In that filial abandonment, we ask the Blessed Mother to direct the footsteps of our family under her mantle of knowledge of what is best for us. She avails to us spiritual protection of our temporal material needs, marriages and children. Our Lady is the Queen of Families. In that trust our plans become realized, there is protection of the home and children, and there is an increase of the practice of Christian virtue in the home. When the family does an Entrustment, grace takes over. This may not happen overnight, but over time as we practice virtue under her mantle, we see wonderful results. Through this transformation, peace and tranquility descend on the home, and the children have a special protection. It is Our Lady who participates in His plan for salvation of all mankind, and she says, we are all, "*apostles of the last times,*" asking for communion with the Father in heaven. Her appointed role at this point in history is the will of heaven. It is under this type of understanding that Saint Maximilian Kolbe, Saint John Paul II, and Saint Faustina were able to understand our times through the grace of the Holy Spirit.

Maximilian Kolbe left the world a treasure of thinking on Marian theology. Perhaps nothing was more profound than when he explained the language of the Immaculate Conception. When the Blessed Mother came to Bernadette Soubirous at Lourdes, France in 1858, she identified herself by saying, "*I am the Immaculate Conception.*" This title intrigued Kolbe his whole life. It is the basis of his thinking and insight into who the Immaculata is. How is it she could say that? She was created by the Eternal Father to physically house His Son, Jesus Christ, to be born into the world for its redemption. She is the daughter of the Father, the Mother of the Son, and the spouse of the Holy Spirit.

The Blessed Mother was the purest vessel ever created by God for His intended purpose for the salvation of mankind. She became the New Eve, the New Ark of the Covenant. Mary was the woman destined to house God, the Tabernacle of God with no stain of original sin. It was she who became the New Ark of the Covenant from the moment of her own conception. No seed of man could produce her as it would have carried the stain and sin of man. It was her own volition to accept her position for all eternity. In her was no vestige of sin's traces—she was total purity.

Kolbe said, "*the Father begets; the Son is begotten; the Spirit is the conception that springs from their love. So Mary too is Their conception, one step removed by being within space/time, and in turn begotten by Their conception, the Holy Spirit. So as all children come from a conception from a man and a woman, Mary and the Holy Spirit are united. They are in essence One.*" Kolbe comments on a profound mystery that few understood except those in the heart of fidelity and union with God:

> *What type of union is this (between the Holy Spirit and Mary)? It is above all an interior union, a union of her essence with the essence of the Holy Spirit. The Holy Spirit dwells in her, lives in her. This was true from the first instant of her existence. It was always true; it will always be true. In what does this life of the spirit in Mary consist? He himself is uncreated love in her; the love of the Father and the Son, the love by which God loves himself, the very love of the Most Holy Trinity. He is a fruitful Love, a "Conception." Among creatures made in God's image, the union brought about by married love is the most intimate of all (Matt 19:6). In a much more precise, more interior, more essential manner, the Holy Spirit lives in the soul of the Immaculata, in the depths of her very being. He makes her fruitful, from the very first instant of her existence, all during her life, and for all eternity.*
>
> *The eternal "Immaculate Conception" (which is the Holy Spirit) produces in an immaculate manner divine life itself in the womb (or depths) of Mary's soul, making her the Immaculate Conception, the human Immaculate Conception. And the virginal womb of Mary's body is kept sacred for Him; there He conceives in time, because everything that is material occurs in time, the human life of the Man God.*
>
> *... If among human beings the wife takes the name of the husband because she belongs to him, is one with him, becomes equal to him and is, with him, the source of new life, with how much greater reason should the name of the Holy Spirit, who is the Divine Immaculate Conception, be used as the name of her in whom he lives as uncreated love, the principle of life in the whole supernatural order of grace.*

If that overwhelms you, you would be in good company because so much of life is a mystery. The Holy Spirit has given us insight and illumination at this point in time because of the evil in our age, for a role the Blessed Mother is carrying out throughout the world as heaven's purest and exalted emissary. The Blessed Mother has been appointed by the Most Holy Trinity for this task. The above quote was written shortly before Kolbe was shipped off to the death camp of Auschwitz. She is the Co-Redemptix (Co means with), Mediatrix, and Advocate for mankind. As Jesus said some serious things to His disciples just before he went to Calvary, the same applies here to Kolbe. Before you know you are to die, only the most important things in life will be said. This is the most important thinking in Kolbe's theology and sums up succinctly Mary's very special role in concert with the Most Holy Trinity. Is it to be fully understood in our intellect? No. It will take a submissive will of littleness and poverty of spirit to accept this doctrine. Unless we become as little children with a heart to the things of heaven, it will be hard to digest this special role of the Blessed Mother in our special age.

In an age where reason has drowned out the message of the heart and the plan God the Father set forth in Scripture, we will not be able to hear His voice. Often, too much intellectualism blocks the work of God. There were those who followed Jesus when he walked physically on earth while others did not. The prophecies of Daniel, Isaiah, Jeremiah, and other prophets foretold of His coming. It appears we are on the threshold of a new era ordained from the very beginning of time. Yes, at this very point in time, we can expect to see the fulfillment of many Scriptural prophecies. If looked at in its entirety, it is nearly overwhelming to comprehend the scope of graces we are privileged to receive.

After the angel appeared to the young virgin handmaiden Mary, Scripture tells us, "*she pondered these things in her heart and told no one*" (Luke 2:19). She knew what God had told her, and kept them in her own heart. In the quiet moments of prayer, after submitting and surrendering to the Will of the Father, wisdom and insight will be mystically given as needed. You will know what you know in your heart, and no one can take it away from you. We are called to have confidence that Heaven has a plan and live peacefully in that knowledge. As the world collapses around us, we are called to have an interior peace.

No one knew this better than the young priest Karol Wojtyla while enduring the challenges of living under the Third Reich, Stalinism, and a Communist regime from youth to being elected Pope in 1979—a total of nearly forty years of foreign oppressive governments being his political and economic master. He understood what it meant to be submissive to the Holy Spirit for survival. It is at the wedding feast of Cana where Saint John Paul II writes so eloquently on the first public miracle of Jesus. The setting is simple. There is a wedding and the wine steward has run out of wine. Mary lets her Son know they have no wine. Her instructions to the steward are the maternal counsel of every age since then, "*do whatever He tells you.*" The story is brief, but powerful (John 2:1-12). It is Mary who opens the public life of Jesus to a new dimension to fulfill why He came to man, ushering in His public ministry through her request of Jesus to fulfill the simple needs of a newlywed couple. She initiates and Jesus willingly complies. Jesus was the Messiah in the flesh, God among men. Saint John Paul II provides deep insight into what is glossed over by many about the Cana event. He writes,

> *Cana clearly outlines the new dimension, the new meaning of Mary's motherhood. It is a new kind of motherhood according to the spirit and not just according to the flesh, that is to say Mary's solicitude for human beings, her coming to them in the wide variety of their wants and needs. At Cana in Galilee there is shown only one concrete aspect of human need, apparently a small one of little importance (They have no wine). But it has a symbolic value: this coming to the aid of human needs means, at the same time, bringing those means within the radius of Christ's messianic mission and salvific power. Thus there is a mediation: Mary places herself between her Son and mankind in the reality of their wants, needs, and sufferings. She puts herself "in the middle," that is to say she acts as a mediatrix not as an outsider, but in her position as mother. She knows that as such she can point out to her Son the needs of mankind, and in fact, she "has the right" to do so. Her mediation is thus in the nature of intercession: Mary intercedes for mankind. And that is not all. As a mother she also wishes the Messianic power of her Son to be manifested, that salvific power of His which is meant to help man in his misfortunes,*

> *to free him from the evil which in various forms and degrees weighs heavily upon his life...*
>
> *Another essential element of Mary's maternal task is found in her words to the servants: "Do whatever He tells you." The mother of Christ presents herself as the spokesperson of her Son's will, pointing out those things which must be done so that the salvific power of the Messiah may be manifested. At Cana, thanks to the intercession of Mary and the obedience of the servants, Jesus begins "His hour." At Cana, Mary appears as believing in Jesus. Her faith evokes His first "sign" and helps to kindle the faith of the disciples... The episode at Cana in Galilee offers us a sort of first announcement of Mary's mediation, wholly oriented toward Christ and tending to the revelation of His salvific power.*

The above ties cleanly into the proposed Fifth Marian Dogma of Co-Redemptrix, Mediatrix, and Advocate, which will usher in unprecedented graces to the world. She participated with the Redeemer for His works of salvation. Until the Blessed Mother is proclaimed as the Queen of Peace, the world will be Peaceless. Therefore, there is nothing more important than to pray for the proclamation of the Fifth Marian Dogma so graces can be unleashed in an unprecedented way.

The locutions received by Father Gobbi for the Marian Movement of Priests are also rich with the treasure of the Blessed Mother's role in our times. Numerous entries could have been provided, but the two below illustrate the importance of the Consecration and her role at this point in history.

> *"You are being called to be the instruments of divine mercy for all this poor humanity, so far from God. For this reason, I ask you to be faithful to your ministry. Be strong witnesses of faith in the time of the great apostasy; of holiness in the moments of great perversion; and of love in the hour of violence and hatred, which is becoming stronger and stronger from day to day.*
>
> *And so I ask you to consecrate yourselves to my Immaculate Heart, because I want to make of you instruments of my motherly mercy. Take my most needy children in your*

> *priestly arms and convert the sinners; heal the sick; comfort the despairing; bring those far away into the house of the Father; give to all the balm of my motherly and merciful love. Let your trust be great. The triumph of my Immaculate Heart is near"* (531).
>
> *"It is my great work of mercy because the merciful love of Jesus wants to manifest itself to you through the motherly means of my Immaculate Heart. To me has been entrusted by Jesus the task of going in search of my wandering children; of leading back the sinners along the road of righteousness; those who are far away, along the road of return to the Lord; the sick, along the way of healing; the despairing, along that of trust; the oppressed, along the road of relief, the lost, along that of salvation"* (562).

For those wishing to explore the subject of Consecration or Entrustment, there are many resources to choose. Getting a book on the Saint Louis Marie de Montfort Consecration will be the first step of the adventure. Saint Louis writes how the gift of Our Lady is to humanity, "*Poor children of Mary, your weakness is extreme, your inconstancy is great, your inward nature is very much corrupted. Yet do not be discouraged. Console yourself and exult because you have the great secret which I will teach you,—a secret unknown to almost all Christians—the secret of True Devotion to Mary.*"

Pope Leo XIII writes of Our Lady, "*Her dignity is so great, God's love to her so immense, that whoever is in need and does not have recourse to her is similar to one that wants to fly without wings*" (Augustissimae Virginis Mariae).

"*The most profound reason, why we want to win Mary's protection through prayer is without doubt because of her office as Mediatrix of divine grace. She acts in this office ever more, because she enjoys His highest esteem by her dignity and by her merit. Her power surpasses all the saints in the heavens by far*" (Jucunda Semper).

Saint Louis de Montfort writes, The Secret of Mary: "*We have to give ourselves over to Mary as instruments. Then she can act in us, through us and in us, however she wishes for greater glory of her Son, and through the Son for the greater glory of the Father."*

It is significant that "*True Devotion to Mary*" by St. Louis de Montfort, written in the early 1700's, was lost and not discovered until 1842, as the Modern Age of Mary had just begun in 1830 with a young Sister Catherine Laboure' and the Miraculous Medal at Rue du Bac in Paris. Near the end of the first chapter, St. Louis describes how during the final battle with Satan, it will be the holy consecrated children of Mary who will form her heel with which she will crush the Serpent's Head, thus fulfilling Genesis 3:15, "*I will put enmity between you and the woman, and between your seed and her seed, he shall bruise your head, and you shall bruise his heel.*" It further emphasizes the Miraculous Medal with Our Lady standing on the Globe of the World with her heel crushing the Serpent's head.

In 1842 an anti-Catholic Jew in Rome, Alphonse Ratisbonne, was instantly converted in the Church of Saint Andrea Della Frate by an apparition of Our Lady of the Miraculous Medal. He immediately received an infusion of all truths of the Catholic faith. He became a Catholic Priest and founded an Order of Priests to minister to the Jews. As his story shows, miracles of grace do indeed occur through Our Lady's intercession.

And thy own soul a sword shall pierce, that, out of many hearts, thoughts may be revealed.

—Luke 2:35, The Prophecy of Simeon

JESUS, I TRUST IN YOU

thirteen

Messages Of Jesus and The Blessed Mother For Our Time

Have no anxiety about anything, but in everything by prayer and supplication with thanksgiving let your requests be made known to God. And the peace of God, which passes all understanding, will keep your hearts and your minds in Christ Jesus. Finally brethren, whatever is true, whatever is honorable, whatever is just, whatever is pure, whatever is lovely, whatever is gracious, if there is any excellence, if there is anything worthy of praise, think about these things.

—Phil. 4:6-8

The validity of a prophecy or prediction can only be determined by looking at it in historical context. Time is the single best barometer of the authenticity and truth of a prophesied event, and filters the authentic from the fraudulent. There are instances where something was prophesied to happen and in fact did, others were conditional warnings of events that might be forestalled or lessened by those messages being heeded, and others still, where events simply did not happen as predicted.

When one looks at the enormous depth of apparitions in the history of the Church, we see clear evidence heaven intervening in the affairs of mankind. The level of such intervention has been accentuated in the last 200 years through Our Lady in her roles as Mother of the Church and Mother of Humanity, assigned to her from the cross by Christ. Heaven sends messengers and messages as an act of love. Most people are not aware of the multiplicity of Our Lady's apparitions because they are rarely spoken of from the Sunday pulpits. Even mainstream Catholic media do not report on them as a general rule. The purpose of presenting the material below is to inform those with a desire either to study heaven's messages to mankind or a willingness to listen and heed the messages in light of the dire consequences predicted should heaven's warnings be ignored. An ounce of caution is worth a pound of cure. Blind skepticism only assures associated graces will be missed. Sadly, the number of people who have listened to heaven's messages throughout history has not been large. The vast majority of Catholic faithful don't concern themselves with what heaven is saying in private revelation and apparitions, nor are they obliged to do so by the Church.

The messages below are a mere sampling of the thousands of pages that could have been provided from many mystics, prophets, stigmatists, saints, Church-approved apparition sites, seers, Popes, and scholars in Church history. Notably, many provide similar language, regarding the near collapse, schism, destruction and apostasy of the Roman Catholic Church in our time. It is macabre, depressing, and often frightening when viewed as one package. However, they are not macabre when viewed in their totality concerning heaven's agenda. The future of the Church is seen also to parallel the destiny of mankind at this point in history. It takes a courageous leap of faith to embrace what is being said. If the messages are true, the world is going to go through seismic changes. People of all professions are openly speaking of the things beyond our control and the events affecting us.

The messages of this selected genre specifically address the apostasy and downfall of the Church, but also speak to some of the larger transformation underway. They are not indicative of the larger body of messages that continuously exhort and confirm the love of God to mankind which is the overwhelming majority. But, they are very important to understand that changes are afoot and we must pay attention to what heaven is asking of us. Why? Because heaven is saying it. Most sense that momentous changes are upon us, and to be spiritually prepared is by far the most important thing we can do for ourselves and our families. Physically preparing can only take us so far, and in the end will fall short of spiritual preparedness. On the other hand, if the Lord is telling you to do something practically, it should be followed. The Lord gave us intellect. If we can see this from heaven's perspective, we will have an easier time adjusting emotionally. Faith will erase the fear of the unknown. The words of the first saint canonized in the new millennium, Saint Faustina, *Jesus I Trust In You,* were intended for times such as these to sustain our spirits.

It is our free choice whether we agree or not with the messages—saying yes or no to heaven's plan. The Blessed Mother provides a model for all mankind and willingness to obey God when the Archangel Gabriel conveyed to her a request she could not comprehend: give birth to a Son, the prophesied Savior, in effect to become the tabernacle that would house God in the flesh. The answer to her question how this could be since she had not known man, was incomprehensible—the Holy Spirit would descend upon her and she would conceive. So trust is called for in viewing heaven's messages and disbelief or unbelief is not unreasonable, at least as a starting point. To critically question is human and reasonable.

Just as God's people have always gone through shifts at pre-appointed times in the biblical narrative, the same applies today. The difficult aspect for us to come to grips with is, "*can this be happening now on our watch, at this very point in history?*" Asking that question is a normal and rational thought.

The Woman Clothed With the Sun

Revelation 12 is the Woman Clothed with the Sun in battle as the Queen of the Universe. Some good Catholics do not understand her role in the salvation of mankind, and reject her words when she speaks; they will only address it in hushed terms for fear of being marginalized. Clergy often move away from her for the same reasons. Some of the faithful will often venerate her as an important person in history, but they will shun her when someone speaks of her majesty and work in the world. Many think her activity stopped at Fatima and refuse to address the last one hundred years. Soon there will be no getting around what she has been saying, as we will know the appointed time(s) by the events themselves. The supernatural events will dictate we look into what has been said at so many apparition sites.

With the Blessed Mother's messages at Fatima, we see messages come true *exactly* as she prophesied to the world. Fatima is still the cornerstone of apparitions for modern times. We have been told by the seers of Medjugorje, that it is an extension and fulfillment of Fatima. Fatima still has significant events yet to be fulfilled. The apparitions at

Fatima were to three young children, that took place in 1917 outside a small Portuguese village. The world still watches what the final outcome will be. To this day, no other messages have such emotional, historical, and spiritual ramifications as it pertains to Russia, and its role in shaping the yet to be determined geopolitical landscape of the world. However, all indications as to what was said point to some terrible events at the hands of an unconverted and unconsecrated Russia.

The ability to look at major prophecies in retrospect provides a unique window into the future, especially when the Church has approved an apparition. Understanding them when they are ongoing is not always easy, but viewing them in historical perspective is quite remarkable once proven true. Often, what is said seems so far removed from reality at the time the message is delivered, it is absurd to the casual observer, so it is often dismissed. This is an important issue to understand as it concerns prophecy and the messages of heaven. The messages are like modern day epistles where heaven is guiding its people. It is a mother telling her children there is danger, and where the path to safety lies. When messages are given so far in advance, it is hard to see how things will evolve, but when the Church does approve an apparition, it can be trusted it is true as the process for approval is wisely rigorous. There is enormous data that our times are indeed unique based on the volume, consistency and intensity of the language of the messages. Below are selected seers and apparition sites with a sampling of messages that are relevant to the depth of change coming to the world. It is by no means meant to be conclusive or definitive. The genre of this book is tiny in comparison to the wider body of heaven's exhortations, messages of love, the New Era, and the New Times that await us. Independent research will allow one to dig deeper for your own edification in subjects of interest.

Queen Esther as Precursor

Nowhere in Scripture do we see a more beautiful story than the Book of Esther. Esther was a young orphan girl who was raised by her older cousin Mordecai, and was living in ancient Persia under the wealthy and powerful King Ahasuerus. King Ahasuerus was married to Queen Vashti who was disobedient to the King. As a result he put out a decree to summon the beautiful women in his kingdom to find a new Queen. Esther's guardian Mordecai served in the King's court and arranged for

Esther to be a candidate. Upon seeing Esther's beauty, the King chose her as his new Queen. A man by the name of Haman had great authority in the King's Court and Mordecai fell out of favor with Haman because he would not bow down in front of him as he rode by on a horse. When Haman found out that Mordecai was Jewish, he decided to have him and all the Jews in the Kingdom of Persia killed. Through a roll of the dice, Haman decided the Jews would die on the 13 day of the month of Adar. Learning of this, Queen Esther asked all the Jews not to eat or drink for three days. She too prayed and fasted for three days and then interceded with the King, and the Jewish people were spared. Going to the King unless summoned was punishable by death, yet she knowingly and courageously did so to save her people. This story is the basis for the Jewish Festival of Purim, which commemorates the deliverance of the Jewish people in ancient Persia. Throughout the Blessed Mother's apparitions, the 13th day of the month is a special day as we know especially from Fatima. Queen Esther is a precursor to the Blessed Mother interceding with Christ the King for her people. The word Esther in Persian means star, and on the hem of the garment at Fatima the Blessed Mother wore a star.

Blessed Elena Aiello, Italy

Sister Elena Aiello from Consenza, Italy was a stigmatist, was born in 1865 and died in 1961. She was the foundress of a charitable order called The Institute of the Orphan Souls and Tertiaries of the Passion of Our Lord. For thirty-eight straight years from 1923 to her death in 1961, she suffered the Passion of Our Lord on Good Friday. Many of her prophecies are a reaffirmation of the authenticity of the Fatima messages. Sister Aiello had similar spiritual ecstatic experiences like those of Saint (Padre) Pio, and Therese Neumann of Germany. She was beatified by Pope Benedict XVI in 2011.

In 1940, Sister Aiello was asked by Jesus to give a message to Premier Benito Mussolini of Italy, telling him not to align himself with Hitler in World War II. Mussolini was told Italy would be defeated and he would suffer a terrible fate. Both came to pass as Sister Aiello had warned. Mussolini was shot by his own countrymen on April 28, 1945, and his body was hung upside down on display like a side of beef for all to see in the center of Milan.

On April 7, 1950, Good Friday, Our Blessed Mother said, "*See how Russia will burn. Before my eyes there extended an immense field covered with flames and smoke, in which souls were submerged as if in a sea of fire. And all this fire, is not that which will fall from the hands of men, but will be hurled directly from the angels (at the time of the great chastisement or 'housecleaning' that will come upon the earth). Therefore, I ask prayers, penance and sacrifice, so I may act as Mediatrix for My Son in order to save souls.*"

On April 16, 1954, The Blessed Mother said, "*Clouds of lightning flashed of fire in the sky and a tempest of fire shall fall upon the world. This terrible scourge never before seen in the history of humanity will last seventy hours. Godless persons will be crushed and wiped out. Many will be lost because they remain in their obstinacy of sin. Then shall be seen the power of light over the power of darkness. Be not silent, my daughter, because the hours of darkness, of abandonment are near. I am bending over the world, holding in suspension the justice of God. Otherwise these things would have now come to pass. Prayers and penances are necessary...*"

On December 8, 1958, Jesus said, "*Italy, my daughter, will be humiliated, purified in blood, and must suffer much, because many are the sins of this beloved country seat of the Vicar of Christ. You cannot imagine what will happen! In those sad days there will be much anguish and weeping. There will be great revolution, and the streets will be red with blood. The Pope will suffer much, and all this suffering will be like an agony, which will shorten his earthly pilgrimage. His successor will guide the boat in the tempest.*"

In 1959, The Blessed Mother said, "*Russia will march upon all the nations of Europe, particularly Italy, and will raise her red flag over the Dome of Saint Peter's. Italy will be severely tried by a great revolution, and Rome will be purified in blood for its many sins, especially those of impurity. The flock is about to be dispersed and the Pope must suffer greatly.*"

August 22, 1960, the Blessed Mother said, "*...If the people do not recognize in these scourges of nature the warnings of Divine Mercy, and do not return to God with a truly Christian living, another terrible war will come from the east to the west. Russia with her armies will* *battle America, and will over run Europe. The Rhine River will be overflowing with corpses and blood, and Italy will be harassed by a great revolution. The Pope will suffer greatly. Speed devotion to my Immaculate Heart, in order that many souls may be conquered by my love, and that many sinners may return to my maternal heart. Do not fear because I will accompany with my maternal protection my faithful ones, and all those who accept my urgent warnings, especially by the recitation of the rosary. All those souls who do this will be saved.*"

On Good Friday 1961, the Blessed Mother said, "*People pay no attention to my motherly warnings… Russia spurred on by Satan, will seek to dominate the whole world, and by bloody revolutions, will propagate her false teachings throughout all the nations, especially in Italy. The church will be persecuted and the Pope and the priests shall suffer much. Oh, what a horrible vision I see! A great revolution is going on in Rome! They are entering the Vatican. The Pope is alone; he is praying. They are holding the Pope. They take him by force. They knock him down to the floor. They are tying him. Oh God! Oh God! They are kicking him. What a horrible scene! How dreadful!*

Our Blessed Mother is drawing near. Like corpses those evil men fall down to the floor. Our Lady helps the Pope to his feet, and taking him by the arm she covers him with her mantle. Flagstaffs ***(flying the Red flag over Saint Peter's Dome and elsewhere)*** *collapse, and power is gone out of the clubs of those evil brutes. These atheists are shouting, we don't want God to rule over us, we want Satan to be our master. My daughter, Rome will not be saved, because the Italian rulers have forsaken the Divine Light and because only a few people really love the Church. But the day is not far off when all the wicked shall perish, under the tremendous blows of Divine Justice.*"

Akita, Japan (Church Approved)

When Cardinal Ratzinger was head of the Congregation for the Doctrine of the Faith (CDF), he said the message of Akita is essentially the same as the message of Fatima and worthy of belief. In the entire history of the Roman Catholic Church, it is difficult to find a message publicly released from an approved apparition more severe than the messages of Akita. On October 13, 1973, The Blessed Mother said,

"The work of the devil will infiltrate even into the Church. One will see cardinals opposing cardinals, bishops confronting other bishops. The priests who venerate me will be scorned and condemned by their confreres; churches and altars will be sacked; the church will be full of those who accept compromises and the demon will tempt many priests and religious to leave the service of the Lord. I alone am able still to help save you from the calamities which approach. Those who place their total confidence in me will be given necessary help. If men do not repent and better themselves, the Heavenly Father will inflict a great punishment on all humanity. It will definitely be a punishment greater than the Deluge, such as has never been seen before. Fire will plunge from the sky and a large part of humanity will perish... The good as well as the bad will perish, sparing neither priests nor the faithful. The survivors will find themselves plunged into such terrible hardships that they will envy the dead. The only arms which remain for you will be the Rosary and the sign left by my Son (Eucharist).

Saint Margaret Mary Alacoque and the French Revolution

In 1689, King Louis XIV was asked to dedicate France publicly and solemnly with the Bishops of France to the Sacred Heart. Jesus instructed a nun by the name of Margaret Mary Alacoque (she later became Saint Margaret Mary) to ask the King to do this to assure peace, and to prevent disasters and war. King Louis was told if he did not do as Jesus asked, terrible conflicts and calamities would come to France. King Louis declined the request, and one hundred years later to the day in 1789 the French Revolution broke out, leading to the execution of King Louis XVI, the persecution of the Church, The Great Terror, and the deaths of many thousands of people.

Our Lady of America (Approved by the Church)

In 1963, Bishop Paul Leibold of Cincinnati, Ohio gave approval of the messages of Sister Mary Ephrem (Mildred Neuzil). Professed as a religious in 1933, she began to have inner locutions in 1938. Many of the supernatural experiences concerned her personal spiritual life and the indwelling of the Holy Trinity, and showed theological understanding beyond her study and experience. Starting in the early 1940's the messages began to focus on the sanctification of the family and a call to faith and purity for America. Then the Host of Heaven began appearing to her for the edification of families. Although there were many messages beyond the death of Bishop Leibold, only the messages up to 1963 are approved. Sister Ephrem died in the year 2000 in Fostoria, Ohio.

The Blessed Mother came as Our Lady of Lourdes and promised great miracles in America if we do as she asked. She then requested that the Basilica of the National Shrine of the Immaculate Conception in Washington, D.C. be made a place of special pilgrimage where the statue of Our Lady of America is to be solemnly carried in by the Bishops, and then placed in the Church and honored there as Our Lady of America—The Immaculate Virgin. On February 11 (Feast of Our Lady of Lourdes), 1958 the Blessed Mother said, "*I am the mother of sacred humanity and it is my special work as Co-Redemptrix of the human race to help souls reach the sanctity of the Father in eternal union by showing them how to put on Christ, to imbibe His Spirit, and thus become one with Him." Saint Joseph then told her that, "spiritual fatherhood extends to all God's children, and together with my Virgin Spouse, I watch over them with great love and solicitude. Fathers must come to me to learn obedience and authority... as fatherhood is from God, it must take once again its rightful place among men.*"

As of the date of this publication, the statue has not been carried in procession as asked. The promise given to Sister Ephrem by the Blessed Mother is that when the statue is processed as asked, America will be restored to purity, and Our Lady will save America. She said America is the key for world peace. Just as graces to the world have been denied because popes have not Consecrated Russia to the Immaculate Heart as asked at Fatima, Our Lady has not been processed into the Shrine of the Immaculate Conception in Washington, D.C. as she asked.

Blessed Anne Catherine Emmerich, Germany (1774-1824)

"*I had another vision of the great tribulation. It seems to me that a concession was demanded from the clergy which could not be granted. ...It was as if people were splitting into camps.* ***I also saw the relationship between the two popes...*** *I saw how baleful would be* *the consequences of this false church. I saw that the Church of Peter was undermined by a plan evolved by the secret sect. They built a large singular extravagant church which was to embrace all creeds with equal rights: Evangelicals, Catholics, and all denominations, a true communion of the unholy with one shepherd and one flock... I saw the fatal consequences of all this counterfeit church: I saw it increase, I saw heretics of all kinds... When the Church had been for the most part been destroyed, and when only the sanctuary and altar were still standing, I saw the wreckers enter the Church with the Beast.*" She had the stigmata or wounds of Our Lord on her body.

Fatima, Portugal, 1917 (Church Approved)

The heart of the message of Fatima is that man's sin has angered God, and heaven has given mankind a prescription to alter God's wrath. Fatima is the cornerstone of all apparitions in the modern era as it concerns the state of the world and the remedy for mankind. Fatima concerns the destiny of the world, and its importance to date is without equal. The Consecration of Russia by name was specifically asked for and has not been done. The Lord told Sister Lucy the Consecration would be done, "*But it will be late.*" God created man with free will, and that free will can influence man's destiny. Unless there is a reversal of man's sin, the Lord said there would be war and the annihilation of nations coming to mankind.

Pope Pius XII said, "*Fatima is the key Marian apparition of the Twentieth Century. Fatima is one of the greatest interventions of God through Mary in world history since the death of the Apostles. Only in the name of God does the Blessed Mother intervene. She does not say a word, does not take a step without the explicit will of God. The message of Fatima cannot be understood if you do not know atheistic communism, if you do not know what happened in Russia.*"

The Blessed Mother told a young Lucia in 1917 that, "*This war will end very soon. If people do not cease offending God, a worse war will break out during the pontificate of Pius XI. When you see a night illumined by an unknown light (January 25, 1938), know that this is the great sign given you by God, He is about to punish the world for its crimes, by means of war, famine, persecutions to the Church and the Holy Father.* ***To prevent this,*** *I shall come to ask for the Consecration* *of Russia to my Immaculate Heart, and the Communion of Reparation on the First Saturdays. If my requests are granted, Russia will be converted, and there will be peace. If not, she will spread her errors throughout the world, provoking wars and persecutions of the Church. The good will be martyred, the Holy Father will have much to suffer, various nations will be annihilated. ...But in the end, my Immaculate Heart will Triumph, the Holy Father will consecrate Russia to me, Russia will be converted, and a certain period of peace will be granted to the world.*" Our Lady asked that the message be kept secret until she gave permission to reveal it. In 1960 it was supposed to be read by the reigning pope, but to date it has never been completely revealed to the faithful.

When this prophecy was given, World War I did not end until a year later, and Pius XI was not elected until 1922. His pontificate lasted until 1939 and saw the beginning of World War II with Germany annexing Austria, and Japan invading China. Hitler had held a secret conference to divulge his war plans to his top leaders unknown to the world in advance of "*the night illumined by an unknown light.*" On January 25, 1938 an aurora illumined all of Europe that was visible for all to see—a year before World War II began. Newspapers worldwide reported on the visible aurora. Sister Lucy saw it and knew this was the sign war was near.

Another warning in the Second Secret was that the economic and political power of Communism would sweep the world if heaven's requests were not met. It would specifically be Russia promoting it. Here is where Our Lady asked for the Consecration of Russia to Her Immaculate Heart. Now that we have nearly one hundred years of observing Russia, we can see just how accurate her words were. People at that time may not have been able to understand due to the enormity of the prophecy, but now we can see the utter destruction caused by Russia because we have not done as Our Lady requested. Is it different today with heaven asking for our attention? All through modern Catholic prophecy, Russia has a pivotal role to play in future events, and Russia again is flexing her muscles as they have took over the Crimea in March of 2014. Crimea is rich in natural gas, oil, and has been the center of Russian Naval Operations for over 200 years. Before

Russia's reign is over, and converted by a True Consecration, Russia will continue to create instability in the world. The former Soviet Union or Russian Federation (USSR) stretches eleven time zones from Vladivostok in the east, to St. Petersburg in the west. Its influence in many areas is unparalleled. Its godlessness, strength of its army, and money from resources will always make it a force in global politics.

Immediately after Benedict XVI became Pope, he stated, "*Pray that I don't flee for fear of the wolves.*" On May 11, 2010 while on a plane trip to Portugal, Benedict was asked about the Third Secret. He said, "*The sufferings of the Church come precisely from within the Church, sins that exist in the Church.*" On May 13, 2010 speaking at Fatima, before 500,000 pilgrims, he said, "*Whoever thinks that the prophetic message of Fatima is over, is deceiving himself.*" Pope Benedict XVI is clearly contradicting what Cardinal Bertone said in the year 2000 that the Third Secret was fully revealed. Pope Benedict then said, "*May these seven years that divide us from the centennial of the apparitions bring forth soon the foreseen Triumph of the Immaculate Heart of Mary.*" Pope Benedict is specifically saying, "*sufferings come precisely from inside the Church.*"

Fatima's Special Role

When one looks at the strength of ecclesiastical freemasonry, the Vatican Bank financial misdeeds, and the widespread moral corruption of pedophilia and sex abuse, these all help illustrate that the Third Secret of Fatima is a living document and has not been fulfilled. If the consecration were done as originally asked by the Blessed Mother, the problems we presently see would not be as they are, and Russia would have assumed another role than it has over the last one hundred years. The consecration has not been done as asked, and there is still more "*future*" in the message of Fatima.

We have also been told gleaning from Fulda, Germany, Sister Lucy, and the narrative coming from the Third Secret over many decades from many sources, it has two dimensions of chastisements. One will be from nature, and the other will be from the hand of man. They both appear to be significant. Data points to events resulting from the sun in some way that will be catastrophic for mankind. If not a solar event explicitly, celestial phenomena of some sort seems to be on the horizon for mankind. Time as always will bring truth to the light of the day.

In Sister Lucy's Fourth Memoir (from the Third Secret) it was said, "*In Portugal, the dogma of the faith will always be preserved, etc.*" This suggests that in other places the dogma of the faith WILL NOT be preserved. We are presently witnessing whole countries losing their faith before our eyes. Truth is being swept aside and relativism and compromise is dominating the culture now on whole continents. Catholic dogma is by and large irrelevant in many countries. This loss of dogma is obviously a critical part of the message of Fatima. What Our Lady prophesied in 1917 has clearly come true due to the requests not being met.

Cardinal Pacelli, who went on to become Pius XII spoke prophetically when he said, "*I am worried by the Blessed Virgin's messages to Lucia of Fatima. The persistence of Mary about the dangers which menace the Church is a divine warning against the suicide of altering the faith, in Her liturgy, Her theology, and Her soul... A day will come when the civilized world will deny its God, when the Church will doubt as Peter doubted. She will tempted to believe that man has become God.*"

Many ask if the March 25, 1984 consecration by Pope John Paul II was done as asked? If it were done as asked, we would have seen different results in the Church and in the world than we have today. We have been told there will be no peace in the world until this is done. It is really that simple. Also, the question must be asked, who are the powerful forces preventing it? Why? What is their agenda to prevent peace? There were specific requests of how it was to be done, and Russia was to be named. Published in *Sol de Fatima* in 1985 the Blue Army of Spain, Sister Lucy was asked several questions:

Q. At what moment of the Fatima mystery do we find ourselves?
A. At the time when Russia is spreading her errors throughout the world.

Q. Are we to understand that Russia will take possession of the whole world?
A. Yes

Q. John Paul II had invited all the bishops to join in the consecration of Russia, which he was going to make at Fatima on May 13, 1982, and which he was to renew at the end of the Holy Year in Rome on March 25, 1984, before the original statue of Our Lady of Fatima. Has he not done therefore what was requested at Tuy?

A. There was no participation of all the bishops, and there was no mention of Russia.

Q. So the consecration was not done as requested by Our Lady?

A. No. Many bishops attached no importance to this act.

Pope John Paul II speaking at Fatima on May 13, 2000 said, "*the message of Fatima is a call to conversion, alerting humanity to have nothing to do with the* ***dragon whose tail swept down a third of the stars of heaven, and cast them to the earth.***" This is reference to the Book of Revelation where Father Stefano of the Marian Movement of Priests says this *third* are the priests or pastors who have been an active part of the apostasy, and do not carry out the truth of the gospel.

The consecration has not been done, and Russia is continuing to spread godless communism and her errors throughout the world. Sister Lucy has said it would be done, "*but late.*" As the King of France was asked in 1689 to consecrate France to the Sacred Heart of Jesus, he rejected the invitation and we know it was not done. In 1789, the French Revolution broke out and King Louis XVI was executed by guillotine altering the French landscape. So the question is how low do we need to go before the pope with the bishops comply with Our Lady's request to consecrate Russia? Will it need to get to the stage of France with blood in the streets?

Pope John Paul I and Sister Lucia

Cardinal Albino Luciani of Venice was on pilgrimage at Fatima in 1977 when he was asked to go meet Sister Lucia. The world had often tried to meet Sister Lucia, but it was she who asked for the meeting. Sister Lucia told him that he would become Pope, and his reign as Pontiff would be very brief. Cardinal Luciano became Pope John Paul I on August 26, 1978. Before Cardinal Karol Wojtyla left to go home to Poland after the Conclave, Pope John Paul 1 met with Cardinal

Wojtyla and gave Wojtyla the rosary his mother had given him when he became a priest. Saint John Paul II took his predecessors name. Heaven communicates with their servants.

The question continues to remain who will Consecrate Russia as the Blessed Mother has asked? No one knows for sure, but with the recent violent activity of Russia, we may not be too distant from the consecration because there are no other alternatives for peace with human solutions.

Saint Faustina, Divine Mercy, 1905-1938, (Church Approved)

The messages of Saint Faustina are the very DNA of the Triune God—Mercy and Trust. There is nothing in the Church that matches their grandeur. The promises are Abrahamic and majestic where the reader is brought to another level of knowing God's love. If we would only listen and partake of the graces which are available to us; if we chose to accept them, our lives and the world would change. They are messages for our sinful age. To get the full dimension of what the Lord is conveying to the young Sister Faustina Kowalska, read from her Diary called, *Divine Mercy in My Soul.* One is encouraged to read what the Lord is saying in the narrative because there is nothing else quite like it.

Some of the messages are of great HOPE and read as follows:

> *"I want this image, Jesus told Sister Faustina, ...to be solemnly blessed on the first Sunday after Easter; that Sunday is to be the Feast of Mercy. I desire that the Feast of Mercy be a refuge and shelter for all souls, and especially poor sinners. On that day, the very depths of My tender mercy are open.* ***I pour a whole ocean of graces upon those souls who approach the fount of My mercy. The soul that will go to Confession and receive Holy Communion shall obtain complete forgiveness of sins and punishment. On that day are open all the divine floodgates through which graces flow. Let no soul fear to draw near to Me, even though its sins be as scarlet. The Feast of My Mercy has issued forth from My very depths for the consolation of the whole world and is confirmed in the vast depths of My tender mercies."***

The scope of what is being said here is breathtaking. In the book of Genesis we see that the Lord made a Covenant with Abraham where the Lord made his descendants promises that would never be broken. This covenant has stood for millennia. The promises that Jesus makes to Faustina here is as close as we ever get to the equivalent of the Abrahamic Covenant. The concept of His Mercy is something no human can fully comprehend. There are no promises like this in the New Testament Church other than the messages of Divine Mercy.

"Before I come as the just Judge, I am coming first as the King Of Mercy. Before the day of justice arrives, there will be given to people a sign in the heavens of this sort: all light will be extinguished, and there will be great darkness over the whole earth. Then the sign of the cross will be seen in the sky, and from the opening where the hands and the feet of the Savior were nailed will come forth great lights which will light up the earth for a period of time. This will take place shortly before the last day" (83).

"*I am not only the Queen of Heaven, but also the Mother of Mercy and your Mother*" (141).

"*It is Jesus' desire that the moment of His death on the cross (3:00pm) be venerated every day; the hour which He said was the hour of grace for the whole world—mercy triumphed over justice. At this hour, we should meditate upon His sorrowful passion because it reveals most fully the love God has for His people. At this time, Jesus wants us to worship and glorify the Mercy of God, and, by the merits of His Passion, to implore the necessary graces for ourselves and the whole world, especially sinners.*"

"*In the evening, when I am praying, the Mother of God told me, Your lives must be like Mine: quiet and hidden, in unceasing union with God, pleading for humanity and preparing the world for the second coming of God*" (625).

"*O, Jesus. Make the fount of Your mercy, gush forth more abundantly, for human kind is seriously ill and thus has more need than ever for Your compassion. You are a bottomless sea of mercy for us sinners; and the greater the mercy: the more right we have to Your mercy. You are a fount which makes all Creatures happy by Your infinite mercy*" (793).

"*While I was saying the chaplet, I heard a voice which said, Oh, what great graces I will grant to souls who say this chaplet; the very depths of my tender mercy are stirred for the sake of those who say the chaplet.*

Write down these words My daughter. Speak to the world about My mercy; let all mankind recognize My unfathomable mercy. It is a sign of the end times; after it will come the day of justice. While there is still time, let them have recourse to the fount of My mercy; let them profit from the Blood and Water which gushed forth for them" (848).

"*Let the greatest sinners place their trust in My mercy... Souls that make an appeal to My mercy delight Me. To such souls I grant even more graces than they ask. I cannot punish even the greatest sinner if he makes an appeal to My compassion, but on the contrary, I justify him in My unfathomable and inscrutable mercy. Write, before I come as a just Judge I first open wide the door of My mercy. He who refuses to pass through the door of My mercy, must pass through the door of My Justice...*" (1146).

"*As I was praying for Poland, I heard the words: I bear a special love for Poland, and if she will be obedient to My will, I will exalt her in might and holiness. From her will come forth the spark that will prepare the world for My final coming*" (1723).

The spark "*that will prepare the world for My final coming*" are the messages of Saint Faustina and her Diary called *Divine Mercy In My Soul.*

Flame of Love of the Immaculate Heart of Mary, Hungary (Approved)

Jesus and Mary speak to Hungarian seer and stigmatist from 1961-1974, Elizabeth Kindelmann. Messages are about the great miracle of light blinding Satan, the power of the Holy Mass, Eucharistic Adoration, the most powerful ways to pray, the importance of family prayer, the power of the Flame of Love Devotion to release souls from purgatory, and the power of the precious blood. Jesus tells Elizabeth Kindelmann the devotion is a great remedy for the evils of our times.

Jesus says, "*Do not stop loving Me all day and night. As Our Dear Mother—She knows how to please Me. Ask for abundant graces. The more you will ask for, the more you will receive. Do not be afraid to ask! Do not restrain yourself in doing so. It makes Me all the happier when I can give more. Your wish alone makes Me happier already. Wish Me a bounty of souls! Renounce yourself! I ask for these things constantly because if you wish to take part in My work of salvation you must live united in Me always. Offer these same things to My Mother for those who have also dedicated their lives to Me. I wish so much to wash away all of your sins. Just come to Me.*

Give yourselves to Me completely. It is the only way in which you can offer sacrifice to Me. Be very humble and small. In this way you will be able to fulfill My wishes. Listen carefully! Do not be afraid; I ask you for great sacrifices. Every Thursday and Friday fast on bread and water and offer it for the souls of priests.

Seek refuge from the temptations behind the cloak of Our Mother. She'll protect you from all the evil which is troubling you continually... Do not worry that you can give Me only little things... Remain little yourself.

To hear My voice you must be very silent because My soft, low voice can be heard only by those who are absorbed in My love. My daughter love is a fire which can only be kept glowing through endless sacrifices..."

Jesus gives a special blessing to parents and mothers, "*All of you mothers who bring pleasure to My heart, the merit of your work is no less than the deeds of the priest in the highest office. You parents, you mothers understand the sublime vocation I have entrusted to you. You are destined to populate My kingdom.*"

The Blessed Mother says the grace of the Flame of Love must go from heart to heart. "*It will be the miracle which will blind Satan. It is the Flame of Love and Unity and we shall extinguish fire with fire: the fire of hate with the fire of love.*"

Fulda, Germany, 1980,
Pope John Paul II Speaks On the Message of Fatima

Fulda is where Akita, Japan and Fatima merge for a lucid and coherent understanding of our times. It was a meeting with the newly elected Pope John Paul II, and Cardinal Ratzinger together in attendance on a visit to Fulda Germany in November 1980 speaking about the Third Secret of Fatima. There was a small gathering of people in extemporaneous conversation. The German magazine *Stimme des Glaubens* published the following account that was unpublished by the Vatican. John Paul II was asked, "*Holy Father, what has become of the Third Secret of Fatima? According to Our Lady's instructions, wasn't it supposed to be revealed in 1960? And what will happen in the Church?*"

The Holy Father responded, "*Because of the seriousness of its contents, in order not to encourage the world wide power of communism, to carry out certain coups, my predecessors in the chair of Peter have diplomatically preferred to withhold its publication. On the other hand it should be sufficient for all Christians to know this much: if there is a message in which it is said that the oceans will flood entire sections of the earth; that, from one moment to the other, millions of people will perish... there is no longer any point in really wanting to publish this secret message. Many want to know out of curiosity or because of their taste for sensationalism, but they forgot that 'to know' implies for them a responsibility. It is dangerous to want to satisfy one's curiosity only, if one is convinced that we can do nothing against a catastrophe that has been predicted. The Church must now be cleansed by the blood of martyrs, that is how it was historically, and it won't be any different this time around. Don't ask anything more, the key to understanding is to recite the rosary.*

We must be prepared to undergo great trials in the not too distant future, trials that will require us to be ready to give up even our lives and a total gift of self to Christ and for Christ. Through your prayer and mine, it is possible to alleviate this tribulation but it is no longer possible to avert it, because it is only in this way that the Church can be effectively renewed. How many times, indeed, has the renewal of the Church been effected in blood? This time again, it will not be otherwise. We must be strong, we must prepare ourselves, we must entrust ourselves to Christ and His Holy Mother, and we must be attentive to the prayer of the Rosary." Cardinal Ratzinger as head of the Congregation for the Doctrine of the Faith (CDF) said about the Third Secret of Fatima, "*The reason the popes since the 1940's have not disclosed the secret is that it could not be fully understood until the close of the 20th Century. There was no sense in offering humanity an indecipherable image which would have created only speculation.*"

Father Stefano Gobbi's (Marian Movement of Priests) message #313 titled, *The Hour of the Public Witness* delivered from Fulda, Germany said, "*Everything that my Pope has said in this place corresponds with the truth.*" The Blessed Mother is validating that Fulda was a real conversation that took place. Message number 313 should be read in its entirety for the full content.

At Fatima the Blessed Mother promised the "*Triumph of the Immaculate Heart.*"

A bold statement indeed that has prompted many a conversation with differing and very diverse views on exactly what that means. No apparition in history has caused as much controversy among the faithful as elements of the Third Secret. Addressed are the Consecration of Russia, a Pope being killed, apostasy of faith, and other important topics.

If one looks at the collective body of messages the Blessed Mother has been giving over the last fifty years, there is no doubt to those educated on the subject, that the Third Secret has not been revealed in total. In the messages to Father Stefano Gobbi, the Blessed Mother has released all anyone would need to know concerning its content.

The very last public message given to the Marian Movements of Priests on December 31, 1997 (# 604), after twenty-five years of messages disseminated around the entire globe, was titled, *All Has Been Revealed To You.* In that message Our Lady says,

> *"This century of yours, which is about to end, has been placed under the sign of a strong power conceded to my Adversary. Thus, humanity has been led astray by the error of theoretical and practical atheism; in the place of God; idols have been built which everyone adores: pleasure, money, amusement, power, pride, and impurity. Truly Satan, with the cup of lust, has succeeded in seducing all the nations of the earth. ...So then, the Most Holy Trinity has decreed that your century be placed under the sign of my powerful, maternal and extraordinary presence. ...As a safe refuge, I offered you my Immaculate Heart. ...All has been revealed to you: my plan has been pointed out to you even in its painful realization. Humanity has fallen under the domination of Satan and of his great power, exercised with the satanic and masonic forces; my Church has become obscured by his smoke which has penetrated into it. Errors are being taught and propagated,*

causing many to lose true faith in Christ and in His gospel; the Holy Law of God is openly violated; sin is committed and even justified, and thus the light of grace and the divine presence is lost; unity is deeply split apart... All has been revealed to you ; my plan has been foretold to you especially in its wonderful and victorious fulfillment. I have announced to you the triumph of my Immaculate Heart in the world. In the end, my Immaculate Heart will triumph. This will come about in the greatest triumph of Jesus, who will bring into the world His glorious reign of love, of justice and of peace, and will make all things new."

This was the last message given to the world by the Marian Movement of Priests, with nearly 1,000 pages of informative and prophetic messages given since 1973. As the Blessed Mother said, "the full and entire truth" was provided to those choosing to listen. There is no guesswork where the world is headed for those walking in the light of Divine Truth. Knowledge of the issues of heaven's agenda is a prescription for attaining peace of mind, body, and soul in troubled times.

Father Stefano Gobbi, Marian Movement Of Priests (1973-1997)

The Marian Movement of Priests has pontifical approbation from Saint John Paul II, who was a close personal friend of Father Gobbi. Saint John Paul II and Father Gobbi concelebrated Mass every December 24th together for many years. Below are brief excerpts from some passages germane to our subject matter. The full title of Father Gobbi's book of messages is *To the Priests, Our Lady's Beloved Sons, The Marian Movement of Priests*. A very tiny targeted portion of the messages is below, and it is greatly encouraged you get the book as there is nothing quite like it for depth and breadth of coverage in diverse subjects. The messages are intended for use primarily by clergy and the faithful, as members of her Marian Movement of Priests in the context of Marian Cenacles of prayer. It conveys comprehensively heaven's understanding, admonitions, wisdom, and guidance for our times along with the ineffable beauty and heaven's plan for a renewed 'church of light' and for a humanity living in the Divine Will in the New Era.

"*At the same moment, in fact, in which humanity is experiencing the greatest rejection of God in all history, you are being immolated on the secret altar of my Immaculate heart, to sing today the glory of the Father, the mercy of the Son and the love of the Holy Spirit: The glory of the new people of Israel, called to prepare humanity for the return of Jesus; The glory of the renewed Church, which will experience the new Pentecost of fire, of grace and of light; The glory of a new humanity purified in the great tribulation, now ready to live the ineffable moment of its complete return to the Lord.*" #220

Speaking to America from Malvern, Pennsylvania, in 1990: "*The great trial has arrived for your church. Those errors which have brought people to the loss of the true faith have continued to spread. Many pastors have been neither attentive nor vigilant and have allowed many rapacious wolves, clothed as lambs, to insinuate themselves into the flock in order to bring disorder and destruction...You continue along the path of division from the Pope and of the rejection of his Magisterium; indeed, in a hidden way, there is in preparation a true schism which could soon become open and proclaimed. And then, there will remain only a small faithful remnant, over which I will keep watch in the garden of my Immaculate Heart...*" #437

"*The great trial has come for the Church, so violated by evil spirits, so divided in its unity, so darkened in its holiness. See how error has flooded throughout it, error which leads to the loss of the true faith. Apostasy is spreading everywhere... The hour of its great trial has above all come for the Church, because it will be shaken by the lack of faith, obscured by apostasy, wounded by betrayal, abandoned by its children, divided by schisms, possessed and dominated by Freemasonry, turned into fertile soil from which will spring up the wicked tree of the man of iniquity, the Antichrist, who will bring his kingdom into its interior...*" #486

"*In the Temple of my Immaculate Heart, I am forming you for the greater splendor of the Church, the New Israel of God. In the time of the great trial for the Church, you become the help which it earnestly awaits, the help which my Immaculate Heart gives it, for these bloody moments of the great tribulation.*" #487

"Satan has succeeded in entering into the Church, the new Israel of God. He has entered there with the smoke of error and sin, of the loss of faith and apostasy, of compromise with the world and the search for pleasure. During these years, he has succeeded in leading astray bishops and priests, religious and faithful. The forces of Masonry have entered into the Church, in a subtle and hidden way, and have set up their stronghold in the very place where the Vicar of my Son Jesus lives and works..." #495

From Fatima, "***My secret concerns the Church.*** *In the Church, the great apostasy, which will spread throughout the whole world, will be brought to its completion; the schism will take place through a general alienation from the Gospel and from the true faith. There will enter into the Church the man of iniquity, who opposes himself to Christ, and who will bring into her interior the abomination of desolation, thus bringing to fulfillment the horrible sacrilege, of which the prophet Daniel has spoken (Matt. 24:15). My secret concerns humanity. Humanity will reach the summit of corruption and impiety, of rebellion against God and of open opposition to His Law of love. It will know the hour of its greatest chastisement, which has already been foretold to you by the prophet Zechariah (Zec. 13: 7-9). Then this place will appear to all as a bright sign of my motherly presence in the supreme hour of your great tribulation. From here my light will spread to every part of the world, and from this fount will gush the water of divine mercy, which will descend to irrigate the barrenness of a world, now reduced to an immense desert..."* #539

Kibeho, Rwanda (Approved)

On November 28, 1981 apparitions began in the country of Rwanda to seven young visionaries. Three of the visionaries messages have been approved, and Rwanda is an approved apparition by the Catholic Church. Never have wc seen happen such a horrific genocide as prophesied by the Blessed Mother when she said, "*Rwanda would become a river of blood.*" Then the world watched in horror from their living rooms on national news as the war broke out. Over 800,000 people were soon dead, with most hacked to death with machetes. An estimated two million were on the march as refugees. More than ten years before the war began, Anathalie (a young visionary), was shown in a vision on four separate occasions of July 1982, August 15, 1982 (Feast of the Assumption), September 4, 1982, and January 1983, what would happen if war broke out. With 20,000 people present during these apparition, Anathalie told people her vision was of "*blood running, people killing each other, fire burning on the hill, mass graves, skulls, beheaded bodies, skulls pulled apart.*" Extraordinary mystical phenomena took place over a several year period, with the emphasis of the messages on amendment of life, humility, reciting the Chaplet of Divine Mercy, reconciliation, repentance, conversion, and being obedient to the most basic tenets of the faith.

The Blessed Mother said to a young visionary by the name of Alphonsine, "*My Son will return to earth soon and our souls must be prepared for His arrival. The world is in a bad way, with a lot of hatred and sin, so she wants us to say the Rosary everyday to cleanse our hearts and show our love for her, for Jesus, and for God. She says that praying the Rosary is the best way to show her our love.*" The name given to the Marian sanctuary at Kibeho is "*The Shrine of Our Lady of Sorrows.*" Our Lady told Marie Claire (young visionary) that she chose Rwanda because "*she wanted to show the world that God sees and hears all of His children—rich or poor, white or black, man or woman.*" It was chosen because "*the people here were humble and had a great faith and respect for God.*" In Kibeho itself, 25,000 people were killed during the genocide including Marie Claire herself.

LaSalette, France, 1846, Leece Version, the Blessed Mother told Melanie on September 19, 1846, "*Rome will loose the faith and become the seat of Antichrist. The Church will be in eclipse. Pagan Rome will disappear.*"

Mother Elena Patricia Leonardi. Born in 1910, she was told by Saint Pio (Padre) on February 4, 1947 that the Blessed Mother would give her a great mission. She was given a message of "*flames and fire falling from heaven and ocean waters turning into vapor and a great war breaking out sowing death and hunger, disease of all kinds.*" She was told about the time of the great trial for the Church when cardinals will oppose cardinals, bishops being against bishops. In 1979, another message spoke of "*communism will triumph, freemasonry in the* *churches, and that cardinals and bishops will confront the Pope accusing and mistreating him.*"

Medjugorje, Bosnia, 1981-Present. The Blessed Mother came as the Queen of Peace and said, "*I have a plan for the salvation of the world, and I come to tell you God exists.*" To date, an estimated 35 million pilgrims have journeyed there. Cardinal Schonborn of Austria has said his "*seminaries would be empty without it.*" The fruit coming from this site is incalculable. There are continued deep mystical phenomena coming from Medjugorje. In a very famous lengthy letter written by Father Tomas Vlasic to Saint John Paul II on December 2, 1983, portions of the letter read,

> "*...Mirjana said that before the visible sign is given to humanity, there will be three warnings to the world. The warnings will be in the form of events on earth. Mirjana will be a witness to them. Three days before one of the admonitions, Mirjana will notify a priest of her choice. The witness of Mirjana will be a confirmation of the apparitions and a stimulus for the conversion of the world. After the admonitions, the visible sign will appear on the site of the apparitions in Medjugorje for all the world to see. The sign will be given as a testimony to the apparitions and in order to call the people back to the faith.*
>
> *The ninth and tenth secrets are serious. They concern chastisement for the sins of the world. Punishment is inevitable, for we cannot expect the whole world to be converted. The punishment can be diminished by prayer and penance, but it cannot be eliminated. Mirjana says that one of the evils that threatened the world, the one contained in the seventh secret, has been averted, thanks to prayer and fasting. That is why the Blessed Virgin continues to encourage prayer and fasting. You have forgotten that through prayer and fasting you can avert war and suspend the laws of nature. After the final admonition, the others will follow in a rather short time. Thus, people will have some time for conversion.*
>
> *That interval will be a period of grace and conversion. After the visible sign appears, those who are still alive will*

> *have little time for conversion. For that reason, the Blessed Virgin invites us to urgent conversion and reconciliation. The invitation to prayer and penance is meant to avert evil and war, but most of all to save souls. According to Mirjana, the events predicted by the Blessed Virgin are near...*
>
> *...Excuse me for this, but you must realize that Satan exists. One day he appeared before the throne of God and asked permission to submit the Church to a period of trial. God gave him permission to try the Church for one century. This century is under the power of the devil; but when the secrets confided to you come to pass, his power will be destroyed. Even now he is beginning to lose his power and has become aggressive. He is destroying marriages, creating division among priests and is responsible for obsessions and murder. You must protect yourselves against these things through fasting and prayer, especially community prayer. Carry blessed objects with you. Put them in your house, and restore the use of holy water.*
>
> *According to certain Catholic experts who have studied these apparitions, this message of Mirjana may shed light on the vision Pope Leo XIII had. According to them, it was after having an apocalyptic vision of the future of the Church that Pope Leo XIII introduced the prayer to Saint Michael which priests used to recite after Mass up to the time of the Second Vatican Council. These experts say that the century of trials foreseen by Leo XIII is about to end..."*
>
> *Father Vlasic said after hearing this message, "The seers say that with the realization of the secrets entrusted to them by Our Lady, life in the world will change. What will change and how it will change, we don't know, given that the seers don't want to say anything about the secrets. Father Tomislav continued, "Life in the world will change. Afterwards men will believe like in ancient times."*

The above vision of People Leo XIII is the conversation in which he heard God grant the devil one hundred years to test the Church, much in the same way the Lord granted Satan the ability to test Job. Medjugorje is about a loving mother admonishing and protecting her children, as she asks people to adhere to the basic and most fundamental aspects of the faith. She stresses year in and year out the key to inner peace of soul is prayer, Mass, fasting, confession, bible reading, conversion and faith. There are literally thousands of messages conveyed to individuals and the peoples of the world through public and private venues resulting from the fruit of Medjugorje. Saint John Paul II and Pope Benedict XVI (Emeritus) were greatly devoted to Medjugorje and protected it from detractors inside and outside the Church.

The messages of Medjugorje are remarkably similar to those from the rest of the valid apparitions sites in the world—Obedience to the gospel message and live what it says.

Sister Natalia, Of Hungary (Church Approved)

The apparition is called *Victorious Queen of the World* and most of the messages were delivered from 1939-1943. Jesus told Sister Natalia (1901-1992) that, "*The Church would only be cleansed and renewed by great sufferings. It will be humble, simple, and will be poor as it was in the beginning. They will live by the Spirit as in the Sermon on the Mount. When the glorious peace arrives, there will be only one fold, and one shepherd.*

There is a coming age of paradise, when humanity will live as without sin. This will be a new world and new age. This will be the age when mankind will get back what it lost in paradise. When My Immaculate Mother will step on the neck of the serpent, the gates of hell will be closed. The host of angels will be part of this fight. ***I have sealed with My seal My own that they shall not be lost in the fight*****.**

I brought peace when I was born, but the world has not yet enjoyed it. The world is entitled to that peace. Men are the children of God. God breathes His own souls into them. God cannot let Himself be put to shame, and that is why the children of God are entitled to enjoy the peace that I promised."

It should be noted that heaven on occasions marks its own people to separate them for what God is doing. They become God's property with a marked seal. Seals are not unique in Scripture. One notable time when the Lord's people were "sealed" is in Ezekiel. The abominations going on were no longer tolerated by the Lord, so He said to Ezekiel,

"*And the Lord said to him, go through the city, through Jerusalem, and put a mark upon the foreheads of the men who sign and groan over all the abominations that are committed in it. And to the others He said in my hearing pass through the city after him, and smite; your eye shall not spare, and you shall show no pity, slay old men outright, young men and maidens, little children and women, but touch no one upon whom is the mark. And begin at My sanctuary*" (Ezk. 9:4-5). Again we see the Lord punishes idolaters and grave unrepentant sin, yet He marks His own for safety. Also, the punishment begins first in His Sanctuary, meaning the House of God—The Church. He begins first in the Church because they know the difference from right and wrong, yet commit grave sin.

Our Lady Of All Nations, Amsterdam, 1945-1959, (Church Approved)

The Blessed Mother appeared to a woman by the name of Ida Peerdeman of Amsterdam, and spoke of a Dogma heaven desires to be proclaimed—The Dogma of Co-Redemptrix, Mediatrix and Advocate. The Blessed Mother foretells that there will be much struggle and controversy over this Dogma, but when this Dogma is proclaimed, a new Era of Peace will begin for humanity. In many messages the Blessed Mother warns the Church of Rome of the seriousness and impending dangers it faces. From May 31st, 1954 onward she appears every May 31st—the old Feast of the Queenship of the World. She points to the Great Miracle of everyday—the Eucharist. On May 31st, 1959, the series of apparitions ends in a magnificent vision, in which the Lady appears in heavenly glory and out of a Host of white fire the figure of the Lord emerges, in all His splendor and majesty.

The Lady draws special attention to the way she appears and asks that an image be made of it. She stands on the globe because she comes for the whole world. As the Lady, she stands in sacrifice before the Cross, clothed with the sun that is Christ; her body translucent as of the Spirit. Out of her hands are coming three rays, the rays of Grace, Redemption, and Peace, that she may bestow upon the nations. She promises to give grace for soul and body—according to the Son's will to all who pray before the image and call upon Mary, The Lady of All Nations. She says her purpose is to, "*urge the Church, the theologians, to wage this battle. For the Father, the Son, and the Holy Spirit, wills to send the Lady, chosen to bear the Redeemer into this world, a Co-Redemptrix, and Advocate. I have said, This Time is Our Time. By this I mean the following: The world is caught up in degeneration and superficiality. It is at a loss. Therefore, the Father sends me to be the Advocate to implore the Holy Spirit to come. For the world is not saved by force, the world will be saved by the Spirit. It is only ideas that rule the world. Know your responsibility then, Church of Rome. Get your ideas across; bring Christ back into the world once more...*

In the sufferings both spiritual and body, the Lady, the Mother has shared. She has always gone on before. As soon as the Father had elected her, she was the Co-Redemptrix with the Redeemer, who came into the world as the Man-God... I know well the struggle will be hard and bitter, but the outcome is already assured... The world is degenerating, so much so, that it was necessary for the Father, and the Son to send me into the world among all the peoples, in order to be their Advocate and save them. ...And then I see the Lady leave and again I hear her say, "This Time is Our Time."

33rd apparition, May 31, 1951. "*...it is the wish of the Father and the Son to send me into the world these times as Co-Redemptrix, Mediatrix, and Advocate." This will constitute a new and last Marian Dogma. This picture will go before it. This dogma will be much disputed; and yet it will prevail!*"

42nd apparition, June 15, 1952. "*The Lady, who once was Mary. Only at the departure of the Lord Jesus Christ did Co-Redemption have its beginning. Only when the Lord Jesus Christ went away, did she become the Mediatrix and Advocate.*"

43rd apparition, October 5, 1952. "*Never has Miriam or Mary in the Community, the Church been officially called Co-Redemptrix. Never has she officially been called Mediatrix. Never has she officially been called Advocate. These three thoughts are not only closely connected, they form one whole. Therefore this will be the keystone of Marian history; it will become the Dogma of Co-Redemptrix, Mediatrix, and Advocate. ...Mary became the Handmaid of the Lord, chosen by the Father and the Holy Spirit. From the beginning she was, in virtue of this choice, the Co-Redemptirx, Mediatrix, and Advocate. When leaving in one final act, the Lord Jesus Christ gave Mary to the nations, gave her as the Lady of All Nations. He spoke the words, Woman behold thy Son; son behold thy Mother. One act! And by this, Mary received this new title. How is it that this new title, The Lady of All Nations, only now enters the world? It is because the Lord reserved it for this time. The other dogmas had to come first: just as her life on earth had to precede the Lady of all Nations. All previous dogmas comprised the mortal life and the leaving of this life by the Lady…*"

47th apparition, October 11, 1953. "*The Lady of All Nations has the power to bring world peace. Yet she has to be asked for it under this title. The Lady of All Nations will assist the Church of Rome…*"

49th apparition, April 4, 1954. "*…I am not bringing a new doctrine, I am now bringing old ideas… Because the Lady is Co-Redemptrix, she is also Mediatrix, and Advocate, not only because she is the Mother of Our Lord Jesus Christ, but—and mark this well—because she is the Immaculate Conception… Do fight and ask for this dogma: it is the crowning of Your Lady…*"

50th apparition, May 31, 1954. "*…When the dogma, the last dogma in Marian history, has been proclaimed, the Lady of all Nations will give peace, true peace to the world.*"

51st apparition, May 31, 1955. "*...Satan is not banished yet. The Lady of All Nations is now permitted to come in order to banish Satan. She comes to announce the Holy Spirit. The Holy Spirit will only now descend over this earth…" Know well that the Holy Spirit is now nearer than ever. The Holy Spirit will come now only, if you pray for His coming. He has always been ready; now, however, the time has come… Once the Dogma has been pronounced, the Lady of All Nations will give her blessing…*"

The Blessed Mother at Amsterdam gave messages that specifically provide the answer for world peace—The Proclamation of the Fifth Marian Dogma. Once the Dogma is proclaimed, graces will shower the earth. We are asked to pray the prayer she gave to the world, which is below:

LORD JESUS CHRIST, SON OF THE FATHER, SEND NOW YOUR SPIRIT OVER THE EARTH. LET THE HOLY SPIRIT LIVE IN THE HEARTS OF ALL NATIONS, THAT THEY MAY BE

PRESERVED FROM DEGENERATION, DISASTER, AND WAR. MAY THE LADY OF ALL NATIONS, WHO ONCE WAS MARY, BE OUR ADVOCATE, AMEN.

Blessed Anna Maria Taigi, 1769-1837, Italy

Anna Marie experienced deep mystical phenomena and had Cardinals and bishops at her doorstep. She had a profound gift of prophecy and reading souls. Today her body is incorrupt at a church in Rome.

> *"There shall come over the whole earth an intense darkness lasting three days and three nights. Nothing can be seen, and the air will be laden with pestilence which will claim mainly, but not only, the enemies of religion. It will be impossible to use any man-made lighting during this darkness, except blessed candles. He, who out of curiosity, opens his windows to look out, or leaves his home, will fall dead on the spot. During these three days, people should remain in their homes, pray the Rosary and beg God for mercy. All the enemies of the Church, whether known or unknown, will perish over the whole earth during that universal darkness, with the exception of a few whom God will soon convert.*
>
> *The air shall be infected by demons who will appear under all sorts of hideous forms. Religion shall be persecuted, and priests massacred. Churches shall be closed, but only for a short time. The Holy Father shall be obliged to leave Rome..." After the three days of darkness, Saint Peter and Saint Paul, having come down from Heaven, will preach in the whole world and designate a new Pope... Christianity will then spread throughout the whole world... Whole nations will come back to the Church and the face of the earth will be renewed. Russia, England, and China will come back to the Church."*

It should be noted that the above message is very severe and is consistent with other Church-approved warnings, and many non-approved mystics have spoken on the Three Days of Darkness. The only message in the Church to come close to a dire warning like this is Akita, Japan. There are stages of the chastisement, and there is little doubt the above event is the very zenith of the Great Chastisement.

There is a lot of ground to cover and events to happen before we get to this stage. The closest we get to this event in Scripture is when the angel of death *Passed Over* the Jewish people living in Egypt during the ten plagues of Moses. Days of darkness over Egypt (Exodus 10:21) was the ninth plague, and the tenth was death to Pharaoh's own son. The plagues built in intensity and severity—much like we are witnessing today. Faithful Hebrews were told exactly what to do by the Lord for safety by painting blood over their doorposts. All who did as Moses instructed lived, and in the Exodus they then left for the Promised Land. In our age our safety and refuge lies in being under the mantle of the Blessed Mother.

Ukraine

In 1987, over 500,000 people saw the Blessed Mother in Hrushiv, as she appeared to Marina Kizyn in a field. The Blessed Mother told her, "*Times are coming which have been foretold as those being of the end times... I shall protect you for the glory and the future of God's kingdom on earth, which will last for a thousand years. The Kingdom of heaven and earth is close at hand. I will come only through penance and the repentance of sin. Ukrainians must become apostles of Christ among the Russian peoples, for if there is not a return to Christianity in Russia, there will be a Third World War. ...Until the West acknowledges its own guilt before the East, Russia will not be able to receive Christ the King.*"

The Catholic Church remains the last remaining obstacle to the complete takeover of the peoples of the world by the one world government movement, and there is a battle to dismantle its moral authority. Satan's last effort is to destroy the Priesthood and the Eucharist—the pillars of Catholicism. Archbishop Fulton J. Sheen gives the reason when he writes,

> *"The acceptance of the fullness of truth will have the unfortunate quality of making you hated by the world... If the grace of God did not give me the fullness of truth, and I were looking for it, I would begin my search by looking through the world for a Church that did not get along with the evil in the world. If that church were accused of countless lies, hated because it refused to compromise, ridiculed because it*

refused to fit the times and not all time, I would suspect that since it was hated by what is evil in the world, it was therefore good and holy; and if it is good and holy, it must be Divine."

No temptation has overtaken you that is not common to man. God is faithful, and he will not let you be tempted beyond your strength, but with the temptation will also provide the way of escape, that you may be able to endure it.

—I Cor. 10:13

JESUS, I TRUST IN YOU

fourteen

Why Some People Grow Spiritually

Enter His gates with thanksgiving, and His courts with praise, give thanks to Him and bless His name.

—Psalm 100:4

Have you ever wondered why some people produce fruit and others don't? Why some people have a positive moral impact on those around them while others do not? Why some people change and thus grow? Why is there joy in some lives but not others? Politics does not change people, but holiness does. Leading someone to a personal life in Jesus Christ makes a real difference, and is truly what matters most in life.

The saints and prophets of old transformed nations because they were holy and bore the image of God. They lived in God's will and exhibited the fruits of the Holy Spirit of love, joy, peace, kindness, and other attributes of God. Holiness is as attractive to people as bees to honey.

Jesus transcends politics. It was through His life that He changed the world, not His social activism, and not His political views. When one follows Jesus, they get the political and social issues correctly. His teachings are not ambiguous on the moral issues, and when following God, you vote and act correctly according to the tenets and precepts of the Gospel message. There are certain things that are political and have no bearing on the gospel as it relates to voting. Do you vote to deny or accept a city bond at the local election as it concerns the construction of a park? This is a morally neutral issue and a matter of personal preference of a city incurring debt for a future obligation providing a public good for children and the enjoyment of all. However, as it concerns the great moral issues of our day like euthanasia, homosexuality, abortion, these are grave sins. There is no moral uncertainty on these issues if you look at what Jesus did address as He taught and lived.

Changed Lives

The principal ministry of Jesus was about changing people—changing their hearts no matter the ethnicity, the background, the culture, or social status. He dealt with the centurion/Roman soldier, who sought Him out for the healing of his son; with Mary Magdalene, who had a refined upbringing but spurned common sense in youth. Peter was a leader of men and a fisherman with a big impulsive giving heart; and James and John of the Zebedee Fishing Company He called the "*Sons of Thunder*" (Mark 3:17). Andrew was a quiet unassuming man and Peter's brother, Matthew was a tax collector, as was a small stout man by the name of Zacchaeus who rigged the books, and wealthy Lazarus was such a dear friend that Jesus wept over him when He heard that he had died. The leper He took pity on; the man by the pool of Bethesda He cured; from the possessed He drove out demons; the woman with the issue of blood; and the woman at the well He gave a new life. With everyone He came into contact—He gave the option of life or death by making a choice on who to follow—Him or the way of the world. One choice was life, the other death. One was light, the other darkness; one way was joy, or a life of sin with fruit of misery.

Jesus was neither left nor right, but was about doing His Father's business. He had no other agenda but to do the Father's will and convert and heal people. There was nothing else that mattered to Him, and of all the names listed above, and all the other names you wish to address in the New Testament, Jesus taught about amending lives. By virtue of the radical message of the avoidance of sin, it is falsely interpreted Jesus was a social activist and philosopher. Blessed Mother Teresa often said she was not a social worker, but it was due to her spiritual commitment she worked with the poorest of the poor. Very often she said if it were not for Eucharistic Adoration and a prayer life, she could not do what she did. Her social activism was born from the time on her knees asking God for His direction. Her love for Jesus transformed those around her. Through Mother Teresa's holiness, people changed and wanted to be better when they saw her holiness. Young women flocked to the Missionaries of Charity at a young age not because their life at that point was well developed theologically or spiritually, but because they saw in Mother Teresa what they wanted for their own life. Holiness is what changes people.

Nothing else has more lasting impact in life than a conversion. If politics were the answer after thousands of years, all of our problems would be solved by now. If you change the soul of a liberal, you will find a changed life. If you change the soul of a conservative, you will likewise find a changed life. If you change the soul of someone who is lost, they will find a new life in Christ. The conversations are endless on social issues, but when the soul is transformed through the light of Jesus, rooms in the mansion of our heart get cleaned out one at a time until the mansion is tidy and better organized.

When the Lord enters a person's life, multiple areas fall into place. That is why Jesus was not a social activist, but had a sole agenda to transform hearts and souls. Yet, the irony is, Jesus was the greatest social reformer the world has ever known. By forming His apostles, they in turn could go into the world to train others, after they received the Holy Spirit. His method was to pour His life into twelve people for three years, preparing them to receive the Holy Spirit. There was clearly a method of discipleship and growth.

Since He is God, and used this approach, there is a lesson in this for all who wish to be called disciples. There are many aspects to the model Jesus used that we should follow for our personal growth. Not speaking to the crowds all the time, but teaching twelve very different men to love one another, pray, do good works, and let things fall by the wayside that didn't matter. The apostles were a disparate group of men who after the death and Resurrection of Jesus, were inspired by the Holy Spirit, and then transformed the world. Observing holiness is what transforms others; then the Holy Spirit can act. Jesus said, "*Seek first God's Kingdom and righteousness, then all these things shall be yours as well*" (Matt. 6:33). Once you have the Holy Spirit, you have everything, and you become like the good soil that brought the harvest of *thirty, sixty, or a hundred fold* (Matt. 13:9).

The Soil For a Soul

In the parable of the sower (Matt. 13:3-9), Jesus gives us His answer for the capture of souls and why some people produce fruit. There are four places where the seed fell—along the path, on rocky ground, amongst thorns, and on good soil. This topic is as rich as anything in Scripture. Some people are just into the intellectual side of the gospel, some see Jesus as a revolutionary as many did with liberation theology and social justice, some are too preoccupied with the cares of the world and the message gets choked off before it can sprout, and the list goes on. The example that Jesus uses covers all the bases, and the only person to produce fruit was the seed that fell in good soil. The condition of the heart is what matters most is the fertile soil. It will endure the test of time, and weather the conditions that come our way. Many come to Jesus unprepared and don't follow the prescriptions necessary to grow. Is the soil cultivated, the right amount of water and sun, the right amount of shade, the right amount of nutrients in the soil? All of these ingredients matter for growth. Is the person growing spiritually doing the correct things? Study Scripture to know the mind of God, pray to know the heart of God, gather in fellowship to follow God, and receive the Sacraments to have the strength to go towards God.

Some people fall away from their faith at some point in their life because a decision often is made in emotion before there is stability of the intellect and a foundation to sustain it. There is not proper time to count the cost of the decision being made, nor a foundation to integrate it. Then, there is often a lack of formation through study of the Scriptures to gain perspective in discerning that God's ways are not our ways. The seed never gets a chance to take root. There is the necessity to know the Scriptures and be able to handle their truths in a workman like fashion where the instruction is "*Study to show thyself approved*" (2 Timothy 2:15). The Word needs to become a part of our being.

Is a person really emotionally ready to accept what Jesus is asking? Are there too many distractions to take the time to grow in the Lord? Is a person spiritually lazy? Are they doing it for a loved one when their heart is not really into a commitment? The reasons are numerous, but Jesus talks about the spiritual ripeness of a soul ready to serve Him. For some there is real enthusiasm at first, but as time moves on, the love grows lukewarm or cold. For some it has been like a child receiving a new toy. The seed that fell on rich soil is the soul that has the best chance to change the world. The desired end result of a journey for any soul is holiness.

The reasons for people growing or not growing are too numerous to name. Some start out strong in their faith, but at the first moment of hardship and trial they wilt under the pressure of an adverse situation. Why do some people go to the lions singing Psalms of joy and thanksgiving when others curse God at the slightest difficulty that comes their way? Why do some people fail in a marriage when it started out with strong faith? There are no really simple answers to these questions, but staying the course is about following the guidelines the Lord has given us. Is there Scripture study, a prayer life, fasting, confession, obedience to the Commandments, obedience to what we are asked to do, fellowship and community, helping those who can't help themselves, an active spiritual life, and obeying the Sabbath, to name only a few elements of discipleship? Jesus said, "*For the gate is narrow and the way is hard, that leads to life, and those who find it are few*" Matt. 7:14). Any priest can tell you as soon as their prayer life lapses, their vocation is in trouble.

The Seed That Takes Root

In 1979, I was a Fellow in a Foundation that was heavily focused on discipleship and Scripture study. It was a nondenominational group of people with a worldwide outreach of changing nations for the Lord. While there, I met a man there by the name of Tommy Tarrants III who had been a former leader of the Klu Klux Klan (KKK) in Mississippi. The story started out many years before where one night he and his girlfriend were going to the home of a businessman where they were planning great harm to a family. The FBI got wind of it, and as he and girlfriend pulled near the family's home, the FBI shot his girlfriend through the head, and she died instantly. Tommy fell out of the car, ran and fell into some bushes. The FBI sprayed the bushes with gunfire and only hit his elbow. How he survived no one knew. He was captured and was sentenced to prison. After spending several years in solitary confinement, he started to read the Scriptures and had a radical turn in thinking. After many years in jail, he was released with the help of Chuck Colson's group Prison Fellowship, a U.S. Senator, and other people fighting for his release due to his amendment of life. Former

Senator Harold Hughes of Iowa called it the greatest conversion story since Saint Paul. Upon prison release he moved to Washington, D.C. to be a part of the Foundation for the reconciliation of nations, and wrote a book called *Conversion of a Klansman.*

Tommy then married, had several children, became an Episcopal priest, pastored a church in Washington, D.C, worked with the inner city poor, and then went on to be President of the C.S. Lewis Institute for many years. For several years we had Thanksgiving dinner together with our young families. I always found it amusing to tell people that I had been a friend and in the wedding of a former leader in the Klu Klux Klan in a state no less than Mississippi! I would often mention this to people, but I wouldn't let on until later in the conversation the circumstances around our relationship! So here I am a surfer dude and Catholic from the coast of New England, and a friend of a man who was a leading Klansman from Mississippi meeting in a small discipleship group. The power of God overcomes all differences when unity is sought for the greater good.

Tommy's conversion came from reading the Scriptures. The seed fell on rich soil and took root. The Scriptures spoke to his heart, mind, and soul while in solitary confinement. The Scriptures are the word of God, and they stand by themselves to instruct us how to live. If we lived the Sermon on the Mount (Matthew 5,6, and 7) most all of our problems would go away. If we are in the Word of God daily with a quiet time asking for direction, we will hear God's voice. This is why there is no good alternative to primarily reading the Scriptures to know God's ways and who He is.

Man In the Arena

The world is full of people with opinions who are not spiritually active. To those who wish to critique the activity of others who get involved in the spiritual fight, it would be advisable to read the speech that President Teddy Roosevelt gave at the Sorbonne in the Grand Amphitheater at the University of Paris in 1910. The name of the speech was called *Citizenship in a Republic.* Roosevelt had been taking on the Robber Barons and tycoons during his presidency and was known as a *"trust buster*" of big, out-of-control businesses that had displayed little morality while building empires.

Roosevelt spoke on the glue that was necessary to make a republic work. He said "*self restraint, self mastery, common sense, the power of accepting individual responsibility, and yet of acting in conjunction with others, courage and resolution, these are the qualities which mark a masterful people. Indeed, it is a sign of marked political weakness in any commonwealth if the people tend to be carried away by mere oratory, if they tend to value words in and for themselves, as divorced from the deeds for which they are supposed to stand. To judge a man merely by success is an abhorrent thing.*" Roosevelt knew that for true leadership, morality counts. He said people will not follow if they see elected leaders abusing their privileges. The most salient part of what is often called *Man in the Arena* is below:

> *It is not the critic who counts, not the man who points out how the strong man stumbles, or where the doer of deeds could have done them better. The credit belongs to the man who is actually in the arena, whose face is marred by dust and sweat and blood, who strives valiantly; who errs, and comes short again and again, because there is no effort without error and shortcoming, but who does not actually strive to do the deeds; who knows the great enthusiasms, the great devotions; who spends himself in a worthy cause; who at the best knows in the end the triumph of high achievement, and who at the worst, if he fails, at least fails while daring greatly, so that his place shall never be with those cold and timid souls who know neither success nor defeat.*

The person next to you at church may have a ministry of doing something different from what you are called to do. This is good and necessary for the mystical body of Christ to function properly. Could you imagine if every person in the world were a plumber? Plumbers have great value when you need them, but it is not the only skill necessary in life. They are not the only trade. The fundamental flaw in our human nature is when someone thinks their ministry or task is greater than another's. It is a question of respecting another's charisms. The needs of the mystical body of Christ are best met, when there is cooperation among the parts of the body. When it is always about another's agenda year after year when you are with someone, it is not a healthy relationship. It is only a matter of time before the relationship ends. We work best when we work and help one another.

In His High Priestly Prayer, Jesus in John 17 prayed "*that not one be lost,*" and that "*they be one.*" Jesus was praying for the new Church that was soon to emerge and petty differences needed to be eliminated if this new Church was to grow. Have you ever noticed how much you enjoy being around holy people? Unity brings friendship, and friendship brings more people to a fulfilled life in Christ. Holiness, unity, warmth of spirit, love, and harmony are attractive to others. People want to be around it, and when they are around it, changes take place.

A Weak and Immature Church

The fact is, most things in life involve personal pride and are not worthy of division. People often argue over things that don't matter and relationships fracture over it. One area of disagreement often is over the authenticity of an apparition or visionary. One apparition is not better than the other, but are like parts of the body. When the Blessed Mother appeared at Fatima in 1917, there was an agenda for the world, and specifically a request about Russia. Her request at Fatima was not followed by the hierarchy in the Church, and what she asked was not done, though the apparition had Church approval. One thing is certain, the scourge of communism did happen and Russia was the principal country spreading its error. The same applies to Our Lady of All Nations, Medjugorje, Garabandal, Akita, and many others. It is a Mother speaking to her children around the world to help all mankind.

Paul also addressed this immaturity to the Corinthians as they squabbled over who was the most important voice when he wrote in his first letter to them:

> *"At the same time, I do appeal to you, brothers, for the sake of our Lord Jesus Christ, to make up the differences between you, and instead of disagreeing among yourselves, to be united again in your belief and practice. From what Chloe's people have been telling me, my dear brothers, it is clear that there are serious differences among you. What I mean are all these slogans that you have, like: I am for Paul, I am for Apollos, I am for Cephas, I am for Christ. Has Christ been*

parceled out? Was it Paul that was crucified for you? Were you baptized in the name of Paul" (I Cor. 1: 10-14).

Paul is clearly addressing a church that is weak, and they must be reminded that it is Christ crucified we are following and squabbles about the non-essentials are for the weak and immature in their faith. Paul is saying what you are arguing about shows your immaturity. The words of Teresa of Avila remind us how a believer should act:

- *Let nothing disturb you*
- *Let nothing frighten you*
- *All things pass away*
- *God never changes*
- *Patience obtains all things*
- *He who has God, Finds he lacks nothing, God alone suffices.*

We need to rise above the irrelevant differences that divide us. As the future becomes more difficult for believers under oppressive government, this will be a key for spiritual vitality in any community. History shows us small differences dissipate in times of stress. There is strength in community. As times get more difficult for many, we will witness a greater maturity on this issue. Embrace unity for the greater good. We should remind ourselves:

- Unity on the Essentials
- Liberty on the Unessentials
- Love Overall

In order to advance the mission of God, the pride of seeing our agenda as more important than another's must end. As we get to know someone on a more personal basis, we will find out why they do what they do. Through friendship comes more understanding. We learn about their background, their life growing up, their community, family life, spouse, and as we learn more, we often grow more sympathetic to them. There are reasons for their behavior. As that happens, we become less judgmental towards them. This is why we must not judge too quickly or too harshly. Heaven is asking us for our cooperation, not division. Proverbs speaks about what the Lord hates: "*There are six things which the Lord hates, seven which are an abomination to him: haughty eyes, a lying tongue, and hands that shed innocent blood, a heart that devises wicked plans, feet that make haste to run to evil, a false witness who breathes out lies, and a man who sows discord among brothers*" (Proverbs 6-16-19). We are all sinners and fall short of the glory of God. So let us take the plank out of our own eye, before we take the splinter out of our neighbor's. Try to look at the good points of a person, instead of their weakness.

The Unknown

Fear is the activator of our faults. Fear is the greatest reason why a godless agenda has been thrust upon peoples of the world. The three basic fears we all have are:

1. We will be destitute, hopeless, helpless, powerless, and defenseless;
2. We will have to live with pain;
3. We will be forgotten with no legacy.

When Jesus was in His forty day fast before He started His public ministry, the devil tempted Him and addressed these issues (Matt. 4:1-11). Satan offered Him power when he said to Jesus, "*all of the Kingdoms in the world are mine to give you.*" With power, wealth and might, these three fears are greatly lessened.

Satan is the author of fear. Satan makes us think an individual voice will not be heard, and nothing can be done to alter the scales of injustice and the direction of society. What if Abraham Lincoln had lacked the courage to tackle slavery? Fear is the reason we are where we are. Fear of what others think, fear of stumbling or falling is why we fail to start. As C.S. Lewis said, "*what are we to do, sit by and concede everything away?*"

The Guilty Bystanders

Several years ago, I met a successful neurosurgeon. He told me when he was younger he had been brought up in a faith-filled home. Now he was living a life of regret and was playing catch up for his inactivity as he watched the culture slip away. After a thirty-five year career as a successful surgeon, he said, "*I looked up one day and saw that we had lost the country.*" He realized he failed to participate in fighting for what was really necessary, and as a result of failing to do so, he said he had lost all that was most important in life—faith in God and the goodness that comes from belief. As a result of not focusing on the only essential thing worth living for, he had lost all that was most dear to him. Seeing the error of not being previously engaged, he spent more time getting involved.

An All-Knowing God

We are dealing with an all-knowing God. We cannot even begin to scratch the surface of His magnificence, yet we continue to question what He does in the universe He made. There are to many mysteries in life to know His mysteries this side of heaven. We each have a body made up of trillions of cells, with a totally unique DNA that no other person in the world possesses. Each of us has totally different fingerprints and a differing eye design, though there are over seven billion people in the world. Scientists tell us there are billions of other galaxies other than our own that we don't even understand in the least, but we know they are there. We are most familiar with ours and we know precious little about even that. We know more about outer space than we even know about the depths of our own oceans. Think of it, each and every snowflake has a different design. The trillions and trillions of snowflakes that fall each year have a different beautiful, unique design. One can only wonder what we don't know, see, or understand about the infinite mercy and love that God has for all of us.

Saint Thomas Aquinas after a lifetime of studying, contemplation and writing, encountered the living God while saying Mass. There was a physical and spiritual manifestation of the living (rhema) God to him versus the logos (word), which he had been accustomed to writing. His utterance was, "*All I have written is mere straw.*" When he had some sort of beatific vision of the living God, Aquinas wasn't able to put into words what he saw. He never wrote again because he said words did not convey the glory of God. It was said Saint Thomas Aquinas spent as much time on his knees praying as he did writing, and he was always on his knees before he wrote.

We are dealing with a God who knows no bounds of mercy and love. If we are to understand that we are in a new dynamic in world history of a large Transformation coming to humanity, we need to embrace His Will—not ours. Our finite minds cannot understand the depths of His mystery. If we fight His plan, we will struggle. If we adapt even though we know it will be difficult, we will do fine because we know God is in control. It is His plan, not ours, and as the author of all life, we will do better in all circumstances living in His Divine Will.

The Tribe Of Issachar Lives Among Us

There are twelve tribes in the nation of Israel that have blood-lines back to Abraham, Isaac, and Jacob. Each tribe is known for certain attributes. Asher, Benjamin, Dan, Judah, Reuben, Zebulun, Joseph, and from Levi came the Levites which is the priestly tribe, and so forth. But there is one tribe, seldom heard from, that few know anything about. It is the tribe of Issachar. In 1 Chronicles 12:32 we get a unique glimpse of their primary attribute. It says, "*Of the sons of Issachar, men who understood the times, with knowledge of what Israel should do, their chiefs were two hundred; and all their kinsmen were at their command.*" They are the tribe of scholars and were the smallest by far in terms of numbers. The Old Testament is primarily about the Hebrew people, much in the same way the New Testament is about one person—Jesus Christ. The role of prophets was very important to the Jews and they relied heavily on them. They were the mouthpiece(s) of God instructing His people as they wandered in the desert and beyond for thousands of years. The Tribe of Issachar "*understood the times,*" and it says King David surrounded himself with them for they understood the times in which they lived.

The word "*understood*" appears 38 times in the Old Testament and derives from the word "binyah," which says a person understands something, its nuances, its deeper meaning, and its subtleties. The Tribe of Issachar had similar traits to the Magi or Wise Men, as they journeyed to lay gifts at the feet of Jesus—a new born King that Scripture had told them about hundreds of years in advance, with the greatest details coming from the prophet Isaiah well in advance of His birth. It would take men of courage and learning to make such a journey. They would have been schooled in the science of the day, the Torah, and been exposed to all the known arts which made them scholars. Concerning the Tribe of Issachar, King David sought their advice. King David truly has a unique distinction among all people as Acts 13:22 says about the Lord's selection of David as King of Israel, "*I have selected David son of Jesse, a man after My own heart, who will carry out My whole purpose.*" That is a significant endorsement for the Lord to say about any person—"*a man after my own heart to carry out my whole purpose.*" So here is the great King David handpicked by the Lord, seeking the counsel of the little known Tribe of Issachar. Many years ago when my son was eleven years old at Mass on Christmas day, a woman pulled out a mirror and started putting on lipstick during Consecration. My son turned to me and said, "*Dad, I wonder what tribe she's from?*" Yes, people do act differently depending on which tribe they are from.

For those Catholics who are in Fidelity to the Magisterium, going to Mass, frequent confession, fasting as requested, studying Scripture, in prayer groups, praying the Rosary, and living life as best one can, the signs of the times are self-evident. You may know of some or all of the writings called *To the Priests Our Lady's Beloved Sons,* the messages of Medjugorje, the Warning and the Miracle foretold at Garabandal, Saint Faustina and the messages of Divine Mercy, Saint Padre Pio, Fatima, Our Lady of All Nations, Our Lady of America, The Divine Will, the lives of the saints, Rosa Mystica, and other spiritual and religious writings. You are attempting to do what God has made known to you. Those who criticize the messages of the Blessed Mother today, knowing very little of what she has been doing for so long now, are like the people in Noah's time who will soon rush to get into the ark for safety. They have been warned, but pay little attention. It is for this reason alone, that formation in the essentials of faith is so important now. Believers today who are moving with the Holy Spirit, and not locked into a regimented formula of thinking and acting, are the modern day version of the Tribe of Issachar.

We are in the midst of a new paradigm in which the times are extraordinarily unique. Heaven has said so in the clearest possible language imaginable if we are willing to listen. The Trinity has sent the Blessed Mother, the Queen of Heaven and Earth as their prophetess to warn and inform us. We are at the end of an age, where a New Jerusalem, New Times, a New Beginning, a New Pentecost is near. A glorious new time awaits us—a time not to fear, but a time to embrace. The rot, stench and corruption of this age is coming to an end. We were never meant to live like this in a sea of filth. Yes, it will be difficult.

Many will not get past just the negative here and fail to see that God has a plan, that these events must take place to usher in the new times.

Stages Of Death and Dying

The death of the world that we are witnessing is similar to the physical death we will all endure at some point. We are being asked to die continually to self as a process of life. Seeing the world devolving is a form of spiritual death especially for the older people. We are being asked to die all the time, everyday to self as Jesus emptied Himself and became the form of a slave.

According to the experts in the field of death and dying, there are five general stages. The scientific study of death is called thanatology or more generally called today, end of life issues. There are five general stages most people go through, and they are:

- Denial
- Anger
- Bargaining
- Depression
- Acceptance

Some people can skip one or two areas, others can go directly to the end stage, but generally people have to go through a sequential process of dealing with them one by one. Our temperament and personality and general spiritual preparedness will determine how we deal with these steps and where we are in them, and the time it takes to pass through each one. People more spiritually formed, and more prepared for death, tend to generally do better with end of life issues. It is because they understand that life is a step to dying and reaching our eternal prize. They realize that this is not our permanent resting place. Life is a test on the way to heaven. We will havc hardship, sufferings, joys, struggles, torments, and every emotion imaginable over a lifetime, but in the end we will pass on. Everyone wants to go to heaven, but no one wants to die.

The same stages of physical death and dying apply to the spiritual world. We all make choices and have to live with them. The spiritual similarities to the physical stages of death and dying are numerous. We are sojourners and pilgrims on the way. As we transition from one world to the next bodily, the mystical world is in Transition/Transformation as well. The steps to come to this realization are not identical, but they do have similarities. They are:

Denial—Many refuse to acknowledge that the world is in this tremendous Transformation or Transition, and think everything is business as usual. There is no amendment of life and focus on the spiritual. The signs of change are all around us, but they are in denial because they are so caught up in the things of the world. They are not equipped to hear the Lord's voice until a crisis of some sort. The older one gets if there has not been spiritual formation, the more difficult it is to hear His voice until there is either a breakdown of marriage, death of a loved one, loss of a job, or illness that changes their worldview. Often it takes a severe uncontrollable crisis in their life for them to awaken from their denial.

Anger—A new thought or way of life disrupts this person and they get angry at an unexpected event. Life is going well and the sudden event puts the brakes on their agenda. If there is spirituality to some degree, they often feel God let them down and He didn't keep His part of the bargain, thus the anger. Often things like, "*Lord how could you do this to me,*" *or* "*if You are a loving God, why do You allow this,*" are common utterances. When it comes to the events prophesied by the major prophets in the world in accordance with Scripture, they refuse to admit anything beyond their realm of comfort. They will consider people religious extremists if they adhere to the issues being discussed in this book. But remember, Noah was considered a madman until it started to rain. Then he was the prophet the Lord commissioned him to be in spite of the previous public ridicule against him.

Bargaining—This applies more to the sick than events that are happening in the world. People cutting deals or making arrangements with God is common. The conversation may go something like this, "*Lord if You do this for me now, I will do this for You.*" Years ago while on a trip to New England, I met a man who was a tireless worker for the Blessed Mother. During the conversation, I asked him how he had the energy to volunteer so much time as he was in his mid 80's. He said lying on Omaha Beach on D Day covered under a dead body, he made a deal with God, that if he lived, he would work for the Blessed Mother until he died. I think as he went up to heaven he may have heard the choir of angels say, "*well done, good and faithful servant*" (Matt. 25:21).

Depression—This is more than understandable in the stage(s) of physical death but the reasons for a spiritual death are somewhat different. There is the famous story of William Wilberforce, the civil rights leader and a member of Parliament in England who is credited with ending the slave trade. As a young Cambridge University graduate it was said he could have had any position he wanted in all of England due to his wide array of noticeable oratorical and intellectual skills. He was called the wittiest man in England. After a profound conversion he uttered a phrase about his conversion when he said, "*how inconvenient.*" The world was his oyster for the taking, and he knew if he committed his life to Christ, certain conveniences and worldly opportunities would pass. He chose the high road from the beginning and transformed the morals of a nation, and altered the destiny of many nations. He gave up nothing in actuality, but the life of nightly conviviality and the frivolous would no longer be his.

Malcolm Muggeridge was the famous editor of the French magazine called *Punch*. In his autobiography called *Chronicles of Wasted Time,* he said life in the flesh and living in the world was like "*licking the earth.*" Often in youth it is perceived as wasted time to devote yourself to Christ, but if you don't, it will often just bring a life of misery and unnecessary pain and hardship. The longer we stay away from the Lord, the greater the pain. So what do we really have to lose? When you are in the world, you will be consumed by the world until you come to the realization we are not all long for this world, and the purpose of living is serving Christ. As Jesus said, "*I tell you most solemnly, unless a grain of wheat falls to the ground and dies, it remains only a single grain; but if it dies, it yields a rich harvest. Anyone who loves his life loses it, anyone who hates his life in this world, will keep it for the eternal life*" (John 12:24-25). Living a life away from the guidance of the Holy Spirit is of little value.

Acceptance—At this point the wide ranges of emotions are varied. The person often feels exhausted from the journey. If it is related to the physical side of life with issues like death, they have no other recourse but to accept the inevitable. Spiritually, it is a different matter. Many fight God kicking and screaming, and losing every step of the way. They refuse to accept the existence of God, but as death comes closer, they often submit their will when no other recourse is available. History shows there are many deathbed changes of heart when earthly options are exhausted. People often surrender only at the last moment. It is why the Chaplet of the Dying (Divine Mercy Chaplet) is so important to recite for people who are dying. Societal structures that have been around for a long time are presently non-functional and badly broken. They are being stripped away one by one, and after decades of irresponsible living away from the Will of God, more and more people are beginning to see that there is something much bigger amiss in society than they previously had thought. People are beginning to see no one has the answers to solve the problems anymore. We have dug a hole so deep, only the Lord can get us out, and most people are deeply stressed.

Saint Padre Pio addressed the solution for stress when he said, "*My brothers and sisters have many ways of dealing with stress in their lives. What heaven is trying to tell you is that much of your stress can be alleviated by a few simple decisions. The first is a decision for Jesus, total and complete. This will actually reduce all of your stress in your life because you will begin to live for heaven and not earth. You will concentrate on your duty, ordained by heaven, and not on the busyness that the world is trying to substitute for your duty. You will decide to live simply, eat simply, love simply, and heaven will surround you with graces each day. Jesus will not be in one box and your life in another. Jesus and your life will be together each day, all day, and each decision will be made in union with Him. This is service to heaven and unity with heaven. Concentrate not on how others are loving you or not loving you. Jesus loves you enough for everyone on the planet with you at any given time. Concentrate on how Jesus is able to flow His love through you to others. This is renewal. This is the process of the Second Coming which has begun. Jesus returns to the earth through each one of His beloved apostles...*

Jesus is calling you and you are called. You must answer. Follow Him and you will find your stress fading away, even in the greatest trials and temptations. I am your friend and heaven is filled with souls like me who are also your friends. We will help you with the process of reducing stress in your life. Acquire a heavenly rhythm to your days and watch what Jesus can do."

Moving With the Holy Spirit

Several years ago, I was by myself and took the ferry from the New Jersey shore to Lewes, Delaware. I parked my car in the bottom of the boat, and since it was such a beautiful summer day, I bought a cup of coffee and went to the very front of the boat. I sat down and just looked ahead. About five minutes after departure, I looked at the shoreline of New Jersey behind me. As I looked up, I saw a seagull floating in the thermal slip stream of the boat not flapping its wings, but just tilting side to side gently to keep in the stream of air the boat was generating as it moved. I sat there just looking at the bird, and it was looking at me. Yes, kind of odd, if someone was watching. Someone would have wondered if I were an ornithologist studying sea gulls.

For the next forty minutes or so, I just watched and was fascinated by what the bird was doing. Maybe this bird was going over to Delaware for lunch and had figured out how to get a free ride with no effort? Maybe there was more food over in Delaware, or too much competition in New Jersey? But nonetheless, this bird traveled for miles without a flap of its wings. What dawned on me is how much less effort there is when we are moving with the Holy Spirit. Limited expense of energy, less problems, less cost, less hassles, less medical bills, less psychiatric bills, less headaches, and less effort all the way around if we are moving in the direction the Lord asks. The Lord doesn't say our life will be problem free if we follow Him, but what He does say is, "*My yoke is easy, and My burden is light*" (Matt. 11:30). Life is difficult, and we can smooth out some of the rough patches by living in the Spirit following Him. As the world tumbles around you, think of the sea gull.

But I will sing of thy might; I will sing aloud of thy steadfast love in the morning. For thou has been to me a fortress and a refuge in the day of my distress.

—Psalm 59:16

JESUS I TRUST IN YOU

fifteen

Evolution To Atheism: Destroyers Of Civilizations, Times Of Diabolical Disorientation

For my thoughts are not your thoughts,
neither are your ways my ways.

—Isaiah 55:8

Several years ago, an event took place that made me look very differently at the issue of evolution. I had never believed that man had evolved from the apes, but I hadn't given a lot of thought to how far evolution had crept into mainstream academia, intellectual life and our institutions. Over time it has trickled its way down to the most elementary level in education throughout the entire world. I, like many others, hadn't thought much about evolution and couldn't argue the points of science. The science and discrepancies of Carbon 14 dating, old earth versus young earth, mysteries of the solar systems and galaxies, rock formations, and so on need study to combat evolution. These issues are not addressed in this chapter as it is not possible to thoroughly address them, and nor is it the intent. But, one thing became very obvious the more I looked into the subject. What I saw is that the more someone believed that man came from the apes, the more I observed godless belief. That was telling how an individual approached life.

There must be a decision by each of us on a personal basis on the major issues on the Origin of Man. If man evolved from the apes, why believe in a Supreme Being? If we came from monkeys, does it matter if we believe in anything spiritual? Did God create man as the Bible states? Was the Lord in the book of Genesis the Creator of the Universe, or was there a Big Bang where man just magically appeared from some green gray goo? Is it possible that nobody plus nothing equals everything? Or, how did it become conscious? Is there a *God Particle* or is that concept bogus, supporting false science for scientists to debunk Creationism? Out of chaos came an ordered universe? Most believers like me know in their hearts, minds, and souls, our origin is from God: but I had not given enough thought to evolution versus the science of Creation.

There is Creation and there is Intelligent Design (ID). There is a difference. Creationism defends a 6000 year age of the universe, and seven literal days of creation. This is not acceptable to many on the modern stage of idea exchange. Intelligent Design is not a religious theory, but it posits a designer and has religious implications. Many have launched attacks on Christian religious belief from a mistaken idea that science "proves" about God. The real question of interest isn't whether religion can live comfortably with science (as we know that it can), but whether religion can live comfortably with scientific ideas that are in error. The atheist will argue because they cannot explain something, it does not exist. Since they cannot provide an answer they dismiss God as a reality—because everything deserves an answer. Therefore, if you cannot "explain" God, He does not exist. Darwinian theory is untenable and the evidence for Intelligent Design is breathtaking. Intelligent Design in science destroys atheism and puts us back on the road to sanity. Revealed religion is also an entirely different subject altogether in the evolution debate.

A conservative person functioning in academia under the auspices of a think tank or university, where their livelihood often depends on what they teach and write, has been well trained that Godly Scriptural thinking is not the way to personal advancement or government grants. The more "sophisticated" the school of higher learning, the more Creationism is denigrated. For the last several generations, authors who are believers have been writing anonymously under nom de plumes (pen names) to protect their careers. The deck is often stacked against believers unless research is independently financed by private philanthropy. The culture as a whole has been moving away from God, not toward Him, and the flow of government funds illustrates this trend.

When the ship *HMS Beagle* left port in England on December 27, 1831, it had a naturalist on board by the name of Charles Darwin. Darwin had won a berth on a trip to transcribe the ship's findings that would eventually take five years doing a survey of many foreign ports of call and looking at animals, birds, plants, fossils, and natural specimens. When the ship returned, science would soon be turned upside down and would have a profoundly diabolical impact on the practice of Christianity. Where Darwin often wrote "LET US ASSUME," that phrase continued to be extrapolated by him time and time again until the ape had become a professor of chemistry at Harvard. Darwin's assumptions have become so blown out of proportion by those that deny God, they often cannot even recite what Darwin actually said and wrote. Deception and lie on top of philosophical lie, as it concerns evolution, has led to a godless pagan world where change is now well past a tipping point in so many areas concerning the way we live. The transition back to the things of God will be disruptive, as we cannot return to a Christ-centered way of living until the present way of thinking is reversed. By its very nature change will be chaotic and will unnerve people.

The world is now in a scientific transition similar to what happened to faith and reason (Fides et Ratio) during the Age of the Enlightenment. Where the early Church Fathers spoke of a young earth, atheists have now swayed church thinking beginning around 1800 to an old earth and no God. Few have seen how profound this thinking has become, and those who do not subscribe to the intellectual thinking of Darwin and its aftermath, are often snubbed, sneered at, shunned, and at worst driven from their chosen professions. They are considered intellectual dimwits and not worthy of the positions of rigorous critical thinking, unless they subscribe to the ideology of evolution, especially in academia.

Evolution's sub-topics are exhaustive and cannot be adequately addressed here. It would require volumes of data to do them justice. I have found that people of good divide on this issue because the terms are not well delineated so they can speak on the same specific topic versus the general subject. Ultimately, it comes down to the issue of "*does God exist*" for both sides, and is He the Creator of the Universe? Your response to that question will determine your world-view and to what journals you subscribe. To the skeptic, He does not exist. So from that thought an ideology and philosophy of life is presented either knowingly or unknowingly by an unbeliever to the general population. Their belief system dictates their actions. Atheism is a belief system—and there is a political agenda with powerful people pushing it. We're at fault for letting humanism get away with imposing their virulent agenda on humanity and saying little. He who is silent consents. Or as Albert Einstein said, "*The world will not be destroyed by those who do evil, but by those who watch them without doing anything.*" Whether people want to say there is a God or isn't, neither group can prove their case definitively. On the basis of what science can, and cannot explain, the door can never be slammed shut on the probability of God's existence. Belief in God is best seen through the eyes of faith, and that decision builds upon itself to greater belief. Faith is like a muscle, the more we use it, the stronger it becomes.

Philosophy Determines the Destiny Of a Nation

A godless agenda is not a neutral philosophy. A regime of activity follows from what you think. Evolution has been used as a significant tool for imposing atheism. The teaching of evolution has been a primary method by atheists and the godless to drive Christianity from the classroom. The data presented is to illustrate the sociological and philosophical roots of widespread atheism. Evolution as a supposed scientific proven fact is not just seriously flawed, it is fatally flawed in areas that are often considered sacred by many people, as it offers no sufficient logical basis to rule out God's presence and engagement in the world. Atheists simply do not want God to have a voice. It is a well thought out agenda to have God removed through science and education even to the youngest age groups. The data shows this thinking has born poisonous fruit upon all mankind. Ultimately "*you know something by its fruit*" (Matt. 12:33). Nearly 160 years of Darwin's godless thinking has bestowed a noisome fetid foul stink upon the schoolrooms of the world. We have seen the destructive effects on the educational system and student morals and behavior. These effects have led to the current breakdown in the family—the basis of a harmonious and functioning society.

The promotion of evolution may have been Satan's biggest conquest of the mind of man. Several years ago, a man by the name of Dr. Gene

Conti, an Emergency Room physician called me and asked to have lunch. He and his wife Barbara had been subscribers to our family magazine called *Signs and Wonders for Our Times* for many years, and we had followed a similar vein of thinking on Catholic issues. We agreed to have lunch, and he said he was four hours away. I said "*why don't we just talk about it over the phone and it will save you a long trip.*" He wanted to sit down and talk, so I agreed. At that lunch he laid out for me in graph and pictorial form what destruction had taken place as a result of the false and diabolical agenda of evolution. He showed me that the thinking of Charles Darwin had spawned a multitude of influential philosophers and scientists to destroy on educational ideology. Destruction is a kind and gentle word when one looks at the damage it has done. Since Darwin took his famous voyage on the Beagle to the Galapagos Islands, a new branch of science emerged that has had a venomous agenda to undermine Scripture and Christian philosophy. Dr. Conti brought scholarly books and material to the lunch and gave me a tutorial on how evolution had caused damage to the entire world and incubated and spawned atheism on a global scale. I listened and knew many of the philosopher's names, but had not really thought about how much damage it had done. Many academics names in the field of evolution were foreign to me, so I had things to learn.

At the end of the lunch I personally liked Dr. Conti and believed him, but I dismissed what he said as "*just unbelief.*" I said at some point people make a choice and they either decide to abide by God or man, and it is just that simple and profound at the same time. I didn't dismiss him personally as there were so many areas of spiritual thinking on heaven's intervention in world history where we could finish each other's sentences. He said he had a lot of DVDs on the subject and he would send a few.

Over the next year he sent me over 35 DVDs on Creation versus evolution thinking. I watched every one of them and clearly saw an insidious agenda by Satan to draw humanity away from God. I saw the destruction that evolution ideology had caused in the world. Evolution has polluted our thinking unknown to so many of us who dismiss it as I had as "*just unbelief.*" Philosophy influences the destiny of nations, and this atheistic philosophy has been the destroyer of civilizations.

The devil's greatest triumph has been a heinous agenda so deceptive and clever few even understand how much destruction it has caused. It is a root cause of unbelief and chaos in our culture. When youth are indoctrinated at such elementary levels, it becomes difficult for them to break away from the educational mindset.

There is not an agenda to get into the polemics of debate of what could be written about the science. There is one significant issue that is absolutely crucial to understand from the Christian and Biblical perspective. Doctrine and canon are clear that there was no death before Adam. The question must be asked, "*Was there death before Adam?*" Death and the fall of man came with Original Sin. The larger question remains, "*what was intended for mankind as designed by God, versus the free will of man and the choices we make?*" All the consequences that came from the fall of Adam in the Garden of Eden like, "man would sweat by his brow, and woman would have pain in childbirth" became the curse of Adam's disobedience of eating from the tree of knowledge. Death and suffering came as a result of Adam's sin. It is not possible looking at this scenario that man came from some primordial soup oozing from the earth tens or millions of years ago.

An example is often used about the Big Bang Theory that it would be like a giant explosion in a print shop, and out pops the Oxford Unabridged Dictionary. Another is that a Boeing 747 would just appear after a tornado rips through a junkyard. This also gets into the issue of was there really a Creation, and the young earth/old earth question. Once you debunk the authority of Scripture, man knows no bounds where it will take him. When man subscribes to something outside of a moral structure as originally designed by God, he will become a tyrant and worse. Godlessness quickly turns to paganism, then barbarism in as little as a generation.

Philosophy, literature, the arts and science in classrooms from the youngest grades have been affected by this godless agenda. Families for the most part don't even know they are fighting it in their children's school curricula. The rubrics and points below are Dr. Conti's thinking as he has done the heavy intellectual lifting with the players, the dates, and the thinking. I have just colorized it. I would also like to point out, the thinking is much broader drawing much more conclusive truths with evidence that demands a verdict on the subject, and families need to look into the role that evolution has played in the destruction of the way the Lord says things happened and what men like Darwin say. The two primary reasons there are over two million home-schooled kids and growing in America, is that parents want more control, and don't want their kids indoctrinated with Darwinian pagan doctrine from Pre K through high school.

Satan initiates what is contrary to God's way. Therefore, an attempt is not made below to include all of people who could be added to the list, just major players at key junctures. Many of the dates are approximate as the thinking that leads to a philosophy being introduced happens much before the actual occurrence of a specific event, as history does not operate in a vacuum of dates. There is always an underground germination first, and something then erupts for the general population to see. It also must be noted that it was Satan, the first great rebel who said, "*I will not serve.*" He has an agenda all his own, one contrary to the things of God at all times. It is the Blessed Mother who crushes the head of the serpent (Rev. 12). At all times she is battling the cohort of evil with the cohort of heaven and she does intercede on behalf of mankind.

Sliding Towards Gomorrah

1600: Francis Bacon. Benjamin Franklin was asked who he thought the Father of America was, and he said Francis Bacon. Bacon believed in God, but he said the Bible was not necessary to understand the world. Bacon was a leading member of the Rosicrucian Order who had deep ties to the cabal of secret societies. Bacon had a vision for America being the new Atlantis where there could be a ruling, working, and a military class. America, being a fresh unblemished continent, could launch that original dream of Plato's *Utopia* into a modern day Atlantis. The battle for the soul of America has always been between people seeing America under the mantle of God versus those like Bacon. This competing ideology is the battle for the soul of America.

1760: Voltaire. Probably no one in France had created such a cynical and comedic effect on the people as Voltaire from his writings and plays breeding ill will and division against the Church. Voltaire in his time was the closest thing to a rock star in France. This general anti-church thinking leads to the Age of the Enlightenment and the French Revolution.

1780: Immanuel Kant. He believed in God, but said there was no proof of God, and reason trumped religion. The constant battle of faith and reason is re-energized. Kant had a huge influence on Georg Hegel of Germany. Hegel and his concept of the "superman" was taught in all the school rooms of Germany with the atheism of Friedrich Nietzsche. These two led the movement of the "superman" and nihilistic "atheism" of the Third Reich under Hitler. It was a perfect dual force of aberrant philosophy that led to Hitler's rise. Nazism just didn't appear one day, people had been brainwashed through godless philosophy for several generations in classrooms.

1785: James Hutton. Father of modern geology who believed in long ages (Lengthy existence of the earth) and that God set up the world, but no longer intervened in it.

1794: Erasmus Darwin. The grandfather of Charles and a major influence on his life. He wrote *Zoonomia,* which believed in long ages and evolution.

1800: Georg Hegel. He discounted supernatural parts of the Bible as myth that had a negative effect on society. He believed a new religion was needed built on scientific reason. His writings were socialistic and were a direct precursor to Marxism.

1800: Christianity begins to look at the Bible's days of Creation as being long ages and defers to evolutionary scientific thinking.

1813: Georges Cuvier. He believed in the old earth and multiple catastrophes, but not in the flood of Noah.

1830: Charles Lyell. Darwin's mentor believed in long ages, no catastrophes, no flood of Noah and no God. Lyell had a major impact on Darwin, and in 1831 gave Darwin his book, *Principles of Geology* before he embarked on the HMS Beagle.

1830: Catherine Laboure' of France. The Blessed Mother comes to a young Sister Laboure' in a convent in France as The Queen of the Globe, and gives the Miraculous Medal to the world. She is seen standing on the globe with rays of light coming from her fingers with the symbol that they are unasked for graces. Millions of medals are distributed in a matter of weeks. Heaven has a different agenda. The apparition is called "the dawn of the Marian Age" where the Blessed Mother as the prophetess of our age becomes more active in world affairs intervening to combat Satan.

1836: Neanderthal Man is discovered and atheists go wild. It is soon proven to be just a man.

1846: The Blessed Mother appears to a peasant shepherdess and shepherd at LaSalette, France. She warns France of widespread famine if the first three Commandments continue to be violated. She foretells of widespread apostasy that will occur in the Church. The Church downplays the messages as it is severe to priests who are not speaking the truth.

1858: The Blessed Mother comes as Our Lady of Lourdes to a young peasant girl in France called Bernadette Soubirous and says, "*I am the Immaculate Conception,*" with Bernadette not knowing what it means. Devotion to Our Lady of Lourdes spreads like none before as a leading political figure has a daughter who is healed, thus opening the way for less political meddling.

1859: Darwin publishes *On the Origin of Species by Means of Natural Selection.* A virtual firestorm erupts. The enemies of God now see an opening to exploit Darwin and distort science.

1860: Thomas Huxley, Darwin's bulldog, debates Bishop "Soapy Sam" Wilberforce in the first Creation/evolution debate, and Wilberforce loses the public opinion. The evolution movement takes on new momentum with leading intellects and scientists backing it. The Huxley family plays a leading role in atheism, secularism, and godless thought.

1864: Francis Galton, a cousin to Charles Darwin, says there is no God and coins the word "eugenics," which is founded upon evolution. It says the feeble nations of the world give way to the nobler and stronger nations of mankind. Germany listens well for a future Aryan brand. Margaret Sanger, the founder of Planned Parenthood takes notes.

1867: Karl Marx, an atheist, writes *Das Capital,* which advocates the redistribution of wealth by governments. Marx gives a signed copy to "*My friend Charles Darwin,*" and dedicates the Second Edition of the book to Darwin. By any standard, this point is of such major importance one must pause here to reflect on what Marxism has done to thinking, politics, and social movements of the world. To understand the atheism of Marx is to understand his writings and their impact on communist countries like Russia and China. His writings became a framework for the execution of an ideological plan and inspire a world without God for generations.

1868: Ernst Haeckel, a proponent of scientific racism, says God is nature alone. Hitler read his writings and was a proponent of his thinking.

1872: Friedrich Nietzsche, an atheist, said, "*God is dead*" and that the science of evolution killed God that led to the loss of coherent objective truth. He heavily criticized Christianity and said people with mental disorders are more likely to believe in God. The New Age movement makes great strides here especially in Western Europe as "*God is dead.*" All sorts of bizarre and occult doctrines gain acceptance throughout Europe.

1879: Wilhelm Wundt, father of "Experimental Psychology," believes man is just an animal with no soul.

1880: Julius Wellhausen writes a theological treatise called *JEDP Hypothesis,* sowing seeds of doubt that the first five books of the Bible, the Pentateuch, have divine authorship. This thought evolved with many Bible scholars rejecting a literal translation of Genesis and the plagues of Egypt as naturally occurring events in nature. People began to look at the Scriptures and the story of Noah as children's fairy tales.

1885: Friedrich Engels, an atheist collaborated with Karl Marx on the *Manifesto of the Communist Party,* and *The Part Played by Labor in the Transition of Ape to Man,* virulent attacks against Christian doctrine.

1890: Andrew Carnegie, a businessman and steel industrialist and for a time the wealthiest man in America said, "*not only had I gotten rid of theology and the supernatural, but I found the truth of evolution.*" The AFL and CIO (labor movements) are direct offshoots of this type of brutal behavior in the Pittsburgh steel mills at the turn of the century. The robber barons saw workers as human slugs and part of machinery as human capital. The Johnstown Flood of May 31, 1889 that killed 2,209 people happened on Carnegie's watch due to inadvertent and careless attention to a dam. Due to public sentiment he fled to Scotland until the outcry subsided.

1891: Java Man discovered by Eugene DuBois. On his deathbed in 1939 he recanted and said they were the bones of an ape.

1895: Sigmund Freud, considered the father of psychiatry, owned and made use of Darwin's writings. He said, "*God is an illusion, religious belief is a childhood neurosis and infantile delusion.*" This is from a man that science ran to for advice.

1907: President Teddy Roosevelt started a eugenics movement. He said, "*I wish the wrong people were prevented from breeding. Nine out of ten Indians should be dead Indians.*"

1912: Piltdown Man discovered. In 1950 it was exposed as a hoax, with the jaw of an ape and the skull of a modern human. Teeth were filed down and the skull stained to look old. Pierre Teilhard de Chardin, a Jesuit priest, was allegedly involved as he was a strong proponent of evolution theory.

1915: Thomas Edison, the U.S. inventor said, "*nature made us, not the gods of religion.*"

1915: The Klu Klux Klan (KKK) believe in evolution and spread their hate against blacks, Jews, Catholics and non-Aryans. Klan members felt Darwin had given them an intellectual basis for their actions to kill off inferior races.

1917: Fatima Portugal, the cornerstone of Marian Apparitions for the 20th Century, takes place from May to October on the 13th day of each month. The Blessed Mother appears to three peasant children and predicts that Russia will become the scourge of the earth and that godless communism will be disastrous for the world. The ramifications of this are still frequently spoken of as there were secrets that were never officially revealed to the world by the Roman Catholic Church. The Blessed Mother asks that Catholics go to Mass and Communion the First Friday and Saturday of the month for the conversion of Russia, as "*Russia will spread her errors throughout the world.*" This takes place before the October 1917 Revolution. The eldest of the children Lucy (she later became a nun) thought Russia was a woman's name when she heard it. On the cover of the *New York Times* it said over 70,000 people were in the field during the phenomenon of the Miracle of the Sun. The Third Secret of Fatima has never been fully released to the world to the great disappointment of faithful Catholics. The question is "why" has the Third Secret not been revealed?

1917: October Revolution occurs in Russia as religion is outlawed and communist thought purges tens of millions of souls. Ukraine is hit hardest and at any time it is estimated over one million people are in rail transport working or on their way to labor camps for those who dissented from the ideology of the revolution, or worse yet, had the wrong blood lines.

1920: John Dewey is considered to be the Father of Modern American Education. He appears to be the single person most responsible for the destruction of the Judeo-Christian ethos of education, with the state taking control of children. America was growing in immigration, industry, and bursting at the seams with economic potential and expansion during this period. Dewey's timing for a godless agenda was perfect. He was an atheist and humanist, and his goal was for the state to control education and incrementally take it away from the parents. His design was that the earliest grades in school be the starting point for teaching socialism, communism, and evolution. He was one of the original signers of the Humanist Manifesto of 1933. Study Dewey and you will see how successful his thinking has become. Many U.S. Supreme Court and lower court decisions on education backed Dewey and made it more difficult for parochial education of all faiths. In the early 1960's, God and the Bible had been successfully removed from classrooms by order of the U.S. Supreme Court. As a result, U.S. classrooms are not value neutral, they are anti-God.

1920: The American Civil Liberties Union (ACLU) is formed by Roger Baldwin and others. It had formerly been called the American Communist Party (ACP). "*Communism is the goal.*" 1981: Before leaving office, President Jimmy Carter presents the Medal of Freedom Award to Roger Baldwin, founder of the American Civil Liberties Union (ACLU). It is the highest civilian medal awarded by the U.S. Government. The American Civil Liberties Union had its roots in the American Communist Part (ACP) before they sanitized its name.

1922: Antonio Gramsci, head of the Italian Communist Party goes to Russia in 1922 and decides the communist model of government won't work long term as it is too violent and against the Russian Christian soul. He devises more socialistic writings that atheists and radicals like. Mussolini throws Gramsci in prison as he sees him as a threat. His thinking is pure genius for overthrowing a government from within by saying whatever needs to be said and infiltrating to gain the inner circle until control is achieved. It is a modified version of Machiavelli, and is an extension of British Fabian socialist tactics. Saul Alinsky in America perfects the manual. This is the form of socialism followed today for state control by a radical element in government. Infiltrate from within, and say whatever is necessary to advance the socialist agenda is the modus operandi of socialism. In many religious circles social justice is the direct path to socialiasm, although it is rarely admitted that is the agenda. Leading Catholic heirarchy have been used by goverments furthering this agenda. America has implemented and perfected the methods of Gramsci's social engineering for the take over of America from within.

1923: Margaret Sanger founds what eventually becomes Planned Parenthood. She was a eugenicist who said, "*the most merciful thing a large family does to one of its infant members is to kill it.*" Her writings and practices heavily influence the rising Nazi Party citing the purpose of birth control as to "*create a race of thoroughbreds, and a woman's physical satisfaction is more important than any marriage vow. We do not want the word to get out that we want to exterminate the Negro population.*" Sanger held contempt for Jews, Catholics, and minorities. Planned Parenthood "clinics" are heavily located in the inner cities.

1925: Adolph Hitler writes *Mein Kampf* (My Struggle), an autobiographical account where he writes a "*the Jew is a sub human, and the Aryan race is the epitome of human evolution.*" The book sells millions in Germany. Hitler rises to power under an Aryan brand of personal identity and godless pursuit of the Motherland and Nationalism over Christianity.

1925: The Scopes, and famous "*Monkey Trial.*" The ACLU defends John Scopes on the issue of Creationism versus evolution being taught in school. It tested the Butler Act in the state of Tennessee, which permitted only Creationism to be taught in school. Creationism won the battle, but lost the war.

1925: Stalin, an avowed hater of the Church, orders the top scientist in Russia to inseminate human females with monkey sperm to "*breed a super warrior.*" It naturally fails, but the pursuit begins by atheistic science towards someday breeding trans-humans through genetic engineering. Over time, the atheist scientist rejects God, tries to play God through science, and in the process destroys civilizations as they breed only societal chaos. Atheism and science reach their zenith when the scientist tries to play God and risks destroying everything around them in the process when their experiments go awry.

1927: Oliver Wendell Holmes, Jr. of the U.S. Supreme Court issues a statement on the decision of Buck v. Bell on why sterilization is necessary, "*three generations of imbeciles are enough.*" A question not asked is, "*Where does it stop? Where does this end?*" The Supreme Court now takes an anti-God view of law that man knows more than God. America is now flexing muscles filled with pride during the "Roaring 20's" which precedes the fall.

1933: The Humanist Manifesto I. "*...humanists regard the universe as self existing and not created. Man has emerged as a result of the continuous process of evolution.*"

1936: Munich Olympics. Hitler leaves the games when Jesse Owens a black track and field runner, wins his fourth gold medal. Hitler says his Aryan supermen were "*running against an animal.*"

1936: The formation of the Pontifical Academy of Sciences (PAS) is created to advise the Pope and the College of Cardinals. Members are of different religions, elected for life, and all on the panel are evolutionists. No papers are allowed which are contrary to evolution, or the millions of years theories (old earth). The British astrophysicist Stephen Hawking in later years is placed on the board as an outspoken atheist.

1941: Germany and the Third Reich are in full stride pursuing the selection of the species. Dr. Josef Mengele, an atheist and a Nazi surgeon, experiments on 1,500 sets of human twins, sewing some together, and interchanging body parts. Less than 200 survived the ordeal. He thought people were animals, so why did it matter? General Heinrich Himmler, the feared leader of the SS had deep roots into the occult from an early age. He was an avowed atheist and the enforcement arm controlling Hitler's secret police—the feared SS.

1947: Everson v. Board of Education. The Supreme Court for the first time in 170 years takes out of context Thomas Jefferson's letter on eight words, "*a wall of separation between church and state.*" The courts sets a new precedent wherein it changes the Founders' meaning of "church" to now mean any religious activity. The court moves to an anti-Christian sentiment, which is without legal precedent. Few see that the courts are stacked with judges who have an anti-Christian view. America has just won World War II, and the young GI's are more interested in getting on with life, and for the next several generations focus on economic prosperity rather than faith. However, the devil never sleeps.

1961: Torcaso v. Watkins. Courts rule that secular humanism is a legitimate religion equivalent to Christianity under the law. A pornographer enjoys more rights now under the First Amendment than a public school, as it is not allowed to put up a Nativity Scene. In public schools today, Ramadan, Halloween, and pagan religions can be observed, but not Easter, Christmas, or a Nativity scene.

1962 and 1963: Murray v. Curlett & Abington v. Schempp: These court rulings ended prayer and Bible reading in the classroom with two separate decisions. The court said, "*If portions of the New Testament were read without explanation they could be and...had been psychologically harmful to the child.*"

1964: President Lyndon B. Johnson says aboard Air Force I to two like-minded Senators, "*I'll have them ni _ _ ers voting democratic for the next 200 years.*" The nation was clearly in need of change to minorities at that time, but *The Great Society* of Johnson and others didn't put the brakes on government. The public largesse created a class of people dependent on welfare, beyond the capacity of the system to support it on a permanent basis. This dependency has grown to such proportions it is hard for any official seeking election to buck the system as welfare recipients and those on the government dole in one way or another (or employed of some kind getting public benefits from tax dollars) are close to the majority of Americans—if not the majority. The present system is not sustainable and will collapse. It will be violent if historical precedent is any guide. As President Ronald Regan said while running for President, "*government is not* *the solution, government is the problem.*" Illegal immigration is being used today to allow the democratic party to have a greater voice in elections and public policy.

1965: The Second Vatican Council and the Blessed Mother's apparitions at Garabandal, Spain come to a close. The Church changed in significant ways after the Council and tens of thousands of clergy eventually left religious life as they did not approve of what happened at the Council. Contemporaneously, the Blessed Mother appeared 2,000 times from 1961-1965 in a remote mountain village in Northern Spain to four young girls. Her message was principally about the importance of the Eucharist and that the priesthood would come under attack. She said a great trial was coming to the world, and when asked what it was, she responded it was communism. One should remember the difference of socialism and communism is that communism is in a hurry to achieve its goals, while socialism is more patient with its agenda of incremental control by infiltrating structures from within to affect change. Communism is socialism when God is expunged from the culture as we saw in Russia and China. Socialism or the Fabian version is incremental change with the same result. God is removed in the end by either approach. The Blessed Mother said at Garabandal there would be some game changing events called, *The Warning and The Great Miracle.* People who are aware of the events at Garabandal are waiting in expectation for them. There were specifics given to the young girls on what to expect. These two events will be the greatest spiritual Transitional and Transformational events of all time.

1970: Earth Day(s) begins on April 22nd, the birthday of Karl Marx. Worship of Gaia as Mother Earth becomes more mainstream thinking. This thinking has morphed into the environmental and green movement in significant ways.

1971: Saul Alinsky publishes *Rules for Radicals* and provides instructions and marching orders for his troops when he says, "*True revolutionaries do not flaunt their radicalism. They cut their hair, put on suits, and infiltrate the system from within.*" Saul Alinsky was a friend and collaborator with the deceased Cardinal Joseph Bernadin (1996) of Chicago for many years. Alinsky dedicates his book to

"*Lucifer, the first radical known to man...*" Alinsky sought out leading clergy over his lifetime and had a significant influence if there was a disposition to socialism. Saul Alinsky and his playbook for radical change is considered the intellectual mentor of President Barack Obama's ideology with social activism and infiltration by any means from within. Alinsky an avowed atheist states his goal at death "*is to organize in hell.*" In the 1960's these people were walking the halls of Congress with backpacks, sandals, and ponytails. Today they are flying on Air Force One.

1972: Pope Paul VI says "The Smoke of Satan Enters the Church," as he quotes Luke 18: 8 which says, "*When the Son of Man returns, will He find faith on earth?" Bella Dodd, a former leading communist, states to Archbishop Fulton Sheen, "In the 1930's we put 1,100 men into the priesthood in order to destroy the Church from within. Right now they are in the highest places.*" Sheen receives Dodd into the Church.

1973: Roe v. Wade: Abortion becomes legal in the USA. The slaughter of the innocents is now funded with taxpayers' dollars. The die is cast for the removal of God's protective hedge around America. America is on its way to judgment. Estimates are that over fifty five million abortions have been performed in the United States alone, not including the abortive effects of the morning after pill or what is now called Plan B. God is a God of love, but there is a price to pay for sin.

1973: Akita, Japan the Blessed Mother appears to a nun and gives the single strongest approved message in the history of the Roman Catholic Church about chastisements and the apostasy (loss of faith) to come. Cardinal Ratzinger, now Pope Benedict XVI Emeritus, when head of the Congregation for the Doctrine of the Faith (CDF), having read the Third Secret of Fatima, said Akita is essentially the same message as what was said at Fatima. Akita speaks of "*fire falling from heaven and a chastisement greater than the flood, that will spare not even the faithful nor priests. The survivors will find themselves so desolate they will envy the dead. Cardinal against Cardinal...*" Throughout Catholic prophecy there are two types of chastisements mentioned. One will be man-made, the other will be sent by God. Either event(s) will alter the destiny of man.

1977: Theriault v. Silber, and Malnak v. Yogi. The courts state atheism is a religion and tax deductions can be taken for donations according to the U.S. tax code.

1980: Stone v. Graham. The court orders copies of the Ten Commandments to be removed from schools. This seals the deal for America's fate. We have officially rejected God and will be left to our own devices.

1981-Present: The Blessed Mother appears in Medjugorje to six young children in what is now Bosnia, and what was then part of the old Yugoslavia governed under President Marshall Tito. She says when the apparitions end, they are the last apparitions on earth as Our Lady articulates what is essential to the faith. She says there will be a Permanent Sign left by her when she stops appearing there. Several visionaries there say her appearances are the fulfillment of Fatima. They are the longest and most numerous in Church history.

1999: Columbine High School, Columbine, CO., school shooting. Eric Harris and Dylan Klebold vent on God in their speech and notes. The day of the shooting, Klebold's T- shirt said, "*Wrath*" and Harris' said, "*Natural Selection.*" They chose to kill on April 20th, as it was Hitler's birthday. Harris and Klebold had been taking psychotropic drugs.

2003: Lawrence v. Texas overturns sodomy rules. Justice Scalia says, "*this effectively decrees the end of all morals legislation.*" The floodgates open the courts to gay marriage, and all sorts of legislation that would have been unthinkable a generation before.

2009: The U.S. Government, as previously stated under Attorney General Janet Reno for President Clinton, lists Christians as enemies and terrorists of the state. The same list prevails under President Barack Obama. However, it is now more virulent towards believers as society slides into greater depravity. Specific targets are people who believe in the U.S Constitution, the Bible, the right to bear arms, homeschoolers, etc.

2011: The United States Air Force Academy in Colorado is planning a Stonehenge like worship center for pagans, druids, witches, and Wiccans, since all religions are now equal in the eyes of the state.

2013: Two former homosexual cadets of the U.S. Military Academy at West Point are married in the chapel.

2013: The Obama Administration lists Evangelical Christianity and Catholicism as terrorist groups. They are in the same grouping of extremists as Hamas, ISIS, Al-Qaeda, and the Muslim Brotherhood.

2014: The U.S. Dept. of Defense plans to offer special marriage benefits to same sex couples, exceeding the benefits to heterosexual couples. Seven days of paid leave are allowed to travel to another state, and expanded to ten days of paid leave for those serving overseas.

Head of the United Nations Climate Change Christiana Figueres says, "*communism is the best system of government to fight climate change.*" Yet, Russia and China are the two biggest polluters on planet earth. The goal of the United Nations is to impose a world tax so they can use the funds for programs they wish to implement, and thus hold a sovereign country hostage through funding requirements.

The Ohio State Supreme Court adjudicated an appeal ruling that an eighth grade science teacher fired in 2011 had no right to have a Bible in his classroom and teach Creationism. The Court ruled he had no religious rights to express his faith.

Governor Cuomo of New York issues a statement there is no place in New York politics for pro-life people.

The Grammy Awards. actress Queen Latifah, deputized by a Los Angeles, CA. official, marries 33 culturally diverse couples including homosexuals to a roaring, boisterous, clapping crowd on live prime time network television. Promoting marriage equality, Madonna and others sing the song *Open Your Heart.* Several songs of the evening were based on the theme *Same Love* and the occult.

The head of the Vatican Guard says the homosexual network in the Vatican are more loyal to each other than the Church.

It is reported in the British Press that aborted babies are used as fuel to heat hospitals. This is an admitted widespread practice.

Amy Dacy, formerly with Emily's List becomes the Chief Executive Officer of the Democratic National Committee. Emily's List raises money for pro-abortion female candidates running for Congressional seats.

The Internal Revenue Service (IRS) allows abortions to be tax deductible.

U.S. Medicare will fund sex change operations for people over 65 at tax-payer expense.

The Obama Administration is pushing hard for transgender people to enter the U.S. Military.

Quebec, Canada approves a bill legalizing euthanasia on demand by more than a 4 to 1 margin in the legislature, and is defined as healthcare for "*end of life care.*"

On October 6, 2014, the United States Supreme Court said they will not rule on same sex marriage as they feel it is best handled by the states. Same sex marriage will now spread like wildfire to more states.

The list goes on…and on…and on…and on. We have to draw the line somewhere, but the point is made on the generational slide towards Gomorrah. Once God is taken from the culture, and especially in the classroom, society moves to eventual moral and societal chaos. As a nation enforces unjust laws upon its people bringing it to a lawless and godless pagan state, it is only a matter of time before the citizenry pushback as the seeds of rebellion lead to revolution.

The Church will go through a great trial, and the material above was presented to show that we are in an epic battle for the very soul of America and the world. Believers are in this situation because they remained silent when they should have spoken out for truth. People will now pay the price by losing liberties and freedoms that were fought for by previous generations for noble and righteous reasons. As the darkness increases, the contrasting light of Christ will be easier to see.

If you have not observed the general downward trend in culture, it is now time to join the fight. God plus one is a majority—in every situation. Prayer and fasting can stop wars and asking for the Lord's mercy is now necessary to turn culture around.

Civil Behavior and Chaos

Civil moral behavior comes from our soul. We abide by a moral code because we know it is good for us, and good for those around us. If abided by, the imposition of good civil law based on natural law is not burdensome on its members. A moral code based on just laws in conformity with natural law enables a society to have order and security, and allows that society to live in economic and spiritual prosperity.

It is a structure that the Lord gave His Hebrew people as they left Egypt so they could have a proper conduct of behavior to govern themselves. This religious code of behavior is an expression of natural law implanted by God in men, became their civil code, and was considered just in the eyes of the Lord. When moral behavior breaks down and no longer functions, it is only a matter of time before chaos consumes that culture. Over time, excessive civil law crushes those it was designed to protect. Man has not reconciled himself to voluntary compliance to even something as basic as the Ten Commandments. Since man's nature has never changed since Cain killed Abel, the same vices have plagued man from the beginning of time. Original Sin has allowed this rebellious nature to flourish until a conscious decision is made by an individual to abide by a higher moral code—God's law. When a decision is in God's favor, a person, a family, and a culture is blessed, and thus protected. The number of words in the Ten Commandments is only seventy-eight words depending on the version of the bible you choose, and the Lord thought that sufficed for mankind rather than a litany of manmade laws that are largely destined to fail.

Unbridled materialism has suffocated spirituality to the point where we have lost all sense of the inner self of what is transcendent, and most important in life. The craze of sports and the inordinate pursuit of money have placed God at a level where it is considered foolish to follow Him. Ridicule, resentment, and marginalization minimize believers, as the practical atheism is so prevalent in our culture. At the moment, the world is consumed with abortion rights and the killing of the innocent, permissive gateway drug use sanctioned and promoted by the state, and rampant homosexuality to the detriment of all rational thought. God is an afterthought that is spoken of, but has no place of primacy in our lives. Virtue is openly scorned that is similar to the angels walking in Sodom and Gomorrah warning Lot and his family of impending danger. It has become the same today. Those not aware of our times are self-absorbed to their enslavement to sin due to excessive distractions and pleasures. Again, this practical and theoretical atheism is everywhere as the sense of sin has been lost. What we are witnessing today is something called *acedia*—a total lack of respect for spiritual things.

A fundamental question must be asked. What is the difference between wisdom and intelligence? We have words like wisdom, justice, truth, intellectualism, rationalism, moralism, socialism, communism, idealism, and many other isms. Does a high IQ constitute intelligence? The fear of the Lord is respect for Divinity and a God whom we can only feel in our spirits and soul. It is a pure soul that allows us to have clarity of mind. A soul cut off from God in mortal sin has no light. It is a clouded soul without clear thinking. We accept sin around us to such a degree because there is no clarity of mind, body, or soul. Those who are the most intelligent know God exists and keep His commands.

New School Prayer

Now I sit me down in school
Where praying is against the rule
For this great nation under God
Finds mention of Him very odd.
If Scripture now the class recites,
It violates the Bill of Rights.
And anytime my head I bow
Becomes a Federal matter now.
Our hair can be purple, orange or green,
That's no offense; it's a freedom scene.
The law is specific, the law is precise.
Prayers spoken aloud are a serious vice.

For praying in a public hall
Might offend someone with no faith at all.
In silence alone we must meditate,
God's name is prohibited by the State.
We're allowed to cuss and dress like freaks,
And pierce our noses, tongues, and cheeks.
They've outlawed guns, but FIRST the Bible.
To quote the Good Book makes me liable.
We can elect a pregnant senior queen
And the unwed daddy or Senior King.
It's inappropriate to teach right from wrong,
We're taught that such judgments do not belong.

Study witchcraft, vampires, and totem poles,
But the Ten Commandments are not allowed,
No word of God must reach this crowd.
It's scary here I must confess,
When chaos reigns the school's a mess.
So, Lord this silent plea I make:
Should I be shot, My Soul please take.

—Amen

The above was written by a 15 year old Canadian who got an A+ for this poem. The Lord's Prayer is not allowed to be read in schools anymore because it has the name of God in it.

Come now, you rich, weep and howl for the miseries that are coming upon you. Your riches have rotted and your garments are moth-eaten. Your gold and silver have rusted, and their rust will be evidence against you and will eat your flesh like fire. You have laid up treasure for the last days. Behold, the wages of the laborers who mowed your fields, which you kept back by fraud, cry out; and the cries of the harvesters have reached the ears of the Lord of Hosts. You have lived on the earth in luxury and in the pleasure you have fattened your hearts in a day of slaughter. You have condemned the righteous man; he does not resist you.

—James 1:1-5

JESUS, I TRUST IN YOU

sixteen

Key Events That Transformed the World

The refusal to take sides on great moral issues is itself a decision. It is a silent acquiescence to evil. The tragedy of our time is that those who still believe in honesty lack fire and conviction, while those who believe in dishonesty are full of passionate conviction.

—Venerable Archbishop Fulton J. Sheen

There are certain events in history that dramatically alter the destiny of nations and civilization itself. That is the history of mankind. We are now living through events that will have lasting impact for many generations to come. A tremendous number of factors are contributing to these sea change events that we are living through, that will affect everything we do and how we conduct our affairs in the future. This chapter is devoted to showing previous events that changed the course of civilization.

Change is a constant, and man adapts to the times in which he lives. Man always adapts no matter the circumstances, and has proven to be very resilient. The USA and the world are at a juncture where seismic shifts are taking place largely through social and language engineering of people that is changing our reality. To say the changes are enormous is an understatement. Our culture has been so intentionally dumbed down, few know the tyranny that awaits us.

The following is a brief but important list of events that have altered history. By no means is the list of key events meant to be exhaustive or inclusive. It is simply not possible. It also has an emphasis on the intersection of political empires and matters of faith and religion versus science and other events, which are important. Everyone will have a list of their own that would be valid as one's view into history is subjective no matter the profession. The primary focus here is the effect these events have had on Judeo Christian culture for centuries. Hundreds of events could be added to this list, but the theme of this book is that there are events that change the world and alter the direction of history—and we are at that place now. See below key events in history.

Abraham becomes the father of Judaism, Christianity, and Islam. The Lord makes a Covenant with Abraham (Genesis 15 and beyond) and His Jewish people that has never been revoked. The significance of this event is secondary only to the Incarnation and Resurrection of Jesus, and the redemption of mankind as it pertains to religion and peoples of the world.

The Exodus of the Hebrew people after nearly 400 years in bondage and captivity in Egypt takes place in approximately 1446 BC. We know from I Kings 6:1 that the Exodus happened approximately 480 years before the building of Solomon's temple so a date can be fairly accurate. Commandments are given by Moses, and 613 precepts of law follow as a method of self rule and self determination that many Jews follow to this day.

Ancient Greece is established from 800-600BC. The City State of Athens emerges into a democracy with civil rule establishing western thought and culture which begins to blossom. Philosophy and classic literature emerge so pure that they are taught in the schools of the world for thousands of years to the present day.

480 BC, the Persian Empire rules the world under King Xerxes and attacks Greece. The Battle of Thermopylae (Hot Gates) and several ensuing battles preserve Western thought, culture and civilization as Persia retreats. The West maintains its own identity as a result and matures into a new culture.

The Birth and Death of Jesus Christ 4BC to approximately 30AD (scholars disagree on exact dates of birth and death) are the single most important events in all of human history. God is born of a virgin woman by the name of Mary for the salvation of all mankind. History is now marked from dates Before Christ (BC) and After Christ, Anno Domini (AD). Christianity begins to spread throughout the world after the life and death of Jesus and has incalculable impact.

The Edict of Milan, or the Edict of Constantine, and the acceptance of Christianity by Constantine, 313 AD. Many historians call this date the end of true Christianity. Up until this time, Christian thinking and ideology had not been tainted by political or socio-economic thought from any governmental body. Since the death of Christ, Christians had been tortured and brutally treated by the Romans. Being fed to the lions for sport and entertainment was a quick and welcome death for many Christians for retaining the purity of their faith. In 313 AD, Emperor Constantine, who ruled over the western part of the Roman Empire, met in Milan with Emperor Licinius who was responsible for the Balkan (eastern) part of the Empire, and agreed to stop the persecution of Christians. Although the Edict did not end all persecution immediately, it was the first step in becoming the legal state religion of Rome by 380 AD. Emperor Constantine was born in 272 AD, and died in 337 AD. He ruled over the whole Roman Empire in 324 AD after several civil wars left him as sole emperor. It was believed that his mother Helena had the most influence on his acceptance of Christianity.

The Fall of the Roman Empire, 454 AD. Never had an empire been so brutal to those who disagreed with the way the Romans wished to rule. Emperors were often referred to as *Your Divinity,* and had despotic rule over their subjects. Roman brutality instilled fear in those they ruled. For a period of time the name given to Emperors was "*The Brutes*" as Rome declined through moral decay from within. Emperor Tiberius was said to have thrown servants off a cliff for the entertainment of his dinner guests. This behavior was tame compared to what took place throughout the Roman Empire, which had no equal in brutality to dissenters of Roman rule.

Mohammad/Muhammad is born in 570AD, and dies in 632. He establishes the seeds of Islam that spreads throughout the Near and Middle East, and all of North Africa quickly. The Koran emerges and gives a code of living. The word "love" is mentioned only once in the entire book as the sword is the model for ideological conquest and advancement. It unites disparate tribes due to an easy to understand doctrine. There is little mystery because there is no Incarnation, Virgin Birth, Trinity, Holy Spirit, Resurrection, and so forth. Islamic thought and culture dominate significant land mass today. Followers of Islam number over an estimated 1.4 billion people today. Islam is growing rapidly due to oil and resource wealth, not believing in abortion, an ideology that is unbending, and other reasons.

Charlemagne (748-814) AD. Charlegmagne unites tribal peoples of what is now Western and some of Central Europe into a region called the Holy Roman Catholic Empire. It is the first time since the fall of the Roman Empire that some form of a united Europe emerges. The Roman Catholic Church provides unity in religious belief for a large region of the known world. Europe is fashioned and molded under Charlemagne as church and state act often as one, establishing the church structure that persists to present times. Charlegmagne is called the Father of Europe.

The invention by the Chinese of Mechanical Printing or Moveable Type today called the Printing Press, 1041-1048 AD. China is credited with the concept but it does not become commonly used until 1450 AD, when Johannes Gutenberg of Germany introduces it in Europe. The first book in English is printed in 1475 AD and by 1500 AD, books were becoming widespread in Europe. In 1620 AD, English philosopher Sir Francis Bacon said "*the printing press changed the whole face and state of the world.*"

The Great Eastern and Western Schism, The Great Schism, 1054. The Roman Church fractures over severe differences that had been in existence since the emergence of the Church as designed by Constantine allowing Christians to practice their faith without persecution. A stated goal of Saint John Paul II was to have "*the Church breathe again with two lungs.*" To date there is still no unity.

The Magna Carta (The Great Charter), June 15, 1215 AD. Accepted by the King of England after feudal landlords sought legal rights against tyrannical laws under English kings, it was designed to limit the king's powers and protect the ordinary rights of British citizens. This led to the basis of English Constitutional Law, which in turn was modified over the centuries, granting more rights to people and the king's subjects. This document paved the way for Constitutional Law in the United States, as so many lawyers had been trained according to British law in the early days of the U.S. colonies. Without the Magna Carta, the United States would probably never have had a Constitution, property rights, or a system of governance like we have enjoyed. The ideology of the United States as a nation was initially based upon Greek logic, Roman and British law, and Christianity. Today that basis of the U.S. system of thinking and execution is increasingly becoming extinct as the U.S. becomes a godless, lawless, pagan nation. As the twenty-third Empire in world history, American power and influence is rapidly giving way to growing power in the East, shifting away from the West.

The Ottoman Empire maintained a dominance for nearly six centuries from 1275 AD to 1700 AD. The Empire ruled much of the surrounding environs, including 32 provinces and many vassal states, through strong fleets and commerce. The capital of Constantinople in what today is Istanbul on the narrow Bosporus Strait, gave the sultans a strategic geographic military advantage against enemies, as ships needed to pass through this narrow waterway.

1347 to 1350 AD, the Black Death/Bubonic Plague. This was an unprecedented disaster in terms of loss of life. It first appeared in Messina/Sicily, Italy, when people were found dead in a beached boat. The concentration of death was centered on a four-year period, but the plague moved to the Islamic world, as well as to the Mongolian Empire and all over Russia later. The areas hit hardest were along the trade routes. In the end it is estimated that more than a third to half of the population of large cities died, having awakened healthy in the morning, and often being dead by nightfall. The disease was thought to have been caused by diseased fleas and rats, and no one was safe. The gentry and those with means moved to the country to get away, and went to great lengths to avoid all human contact. In the end, 75 to 200 million perished, altering the population of Europe for the next 150 years. The Church lost influence as people looked to science and medicine rather than to the clergy who were also defenseless and died in proportional numbers. This set the stage by the time of Darwin (see Evolution chapter), for inroads by an anti-church, anti-faith mentality. New public health laws were enacted to curb disease from spreading again. The population was so drastically changed, peasants became landowners and a merchant class developed. People now began to think more independently after seeing whole villages and cities decimated, believing they had nothing to lose by venturing out pursuing new endeavors of all kinds. Death changed every family, village, and city where the plague was present.

Christopher Columbus set sail in 1492 AD for a New World that he believed existed, with three ships named the Nina, Pinta, and Santa Maria. Although many said the world was flat, Columbus thought otherwise. Financed by Queen Isabella of Spain, he planted a flag for Spain on Latin American soil. While he may have hoped for the best, the New World got only a blend of goodness from those seeking to evangelize and bring Christianity, interspersed with plunder and domination by those with gold on their minds. South America and Mexico were subjugated by a mixture of the Christo-pagan culture of the Conquistadors. When Indians of the Americas were strong enough to battle the better-equipped Spanish and Portuguese rivals, they obliged by pouring molten gold down their throats to give them all they wanted. Entire continents were changed by this single voyage. The Franciscan Friars of Saint Francis came and eventually the mission fields of California were opened up as Christianity moved north into America. In time, America becomes an empire like no other as agriculture and commerce bring a new dimension to the world.

The Protestant Reformation of 1517 AD. Although there had been previous attempts by John Wycliffe and Hus to overthrow Roman Catholic doctrine and thinking, under John Calvin and Luther a seminal moment in history occurred when Martin Luther, an Augustinian monk, posted his 95 dissenting theses on the Cathedral door in Wittenberg for all to publicly observe and a split of Christian unity took place in the West. Luther had not originally intended to revolt against the Church, but his public opposition to certain religious abuses set off a chain reaction of societal, economic, and political upheavals whose effects are still being felt today. Europe went into revolt and wars broke out all over Europe due to religious differences. Freemasonry was born in Europe in 1717, asserting the spirit of the Enlightenment. Peace would now be elusive.

Our Lady of Guadalupe, 1531 AD. The Spanish had heavily colonized Mexico but the Indian population had not been converted. In what is considered one of the greatest acts by the Blessed Mother in world history, she appeared to a peasant by the name of Juan Diego on December 9, 1531. Juan Diego was asked by the Blessed Mother to tell the local bishop what he had seen and heard. The bishop asked for a sign of the apparition's authenticity. Our Lady worked a miracle by placing an image of herself on a cactus fiber that was called a Tilma. When Juan Diego arrived at the Bishop's residence, he opened his cloak and the bishop saw the image, and a dozen Castilian roses fell from the mantle of the Tilma and onto the floor—a rose not indigenous to Mexico, especially for that time of year. The Blessed Mother appeared as a woman clothed with the sun (Revelation 12:1) in the colors of the Aztec godess. Over the next ten years, nine million Mexican Indians converted under the title given to her, *The Patroness of the Americas and the Philippine Islands.* Christianity had taken deeper root with an event initiated by the Queen of the Universe in the Americas. Many more apparitions would follow with similar circumstances of her intervention into the affairs of mankind. The Tilma should have deteriorated and rotted in a short period of time, but exists today as it did in 1531, nearly 450 years later.

The Battle of Lepanto, 1571 AD. The Ottoman Empire, at the peak of its strength assembled oarsmen, soldiers, and sailors against an armada from the Holy League for a battle on October 7, 1571. In what is considered by historians up to this day to be the single most decisive battle to preserve Christianity from the expanding Muslim Ottomans along the Mediterranean into Europe, the future of the world map would be decided. A battle was waged for the soul of Christianity in what was the last of the great battles of galley ships. Some estimates have the Christian fleet of boats outnumbered nearly three to one. Saint Pope Pius V asked the Blessed Virgin to intercede for victory with all of Europe praying the rosary. When it appeared the Muslims would win, violent winds shifted unexpectedly in favor of the Holy League, and Ottoman ships collided and sank each other. The Holy League lost about 8,000 men and 17 of the 100 Christian ships sank before saving 15,000 Christian slaves on Turkish ships. The Sultan lost 260 of his 300 ships and over 30,000 men. Commander Andrea Doria had been given an image of Our Lady of Guadalupe by King Philip II of Spain that he kept in the stateroom of his ship. Saint Pope Pius V named October 7th the *Feast of Our Lady of Victory,* which in time became the Feast of the *Most Holy Rosary*. The Holy League and Europe credited the Blessed

Mother with the victory. With the emergence of the new Islamic State (IS) in 2014, it is the first time there is a Caliphate since the demise of the Ottoman Empire. The caliph has a well defined ideology and he has a Ph.D in Islamic Studies. The goal of the Islamic State (IS) is to take over the world for Allah.

The Treaty of Westphalia, 1648 AD. Europe is established as a disparate group of people with borders. Wars and disputes had been fought among neighboring tribes of the Swedish, the French, the Netherlands, the Germanic, and the Hapsburgs for the previous three decades (The Thirty Years' War). Wars over religious differences and borders were resolved for the time being. The truce of wars had established permanent distribution of land for some time. What is now called Old Europe is formally established.

Battle/Siege of Vienna, September 11 (9/11) 1683 AD. The three hundred year battle of the Holy Roman Empire with Islam reached a turning point with the defeat of the Muslim Ottomans outside Vienna. This event established the Hapsburg Dynasty as a part of the Holy Roman Empire in Central Europe and solidified a far wider reach for the Catholic Church. The Ottoman Empire had been trying for the expansion into Vienna and failed. The Twin Towers of New York and the Pentagon in Washington, D.C. were attacked on September 11, 2001—the significance of the date not being missed by scholars. September 12th is the Feast of the Holy Name of Mary.

The Industrial Revolution, 1760-1840 AD. Historians disagree on the exact dates for its beginning, but civilization started to change rapidly as the world began to mechanize. An agricultural economy that had stood for thousands of years began to industrialize like never before, and yield per acre skyrocketed with the spread of mechanization and crops like the potato from Peru. The Industrial Revolution freed labor to work in industry with people being fed in large cities. Many people were able to move away from farms and still sustain themselves. Through the exodus from the countryside to the cities led to new problems, including the loss of a sense of community, a decline in morals, and a decrease in health and sanitation. Hand tools and back breaking plowing the ground behind a team of oxen or horses gave way to farm mechanization. The general mechanization of large and small industry changed the landscape forever. For civilization this was a quantum leap in which machinery replaced animals and the human back as the primary sources of power to produce products. All modern agriculture and industry can be traced to what happened in this time frame as more efficient industrial methods changed the plight of mankind.

1776 AD, The Declaration of Independence of the United States from British rule is written and distributed. Documents written by the Founding Fathers of the young colonies were divinely inspired for the enrichment of mankind. In the history of the American Empire, this date of July 4th can be traced to the official origin of a nation ascending in prominence and significance, with parades and fireworks still celebrating it today. It was the birth of this idea that is considered the origin of the country. The Bill of Rights and Constitution then assigned God-given rights to its citizens regardless of class or distinction something no nation had ever done in world history. The famous poem etched into the Statue of Liberty by Emma Lazarus called *The New Colossus* would evolve from this thinking on the independence of mankind in a new land with liberties and freedoms within a nation bound by law. It reads in part:

> *"...From her beacon-hand Glows world-wide welcome; her mild eyes command the air bridged harbor that twin cities frame. Keep ancient lands, your storied pomp cries she with silent lips. Give me your tired, your poor, your huddled masses yearning to breathe free, the wretched refuse of your teeming shore. Send these, the homeless, tempest-tost to me, I lift my lamp beside the golden door!"*

A new America and new experiment emerges, altering life and inspiring all peoples throughout the earth.

1789, the French Revolution, The Age of Enlightenment, the Age of Reason, and the humanistic and anti-church writings and philosophies of Voltaire and Rousseau. The rule of the monarchy ends in France and the working class proletariat takes control. These noble ideals are quickly replaced by the guillotine, class warfare, persecution of the Church, and the Reign of Terror. Liberty, equality, and fraternity became the new ideology for France. Faith is questioned, reason takes a new shape that challenges Church authority, science takes a new emphasis, and a new moral structure shapes culture and society. The role of the Church is lessened, and France as the elder daughter of the faith loses orthodoxy. In 1689, 100 years before the Revolution, the King of France was asked by Saint Margaret Mary Alacoque to Consecrate France to the Sacred Heart of Jesus. It was not done and the French Revolution took place exactly 100 years later to the day.

The Establishment of the U.S. Federal Reserve, 1913. In a stealth vote that passed on Christmas Eve, December 24th 1913, President Woodrow Wilson allowed the sovereign government of the United States to be placed into the hands of private bankers creating fiat money backed by nothing other than thin air. The significance of this event is seen in the role that central bankers and the Bank of International Settlements (BIS) located in Switzerland have in controlling the destiny of nations via the expansion and contraction of credit. Bankers were placed in a position to control the destiny of nations. Thomas Jefferson fought his whole life against a central bank as he said it was worse than a standing army working against its citizens. It is for this reason he fought so hard for states' rights (the Tenth Amendment), which would limit the size and the authority of the Federal Government. At the end of his life, Woodrow Wilson regretted allowing the U.S. Federal Reserve to become enshrined in law and admitted he made a mistake.

Early 1900's. Nikola Tesla, a Serbian immigrant, and Thomas Edison reinvented the world in the early 20th Century. Tesla solved a problem for Edison, and Edison grew rich and famous while Tesla died broke. Direct Current (DC) and Alternating Current (AC) soon allowed electricity to play a vital role in the transformation of the entire world. Darkness turned into light and technology and innovation took a new turn after the Industrial Revolution as electrical power generation built new cities, and permanently altered the lifestyles of billions of people.

World War I and the Guns of August, 1914. The first world conflict between major powers occurred, as nations took sides over an ideology on how the world should operate and who should rule it. Weapons were more sophisticated and deadly than in previous wars. Ships and large numbers of troops crossed oceans to participate in a global war.

The Bolshevik Revolution in Russia, October/November 1917. Similar to the French Revolution, a monarchy was toppled and the people took over, and soon the working class were betrayed by their leaders. It was a bloody war where the terrain of a country with eleven time zones changed color and political leanings. Communism began its campaign throughout the world with an agenda to expel Christianity and sacred thought from any role in the state, families, or education. The Blessed Mother appeared at Fatima, Portugal, from May 13 to October 13, 1917, before the October 1917 Revolution in Russia, prophesying exactly what would take place if her requests were not heeded. She said Russia would become the scourge of the earth unless it was consecrated to her Immaculate Heart, and Russia would spread her errors throughout the world. The world gradually is colored pink and red with communist and socialist thought. The fact that the Blessed Mother asked specifically for the Consecration of Russia to prevent a global war and a generalized apostasy of faith is a major event by itself that has continuing ramifications today.

World War II, 1938-1939. Hitler moved into Austria and Poland and a second great war commenced that involved nearly the whole world. Japan attacked Pearl Harbor on December 7, 1941, forcing America into the war and setting the stage for its emergence as a military, industrial, and economic superpower. An estimated sixty million people die in World War II in all theaters of battle. The Blessed Mother said at Fatima, "*wars are punishments for the sins of mankind.*" Sister Lucy of Fatima spoke of the aurora over Europe as an omen of war in advance of the German invasion of Poland, which she saw. Germany then invaded Poland in September of 1939.

1944. At a hotel resort named Bretton Woods in the White Mountains of New Hampshire, the World Bank was created, forming the underpinnings of a global post-war system for dispensing money and policy to nations. An interconnected and formal systematic approach to banking and lending began to be administered more formally than at any other time in history by nations acting collectively with greater cooperation among developed countries. A host of international agreements and organizations gradually emerged at regional levels as components of a more centralized financial system of government, with decisions made by unelected bankers and officials determining what countries and types of projects would be financed. Pressure began to be put on nations to conform to social as well as economic policies that financial institutions deemed acceptable if nations expected to be loaned money. As a result of World War II, new structures were needed to govern and operate in a global and fast moving world with cooperation among nations in an attempt to avoid conflict that leads to wars. At all times the question must be asked, "*under what ideology is a plan of action administered and executed? Who runs it?*" With God increasingly being expelled from the public square, public policy is flawed.

Israel becomes a State, 1948. After several thousand years of the Jews not having a homeland, a Zionist named David Ben-Gurion secured a homeland for the Jewish people. On May 14, 1948, the last day of the British Mandate, Ben-Gurion declared Israel a nation, and President Harry Truman of the U.S. formally recognized the State the next day. Ben-Gurion became the first Prime Minister of Israel. The politics of the Near and Middle East is in constant conflict between the sons of Ishmael and those of Abraham, Isaac, and Jacob, with no human solution for peaceful coexistence. Global politics continue to center around a nation approximately the size of New Jersey, as the world is at a complete loss how to solve geopolitical issues in the region.

India (1948) changes hands. India had been under British control and a movement of non-violent, non-cooperation began under the spiritual, moral, and civil direction of Mohandas (Mahatma–the Great One) Gandhi, which gradually gained national momentum. Returning from South Africa as a British educated lawyer, Gandhi began to work on Indian self-rule independent of British intervention. Gandhi was assassinated in 1948 after the partition of India had created the Muslim state of Pakistan. India today has a population of approximately 1.2 billion people.

Mao Tse-tung or Chairman Mao Zedong of China, 1949. Chairman Mao was responsible for creating the Peoples Republic of China (PRC) under brutal circumstances of violence and suppression, using a Marxist Leninist philosophy called Maoism. It is estimated 50 million people were purged to bring the new system of government to fruition.

China discarded all foreign influences in its new government but opened its economy to foreign investment and ingenuity in the 1970s. China then became the world's cheapest provider of manufactured and assembled products. In the last several decades, China has grown into an enormously wealthy superpower that has oppressive social and environmental conditions for its citizens with no freedom of worship and forced abortion. China's population is estimated at nearly 1.3 billion people, roughly four times the population of the United States. The power structure of global politics continues to move East to China as Western nations lose their Christian identity.

2008—, The Meltdown and Restructuring of the 20th Century Financial System has a profound impact on all governments of the world. The industrial world, in particular the U.S., began printing fiat money at an unprecedented scale (currency just printed backed by nothing—called Quantitative Easing, QE) thereby raising government debt to unsustainable levels as part of the attempt to eliminate the possibility of the collapse of U.S. and world financial markets in September, 2008. The financial world nearly collapsed at that time under its own weight and corruption. The USA and several other countries print billions/trillions of dollars to sustain their lifestyle. Due to the convergence and interconnectivity of the world economy in a digital age, it was not prudent to let banks fail that could bring down the financial system that had operated for so many decades. The term "*too big to fail*" was commonly used. It is generally now recognized by many foreign nations that the world wants a new international monetary system no longer solely reliant on the U.S. dollar as the international reserve currency. It remains unclear what the outcome will be, but it appears probable that the end result will be strengthened centralized control of governments and banks over the citizens of the world. In one scenario, a new global currency could emerge, administered by an elite group of central bankers. Governments are ready to administer a new structure, but it will need a catalyst of significant proportion. People will voluntarily accept, even welcome, a new system should circumstances become so dire in the world where people feel boxed in and helpless by the failure of existing financial and civil system of government. The destruction of the United States is happening by design. In the future, one will be either "*In*" or "*Out*" of the new order, but it will be impossible to be both, and still maintain one's faith. Personal decisions as to whom we serve will become necessary, urgent, and life changing—even to the extent of determining our personal destiny. The love of money is the root of all evil, and to know the future of mankind is to "*follow the money.*" People with power do not give it up easily.

A new paradigm and a Great Transformation is upon us.

His disciples remembered that it was written, "Zeal for thy house will consume me."

—John 2:17

JESUS, I TRUST IN YOU

Bibliography

Bebie, Father Philip, C.P., *The Warning,* A booklet printed in 1986.

Catechism of the Catholic Church, Ignatius Press, Latin text copyright, 1994, Libreria Editrice, Vaticana, Citta del Vaticano.

Conti, Dr. Gene, *Original Outline* of key figures and dates in the evolution/ atheist deception.

Crocker, H.W. III, *Triumph, The Power and the Glory of the Catholic Church,* A 2000 Year History, Three Rivers Press, NY, 2001

Delaney, John, *The Woman Clothed with the Sun,* Image Books, 1960.

De Marchi, IMC, John, *The Immaculate Heart, The True Story of Fatima,* Farrar, Strauss, and Young, NY, 1952.

De Montfort, Saint Louis Marie Grignion, *The Secret of the Rosary,* TOP, Montfort Publications, Bayshore, NY, 1965, See also, *True Devotion to Mary,* and *Letter to His Missionaries,* same source.

DuPont, Yves, *Catholic Prophecy,* TAN Books, Rockford, IL, 1970.

Estulin, Daniel, *The True Story of the Bilderberg Group,* Revised, North American Union Edition, 2009, PO Box 577, Waterville, OR, 97489.

Evans, Richard, *The Third Reich in Power,* Penguin Books, 2005.

Fatima Family Messenger, through the years

Fatima in Lucia's Own Words, Population Center, Fatima Portugal.

Flynn, Ted, *Hope of the Wicked, The Master Plan to Rule the World,* MaxKol Communciations, A book on the political philosophy of the New World Order, 2000, Herndon, VA. 20170. See Sign.Org

Flynn, Ted, *Idols in the House,* MaxKol Communications, 2002, Herndon, VA. 20170

Flynn, Ted and Maureen, *The Thunder of Justice, The Warning, The Miracle, The Chastisement, The Era of Peace,* MaxKol Communciations, 1993, revised 2010, MaxKol Communications, Herndon, VA. 20170. Distributed by Signs and Wonders for Our Time. See Sign.Org

Flame of Love of the Immaculate Heart of Mary, Diary of a Third Order Carmelite, and The Victorious Queen of the World. Sister Natalie of Hungary, Second Edition, Two Hearts Books, Mountain View, CA, 1991.

Francois, Robert, *O Children Listen to Me, Our Lady Teaches at Garabandal.* The Workers of Our lady of Mount Carmel, PO Box 606, Lindenhurst, NY.

Freemasonry, Human Genus, Encyclical Letter by Pope Leo XIII, April 20, 1834, Servants of Jesus and Mary, Box 258, Constable, NY.

Frere Michel de la Sainte Trinite', The Whole Truth About Fatima, all volumes, Bufffalo, NY, Immaculate Heart Publications.

Garabandal, The Warning and the Miracle, A Summary of Events, 1961-1965, Workers of Our Lady of Mount Carmel, PO Box, 606, Lindenhurst, NY. In addition, the author has past copies of the magazines published by the same group originally called *Needles,* and then *Garabandal Magazine* over nearly a thirty-year period.

Golitsyn, Anatoli, *New Lies for Old,* Dodd Publishers, 1984.

Gouin, Abbe, *Sister Mary of the Cross, Shepherdess of LaSalette,* Melanie Calvat, Marian Center for Unitas, Catolica, 31 Parkdale, Wolverhampton, WVI 4TE, England.

Internet. There is little that is not available on the internet. It has changed writing, bibliographies, and publishing. There are many sites, which are highly questionable presenting information, while others that are official sites on subjects worthy of quoting where data can be considered valid. There was information in this book from many internet sites where people are quoted.

Interviews and Conversations, The author has written about, filmed, spoken to and met with many people on this subject worldwide for over twenty-five years. There has also been a family magazine called *Signs and Wonders For Our Times* based in Northern Virginia since 1988 on this genre that is published several times a year. There are stories, interviews, and messages posted in the magazine. See Sign.Org

Kondor, Fr. Louis, editor, *Fatima in Lucia's Own Words, Sister Lucia's Memoirs,* Ravengate Press, Box 49, Still Water, MA, 01467

Kowalska, Saint/Sister Faustina, Apostle of Divine Mercy, *Divine Mercy in My Soul—A Diary,* Marian Fathers, Stockbridge, MA.

Kramer, Father Paul, *The Devil's Final Battle,* The Missionary Association, Terryville, Conn., 2010

Laffineur, Fr., Mateme, and Pelletier, M.T., *Star on the Mountain, Our Lady of Mount Carmel, de Garabandal,* Lindenhurst, NY.

Lliibagiza, Immaculee, *Our Lady of Kibeho, Rwanda,* with Steve Erwin, Hay House, Inc. 2008.

Marian Movement of Priests, *Our Lady Speaks to Her Beloved Sons,* Locutions to Father Stefan Gobbi of Milan, Italy, Saint Francis, ME, 04774.

Peerdeman, Ida of Amsterdam, *Our Lady of All Nations,* and the links to Akita, Japan, Signs and Wonders for Our Time Magazine, Herndon, VA. 20170. See Sign.Org

Peerdeman, Ida, Visionary of Amsterdam, *The Hour of the Lady of All Peoples*, Earl Massecar, L'Armee de Marie, PO Box 95 Limoilou, Quebec, Canada, GIL 4TB, 1978.

Ratzinger, Cardinal Joseph, *The Ratzinger Report,* Messori Vittorio, Ignatius Press, San Francisco, CA., 1985.

Socci, Antonio, *The Fourth Secret of Fatima,* Loreto Publications, PO Box 603, Fitzwilliam, NH, 03470.

The Syllabus of Errors, The Encyclical of Quanta Cara, issued by Pope Pius the IX, 1864, and *A Syllabus Condemning Modernism (Lamentabili Sane),* issued by Pope Pius X in 1907, The Remnant 2539 Morrison Ave., Saint Paul, MN, 55117.

Wynne, John W, Stephen A, *Repairing the Breach, Explaining the Systematic Deception Behind the War on Worldviews, and How Christendom Can Turn the Tide,* P3 Printing, Dallas, Texas, 2008. This is an 800 page textbook on evolution, Intelligent Design, and many other topics.

Index

D

E

F

G

H

I

J

K

L

M

N

O

P

Q

R

S

T

U

V

W

Z